THE BUSINESS OF
MAJOR LEAGUE BASEBALL

THE UNIVERSITY OF CHICAGO PRESS Chicago and London

THE BUSINESS OF
MAJOR LEAGUE BASEBALL

GERALD W. SCULLY

GERALD W. SCULLY is professor of management at the
University of Texas at Dallas.

The University of Chicago Press, Chicago 60637
The University of Chicago Press, Ltd., London
© 1989 by The University of Chicago
All rights reserved. Published 1989
Printed in the United States of America
98 97 96 95 94 93 92 91 90 89   5 4 3 2 1

Library of Congress Cataloging-in-Publication Data

Scully, Gerald W.
     The business of major league baseball / Gerald W. Scully.
        p.   cm.
     Bibliography.
     Includes index.
     ISBN 0–226–74389–6 (alk. paper)
     1. Baseball—United States—Clubs—Economic
aspects.   I. Title.
     GV880.S38   1989
     338.4'7796357'0973—dc20   89–32840
                                                          CIP

For my daughters Deirdre Koren and Audra Laine

Contents

Preface

Nearly twenty years ago I participated with a few other economists in a research effort that greatly increased our understanding of the operation of professional sports leagues. Since then, enormous changes have occurred—particularly in baseball—that date much of those findings. The last decade, during which baseball has struggled with free agency, has been turbulent; moreover, many of the agreements that govern baseball's relations with the players, television, and the minor leagues have been, and will continue to be, subject to frequent renegotiation.

I have written this book for those who would like to understand the economics behind these developments. Such an audience presumably includes more than economists. To the largest practical extent, therefore, I have attempted to avoid technical expressions and professional jargon, hoping that the compromise between rigor and readability will satisfy economist and noneconomist alike.

C. A. Knox Lovell and Philip K. Porter read two preliminary chapters of the book. I benefited from their comments. Roger G. Noll read the entire first draft of the manuscript and cheerfully gave me the benefit of his encyclopedic knowledge of and insight into the sport. He also provided the data on profits in baseball.

Introduction

The purpose of this book is to analyze modern baseball from an economic perspective. Much has been written about the history of the game, and about its sociological and psychological aspects, but only recently have economists turned their attention to the subject. To an economist, the study of the game and the industry is rewarding, because individual decision-making units can be closely observed and their reactions to a variety of economic incentives measured. To a fan, an understanding of the economic aspects of baseball is quite indispensable now, because economic factors play a very large role in the quality of the games. Over the years, I have shared with other fans a sense of perplexity about whether the economic pressures on baseball are consistent with the objective of attaining the maximum degree of quality on the playing field. Some of the economic issues in baseball are fundamental and widely debated. For example, are amateur drafting and restrictions on player movement making play more competitive among the clubs or are they just devices for holding down team costs? Is ownership of a franchise a profitable undertaking or are the owners merely civic-minded individuals providing a public service? How are we to evaluate the seemingly ungracious complaints of many $500,000-plus ballplayers that they are underpaid? While baseball has been integrated on the playing field for 40 years, why are there so few black coaches and managers in the game?

Part 1 of the book examines the organization and structure of baseball and the effect of various league operating rules on the level of team performance and on the distribution of team playing strengths. In chapter 2, the organization and structure of the baseball leagues are outlined in considerable detail for the purpose of identifying those aspects of league structure that are necessary for the provision of quality games and those league operating rules that serve only to enlarge profits, sometimes to the detriment of the games. A league is an association of clubs (firms) that act in concert according to a set of written agreements. This type of arrangement is legal in baseball but is per se illegal as a business form in the United States. The leagues enjoy, at the public pleasure, the opportunity to engage in a number of collusive arrangements that restrict competition in their various markets. The range of these collusive restrictions is quite wide, from defining the exclusive home territory of a team, to specifying the manner in which players are to be assigned to the clubs, to negotiating the national broadcast contracts with the TV networks. Many of these rules and agreements have been challenged in the courts and by the Players Association. The most dramatic structural change has been in the players' market. Since 1974 the players have had binding final-offer salary arbitration and, since 1976, there has been free agency for eligible veteran players. However, there is some evidence that by the mid-1980s owners openly were colluding to restrict the market for free agents.

Chapters 3 and 4, respectively, analyze the effects of league operating rules on the absolute level of play and on the closeness of club standings within a league. There have been improvements in the quality of athletes over time. Veteran players are better than novice players. Large sums are expended training players in the farm system. League expansion, player roster limits, and playing rules affect the absolute level of play. Also, in chapter 3, the effects of various playing rule changes (e.g., the lively ball, changes in the strike zone, the designated hitter, etc.) on hitting and pitching performance and on scoring are measured. In chapter 4, the various league rules, which divide territory and gate receipts, socialize national broadcast fees, control the sale and movement of clubs, and allocate players through drafting, reservation, and assignment, are shown in general to have important implications for the distribution of club competitive strengths (win records), because of their financial effects on teams. Historical evidence on trends in competitiveness within the leagues is examined, and the effect of free agency on the distribution of playing talent is determined. In 1976, the owners lamented that free agency would marshal in an era dominated by big city clubs. Has this happened?

The business of baseball is examined in part 2 of the book. Chapter 5 documents the rise in popularity of the game, particularly since the mid-1970s. Much of this growth is due to increased ticket purchases by businesses as part of customer and employee entertainment. The wide disparity in attendance among clubs is documented. Using data for 1984, the determinants of club attendance are analyzed. An important finding in this chapter is that clubs appear to charge ticket prices consistent with maximizing club revenue. This finding contrasts sharply with the myth that owners are committed to winning at any price and set ticket prices more or less to defray expenses.

A remarkable body of club financial accounting data from 1980–84 is used in chapters 6 and 7 to examine team revenue, costs, and profits. The data, revealed here publicly for the first time, permit a much clearer evaluation of the financial status of the industry. However, because of the special tax treatment that sports franchises receive (e.g., depreciation of player contracts and other intangible assets), the integrated ownership structure in baseball (e.g., Ted Turner owns both the Braves and WTBS-TV), and the particular practices of sports accounting, it is extraordinarily difficult to compare the profits of one club with those of another. The tax treatment and ownership structure of baseball franchises distort club finances. Thus player, franchise, and lease agreement depreciation, which are not economic costs that need to be recovered to make the asset whole, are treated as a deduction from income when they are in fact a cash flow to the owner. And Ted Turner's sale of his club's broadcast rights to his own television station at a price below their market worth transfers income from the Braves to WTBS-TV. Exactly where the profits for Turner emerge is a matter of corporate tax strategy. But this type of practice, now common in baseball, makes baseball franchises look a lot less profitable than they are in fact.

Part 3 examines the players' market, race discrimination, and the quality of managing in the major leagues. In chapter 8, player contribution to club revenue is estimated and compared with player compensation. Player pay is shown to be closely related to player performance. Players of the caliber of Dan Quisenberry, George Brett, Mike Schmidt, and Gary Carter, who are paid $2 million or so per season, are shown to contribute $2 to $3 million in revenues to their clubs. Ballplayers may be highly paid, but, in general, it appears that they are not overpaid. Also, in this chapter, I attempt to determine whether club owners colluded to suppress the market for free agents during 1986 and 1987.

In an earlier paper, which examined the extent of the problem in the late 1960s, I found evidence of race discrimination in baseball. Happily, today, there is no evidence of racial salary discrimination. But there is some evidence of continued positional segregation (e.g., blacks overrepresented in the outfield and underrepresented in the battery) and continued but narrowing racial performance differentials, which are consistent with discriminatory behavior. A novel theory of why there are so few black coaches and managers in baseball is provided in chapter 9.

Obviously, managers perform an extremely important function in baseball. Managers select new playing talent, supervise player training and development, develop game strategies, select the starting pitcher, and so on. In chapter 10, I develop a methodology for estimating precisely the contributions that managers make to team win records. The performance records of all baseball managers with five or more years of experience over the period 1961–80 are determined. A manager of the quality of Earl Weaver is found to be worth 10 to 11 games to the club's win record. Such managers contribute as much to teams' winning as superstar ballplayers, but are paid only a fraction of their salaries.

Chapter 11 presents a summary and draws some conclusions.

1

Baseball: An Overview of the Major Economic Issues

In the beginning, around 1845, in New York City, baseball was played among gentlemen's clubs. By the end of the Civil War, however, the sport was a national pastime with commercial prospects. In 1870, over 400 amateur and professional baseball clubs were represented in the National Association of Baseball Players.[1] In 1871, the professional clubs withdrew from the association and formed the National Association of Professional Baseball Players. During the five chaotic years of existence of this first professional league, a total of 25 clubs were formed and competed, although financial pressures forced most of them sooner or later to disband. Of those clubs that wanted to win and had the resources to achieve that goal, the financially stronger inevitably stripped the weaker of their better players. Early professional baseball was thus often more of an exhibition than a contest between matched clubs. For example, in 1875, the Boston Red Stockings, which were owned by Harry Wright, a successful early baseball promoter, finished with a record of 71 games won to 8 lost. The lowly Brooklyn Atlantics, on the other hand, won only two games during that season.

In Chicago, in 1876, for 50 cents fans could see Al Spalding's White Stockings take on Wright's Red Stockings. Chicago had a 12-man club, while Boston had fourteen players on its roster. There were nine innings of play, but much else about the game would be unfamiliar to today's fans. The baseball had a wood center and the gloves were fingerless. The pitcher's mound was 45 feet from home plate. Nine pitched balls outside of the strike zone constituted a walk, and the hitter could call for a high or a low pitch.

The financial structure of professional baseball in those days was also quite different from that of the sport today. While the players were free to sign for the following season with any club they pleased, the owners deducted $30 from the player's pay for uniforms and 50 cents a day for road expenses. The average player on the Red Stockings made $1,380 for the season. The umpire was paid $5 for calling the game. Harry Wright reported a profit of $65.20 in 1874, despite a season during which his team compiled fifty-two wins versus eighteen defeats (an impressive .743 record). The net worth of the club was $833.13.[2]

The Origin of Restrictive Practices in Baseball

The National League was formed in 1876 by a group of clubs which sought to bring greater financial stability to the game. Low fan turn-out in small cities and high player salaries were the new league's most pressing financial concerns. Certain collusive practices emerged immediately as a means of relieving those pressures. The league sought to stabilize market size by granting exclusive territorial rights to franchises and stipulating minimum size for a city as one condition of league entry. A visitor gate share of 30 percent helped redistribute revenue from clubs in the larger markets to those in the smaller markets. Player salaries were two-thirds of team costs. Winning teams of course draw more fans and the wealthier clubs continued to buy the best playing talent. Indeed, the richer clubs were so dominant on the playing field that membership in the league continued to be volatile.

Concerned with the financial consequences of unrestrained competition for players, the league in 1879 secretly introduced a player reservation rule. Under this collusive agreement, exclusive property rights to five players (about one-half of the roster) were assigned to each club. Clubs were forbidden to compete for the contracts of the reserved players; players who jumped their contracts were blacklisted, and clubs that employed such players were boycotted. Reserved players thus either played on the club that held their reservation rights or they did not play professional baseball at all. Blacklisting and boycotting, which are illegal business practices, were effective instruments of fiscal discipline in baseball. Club roster costs fell significantly after the assignment to the clubs of reservation rights to players. During the 1880s, for the first time, many clubs began to make a profit, and a semblance of stability emerged in the league.

While the player reservation system protected the team's roster, there was no mechanism for transferring players between clubs. In 1884, the St. Louis Browns of the American Association wanted to transfer the contract of pitcher Tony Mullane to Toledo, but there existed no method of releasing him from reservation without giving clubs other than Toledo the right to sign him. A. G. Mills, then president of the National League, ruled that a qualified release was not possible under 1883 Tripartite Pact or National Agreement between the National League and the American Association, but that a letter circulated among the clubs stating the Browns' intention and pledging the clubs not to negotiate with Mullane was legal.[3] Although it was later often honored in the breach, a crude waiver rule in the form of gentlemen's agreements had thus been established.

By 1883, the entire player roster was protected under what has become known as the reserve rule (or reserve clause). As a result, new talent could only be acquired through transfers under dubious gentlemen's agreements or through the outright purchase of the entire roster of a failing club. These methods of acquiring players were uncertain and expensive. In 1885, Cleveland sought to recoup some of its financial losses by selling its players to Brooklyn. To avoid interference in the deal by other clubs, Cleveland sequestered its players in a small town on the Canadian border, until they could be legally signed by Brooklyn.[4] A formal waiver rule was adopted in 1885. For a ten-day period after a player was released from reservation, only clubs within the league could negotiate with him. Thereafter, the player had an unconditional right to sign with any club he pleased. The waiver rule increased the value of player contracts to the clubs. Beyond playing the reserved players, clubs had assets that could be sold for cash or traded for other players. This procedure greatly simplified the movement of major league players among the clubs.

Rules governing the relationships of major league clubs within a league, between clubs in different leagues, and between major and minor leagues are contained in the National Agreement, which has changed periodically. The National Agreement of 1883 recognized reservation rights to minor league players. Minor league players were brought into the majors through the purchase of their contracts. This method of acquiring new playing talent was expensive. In 1892, the National League refused to grant continued recognition of minor league reservation rights. Confronted with the complete loss of a property right, under the National Agreement of 1892, the minor leagues agreed to a player draft. Players were drafted at fixed prices, depending on the minor league classification. Additionally, there were no limits on the number of players on a club's roster. And, players were farmed out to or placed in "cold storage" on other teams, to be recalled when required.

The competition for players intensified in 1890–91, when new leagues emerged that did not honor the reservation rights of the National League clubs. In 1890, mainly as a reaction to a new player salary classification scheme imposed by management, the short-lived Players' League was formed. Unable to agree on a method of reassigning the players who had jumped their contracts to the defunct league, the American Association withdrew from the National Agreement. The rise in player salaries, the decline in league revenue, and the costs of absorbing weak clubs from the Players' League in settlement of the "war" among the leagues greatly weakened the National League. Wealthy clubs were forced to aid the weaker franchises financially. By the turn of the century, nearly all clubs were part owners of other clubs. In 1901, the surviving clubs in the league formed a syndicate. Syndicated baseball was not popular with the fans, since the lack of independence among the clubs made the outcome of the games suspect. Loss of fan confidence in the National League contributed to the rise of the rival American League. A. G. Spaulding, who had retired from an active role in league affairs to pursue his business interests in sporting goods and bicycles, responded to this competition and succeeded in ending the "trust" or multiple-club ownership arrangement in the National League in 1902.[5]

By 1903, with the signing of a peace treaty between the National and American Leagues, the governance structure of baseball and the collusive arrangements among the clubs that characterize modern baseball largely were in place. Each club wanted to monopolize playing talent by controlling the largest number of players at the lowest possible cost. Under the 1903 agreement, the practice of farming was prohibited. The ban on farming led to a rule of optional assignment, increases in the size of clubs' rosters, and the widespread purchase of minor league clubs. Under an optional assignment, the contract of a major league player was sold to a minor league club with a repurchase option, a method of transferring a player back to the minors while retaining a future interest in him that was subject to abuse. The practice became so abused that restrictions were imposed in 1907–08. Restrained by these limitations on farming and optional assignment, club rosters ballooned. Brooklyn had 61 reserved players in 1909, while Washington had 29. In 1912, the major league clubs agreed to an overall limit of 35 reserved players, with a limit of 25 during the regular playing season. Major league clubs then sought to control players by owning minor league clubs. The National Commission (the presidents of the American and National Leagues and a selected chairman) ruled that direct ownership of these clubs violated the ban on farming, and the clubs were forced to liquidate these holdings.[6]

Branch Rickey, general manager of the St. Louis Cardinals, revived the practice of farming shortly after the 1919 "Black Sox" scandal. At one time the St. Louis Cardinals owned outright or had controlling interest in 33 minor league clubs, or about 600 players.[7] The post-World War II domination of the New York Yankees largely was due to the growth of the farm system. The elaborate arrangements with the minor league clubs choked off the competitive supply of new playing talent. Clubs either grew their own talent on the farms or bought whatever talent other clubs were willing to supply. Lacking restrictions on the number of players that could be controlled, the wealthy clubs dominated baseball by monopolizing playing talent.

Self-Regulation in Baseball

Baseball is self-regulated. The collusive practices in the sport are entirely legal, having been sanctioned by the Supreme Court of the United States in *Federal Baseball Club of Baltimore v. National League et al.* [259 U.S. 200 (1922)] and reaffirmed in several decisions since then. Writing for the Court of Appeals of the District of Columbia (269 Fed. 681 and 50 App. D.C. 165), prior to the Supreme Court hearing, Chief Justice Smyth remarked: "If the reserve clause did not exist, the highly skillful players would be absorbed by the more wealthy clubs, and thus some clubs in the league would so far outstrip others in playing ability that the contests between the superior and the inferior clubs would be uninteresting and the public would refuse to patronize them."[8]

Until recently nearly everyone in and out of baseball subscribed to the view that the collusive practices in baseball were reasonable and utterly necessary for the equalization of playing strengths on the field. In 1887, the players themselves had been so convinced of this that they agreed to the stipulation of the reserve clause in their contracts. A Congressional investigation into the sport in 1951 recommended that no legislative action be undertaken with respect to the practice of reservation. The report that emerged from this investigation—*Organized Baseball* (1952) prepared by Peter S. Craig, the leading authority on the economic aspects of baseball at the time—accepted the view that while organized baseball was a monopoly, club owners were sportsmen who were not particularly interested in profits, which didn't amount to much in any case, and that the restrictive product and labor market practices were necessary methods of equalizing playing competition.[9] Branch Rickey reflected the owners' sentiments: "Every thinking person will shortly take judicial notice that the reserve clause is the sine qua non to the existence of baseball as a professional sport."[10] Fred Hutchinson and "Pee Wee" Reese as league player representatives testified to the necessity and reasonableness of the reserve clause.[11] Of 105 sportswriters surveyed by the Committee, nearly all found the reserve clause to be both necessary and desirable.

During the late 1960s and through the 1970s the players lost their naiveté about the reserve clause and were organized under a very strong and directed players' union. The unanimous assault of economists on the owners' defense of the reserve clause legitimized player opposition to these restrictive labor market practices.

Economists' Views of Baseball's Restrictive Practices

The main concern of economic analysis is the allocation of scarce resources within decision-making units and the rules or framework governing transactions within these units. The economic analysis of baseball is particularly attractive, because the rules which govern resource allocation within the industry are known with certainty. The *Baseball Blue Book*, a compendium of every agreement among the clubs in organized baseball, is published annually, although written agreements within cartels on the division of markets and the arrangements governing transactions among the members have not been released for other industries since the passage of the Sherman Act in 1890. Moreover, considerable data is available to test the allocation effects of these rules. Figures are compiled on output (club records), sales (attendance, ticket prices, broadcast receipts, etc.), player inputs (performance statistics), and so on, and are available to the analyst.

Simon Rottenberg was the first economist to recognize that the reserve clause was a restriction on player movement that served to suppress player salaries but did little to contribute to the stated goal of equalizing club playing strengths.[12] His analysis was inferential, since available data were inadequate to support a conclusion that players were paid less than their market value. The fact that ballplayers made more money, and sometimes a great deal more money, than the working population, allowed baseball spokesmen to deflect the charge that the player allocation system was inherently unfair. The challenge of new leagues in football and basketball during the 1960s led to an enormous increase in players' salaries in these sports. While their teams' owners chafed under the financial pressure, football and basketball survived and ultimately prospered. The survival of these sports in a regime of dramatically higher player salaries weakened the general conviction of the need for the reserve clause in baseball.

The way in which the restrictive practices in organized baseball affect the allocation of playing talent within the leagues was studied by economists Mohamed El-Hodiri and James Quirk.[13] They found that under baseball's operational rules equalization of playing strengths theoretically could not be achieved by the natural activities of profit-maximizing teams, since revenue inequality among clubs made playing talent more valuable in some locations than in others. The rule which permits the sale of player contracts guaranteed that rich clubs could purchase the playing talent that was of more value in their location from the weaker franchises that held the reservation rights. The weak clubs would sell these contracts because the revenues from player sales were higher than the revenues from player services on these clubs. Only if all teams had equal revenues or if a ban were imposed on the sale of player contracts would equalization of playing strengths emerge under a system of player reservation.

Roger Noll, while at the Brookings Institution in Washington, gathered a group of scholars in 1971 who examined a number of important policy issues related to professional team sports. Among the topics analyzed were player reservation and comparative team playing strengths, the rising militancy of players' unions and its effect on sports, race discrimination in both pay and in positional assignment, ticket price setting and the motivation of ownership (i.e., sport or business), tax benefits (player depreciation) and subsidies to professional team sports, broadcasting policy (i.e., blackout rules, etc.), and franchise shifts and league expansion. *Government and the Sports Business*, the report that was issued in conjunction with this study in 1974, represented a remarkable theoretical advance in the understanding of the organization and structure of professional team sports and the effect that the various operational rules of the leagues had on the economics of the sports and on the quality of the games. In the same year that the Noll volume was published, I published a paper that compared the actual contribution of players to club revenues and the salaries that they received.[14] I was able to show that the players were paid about 10 to 20 percent of their contribution to club revenue. In 1975, as a result of the Messersmith arbitration decision, the players succeeded in obtaining free agency. While no direct link between economists' thinking on professional team sports and the achievement of the players' union is claimed, there was considerable formal and informal exchange of views between these economists and the members of the sports industry at conferences, meetings, and in Congressional hearings.

The Major Economic Issues Facing Baseball in the Late 1980s

In recent years, there has been considerable discussion of the changing nature of baseball. A most important change has been its growing commercialization. Whether this change is due to the enormous and growing popularity of spectator sports in America, or to the impact of television, or to the increased financial opportunities of franchise ownership, the result has been that the era of philanthropic sportsmen providing contests for the public's pleasure has long ended. Now, team owners hawk games for fame and profit. There is no moral imperative in the commercialization of baseball. In fact, placing the game on a paying basis may very well have improved the overall quality of the contests. However, government has fashioned a public policy (the antitrust exemption) for the leagues based on the premise that such games are more sporting than business ventures. But this is the era of big-money baseball. Average players command nearly half a million dollars in pay, while superstars make $2 million and more. Umpires go to umpire school and make up to $117,500 for six months of work.[15] The industry grosses nearly a billion dollars a year from ticket sales, concessions, parking and licensing receipts, and from broadcast fees. Clubs have been sold for over $100 million.

Along with the rise in popularity has been the emergence of a strong players' union and a dramatic change in the contractual structure of the players' market. Prior to 1976, players were bound indefinitely to their clubs. Interteam competition for veteran free agents has increased player salaries enormously. Average pay today is ten times that of 1975. The increased share of player salaries out of club revenue (roughly a doubling) has brought recent attempts by club owners to collude by not signing free agents from other clubs. The clashes between a militant players' union and strong-willed owners have grown in intensity and in frequency. Baseball had its first players' strike in 1972. The players' strike of 1981 lasted nearly two months and resulted in a split season. Because of the threat it poses to the enjoyment of the games, fans increasingly are uneasy about player-management disputes and other problems of an economic nature (e.g., franchise shifts, competitive balance within a league, etc.).

The years 1989–90 will be crucial for baseball. Several agreements, which shape the financial structure of the sport, expire at that time. The Basic Agreement between the Major League Baseball Players Association and the club owners expires at the end of the 1989 season. The collective bargaining issues are club compensation for lost free agents and the attempt by the owners to reimpose the indefinite reserve clause de facto by restricting contract offers to one year and by refusing to bid for free agents unless the club owning the free agent's contract expresses no interest in re-signing the player. Player concession to owner wishes would result in a sharp decline in compensation.

At the end of the 1989 season the national broadcast contract also expires. In 1988, the clubs received about $8 million a year from the sale of national TV rights. Broadcast fees from all sources represented 35 to 40 percent of club revenues. The new 1990–93 national contract with CBS-TV is worth $1.06 billion for the four-year period. Each club will receive $10.2 million per year from the broadcast rights to 12 season games, the league playoffs, the World Series, and the All-Star

Game. Additionally, ESPN cable network bought the broadcast rights to 175 regular season games for the 1990 through 1993 seasons for $400 million. Combined CBS-TV and ESPN cable revenues are $14 million per club beginning with the 1990 playing season. The deregulation of broadcasting and the rise of the cable television networks offer substantial commercial opportunities to both the broadcast and the sports industries. Baseball could make its own broadcasting arrangements with cable TV or pay TV and televise its home games. The revenue potential from the sale of such games is very large. The New York Yankees sold the broadcast rights to 150 regular season games for a 12-year period beginning with the 1991 season to Madison Square Garden cable television for $500 million, an amount that represents an enormous increase in the per-year value of such rights over that of the Yankees' current contract with WPIX. The Yankee deal is expected to set the standard for other teams' negotiations in other cable markets. Of course, the consequence of cable sales, which include the broadcast of home games, could be reduced attendance at the parks. For the television networks to increase their future contract offers significantly it is widely believed that the clubs would have to agree to expansion, league realignment, and interleague play.[16] But expansion to the envisioned 32 clubs would encroach on some of the remaining viable territories of minor league clubs.

The National Association Agreement, which controls relations between the major and minor leagues, expires at the end of 1990. The viability of the minor leagues remains an important concern. It is true that college baseball is an increasing source of supply of major league talent. In the period 1972–88, 6,067 of 8,481 (71.5 percent) amateur players selected in the June draft were college players. However, in the last All-Star balloting, 56 percent of the stars were signed as high school draftees, and in the last ten years only two Most Valuable Player awards have gone to former college players (Mike Schmidt and Roger Clemens).[17] The farm system is a superior means of developing playing skills and further erosion of its strength could have a long-term damaging effect on the quality of play in the big leagues.

1

THE RULES OF BASEBALL
AND THEIR EFFECTS

2

The Organization and Structure of the Baseball Market

No other business in America operates with quite the special privilege of baseball. A baseball team produces nothing of value beyond the entertainment derivable from watching it compete with other teams. By its nature, then, baseball is a cooperative activity. For the contests to be sporting, the teams must agree on a framework that gives structure to the competition on the playing field. Agreements are required for playing and scoring rules, the number of players on a team, equipment, division of receipts, and so on. These formalized agreements give baseball some of the attributes of a cartel.

The Sherman Act, passed by Congress in 1890, made business combinations formed with the intention of restricting trade illegal. Baseball has been exempt from the provisions of such antitrust statutes since 1922, despite a number of court cases and more than 50 bills introduced in Congress seeking to remove or weaken that exemption.[1]

Spokesmen for the industry remain steadfast in their claim that the collusive agreements are crucial for maintaining competitive balance on the playing field and financial stability of the franchises.[2] Generally, sportswriters, whose access to the teams is at the sufferance of the management, tend to pass on this view to their readers uncritically. Naturally, the Major League Baseball Players Association has argued that control over player movement has more to do with the suppression of player salaries than with competitive balance.[3] Economists have shown that a number of the industry's agreements and practices have little to do with the quality of the contests.[4]

An understanding of the agreements that structure and govern baseball is crucial to an appreciation of the economics of the sport. Broadly, these agreements either impose restrictions on the teams' relations with one another or on their relationships with the players. These agreements, which have important implications for fans and players as well, affect both the absolute level of play and the competitive balance among the teams. These subjects are discussed in the next two chapters. Moreover, the agreements have implications for fan interest (chapter 5), team revenues and costs (chapter 6), team profits (chapter 7), and player salaries (chapter 8).

Governance Structure of Baseball

The war that raged between the National and American Leagues between 1901 and 1903 was settled when the leagues agreed to respect each other's player reservation rights and to effect a division of geographical markets. A National Commission, composed of the league presidents and an independent chairman, was established to govern the agreement. The first and sole chairman was August (Garry) Herrmann, President of the Cincinnati Reds. When the Chicago White Sox players threw the 1919 World Series to the Reds, the integrity of the game was called seriously into doubt. In 1921, the leagues committed themselves to a new governance structure, which remains in effect today. The office of Commissioner of Baseball was established, and the person appointed first commissioner was Judge Kenesaw M. Landis, who had been the trial judge in the *Federal League* case. Landis ruled baseball with a firm hand.

Subsequent commissioners from Happy Chandler to Bowie Kuhn were not nearly as strong as Landis. Seeking to restore baseball's image, which had been tarnished by the 1919 scandal, the club owners had granted Landis broad powers to act against practices "detrimental to baseball." Landis exercised that power frequently, to much owner complaint. When Landis died, the owners reasserted their powers over the commissioner, adopting in 1945 a three-fourths vote rule for electing a new commissioner.[5] This rule assured that the commissioner would be a compromise candidate with limited ability to make changes independently of the owners.

Under what is called the Major League Agreement, the commissioner has broad powers to investigate and formulate remedies on matters suspected of not being in the best interests of organized baseball. The commissioner can reprimand, exclude, suspend, disenfranchise, and fine leagues, clubs, officers, employees, and players for offenses. Fines are set at a maximum of $250,000 for leagues and clubs and $25,000 for officers and employees. Fines on players are generally much smaller, although suspension without pay is costly. Commissioners have not been reluctant to use this power. For example, in 1987, Eddie Childs, the owner of the Texas Rangers, was fined $250,000 for reinstating pitcher Steve Howe, who had been suspended for repeated drug use and was ineligible to play. (On 17 January 1988 Howe was released by the Rangers after failing a drug test.)

The commissioner's office is financed by agreement with the leagues and must submit audited financial reports. While Landis served on a renewable seven year contract, the owners have recently begun to reduce the length of the commissioner's term. Peter Ueberroth, commissioner through 1 April 1989, served on a five-year contract, as does his successor, A. Bartlett Giamatti, former professor of Renaissance literature, former president of Yale University, and former president of the National League.

The commissioner is the chief executive officer of major league baseball, but owner authority is asserted through the Major League Executive Council. The council is composed of the commissioner, the league presidents, and eight club members, four from each league. Decisions are by majority rule, and, in interleague disputes, the commissioner's vote is decisive. The major responsibilities of the Executive Council are to recommend changes in rules, regulations, and agreements between players and clubs, between clubs and leagues, and in all matters concerning players' contracts and regulations.

In business matters vote may be by simple majority or by a three-fourths rule. For matters relating to the scheduling of games, playing or scoring rule changes, and industry-wide radio and television broadcast rights, vote is by simple majority of the clubs. A vote of three-quarters of the clubs in each league is required with respect to interleague championship play, any change in the present form of two-division play in the leagues, league expansion, the sale or transfer of a club, the relocation of a club, any provisions affecting the sharing of revenues among the clubs, and any change in the Major League Agreement.

All parties to the Agreement commit themselves contractually to submit all disputes and controversies among themselves to the commissioner for arbitration, to accept the commissioner's judgment as binding, and to waive any right to recourse in the courts. The Agreement further stipulates that the players' contract and all club contracts shall contain a clause submitting them to the discipline of the commissioner.

All of the clubs signed the current version of the Major League Agreement on 1 January 1975. The Agreement is to remain in effect until 1 January 1990.[6] Article IV of the Agreement creates the authority for the institution and enforcement of the rules and regulations that govern clubs. These are known as the Major League Rules.[7] The minor leagues are governed by the National Agreement of Professional Baseball Leagues, first adopted at Chicago in 1901.[8] The relationship between the major leagues and the minor leagues is structured and governed in the Professional Baseball Agreement.[9] The current five-year agreement went into effect in 1983. Article IV of this agreement provides for uniform rules and regulations between the major and the minor leagues known as the Professional Baseball Rules.[10] These five sets of agreements define the structure and governance of organized baseball.

Restrictions Among Clubs in the Product Market

Teams collude to divide up the market for games and to insure even-handedness on the playing field. Market division is accomplished by the agreements on conditions for entry into the league, franchise relocation, team territorial rights, and revenue division among the contestants. There are a variety of agreements to assure that only playing skills determine game outcomes. The leagues regulate equipment, playing surfaces, the length of spring training, the number of championship games, the procedures for make-up games, and so on. Some of these rules and procedures merit elaboration.

Entry Restrictions and Territorial Rights

Each league allocates territory, restricts entry, and controls franchise transfer. The leagues are closed organizations. Membership is restricted to the original signatories, who attempt to stringently self-regulate. Expansion or franchise relocation is at the sufferance of the teams within the league. Three-fourths of the clubs must appove an application for new membership. The owner must present satisfactory bona fides on his or her moral character and financial ability to operate on a long-term basis. If the proposed location is in the territory of a current member, the affected franchise must approve the site. Compensation to existing members for lost revenues is required.

A special rule exists for a change in the circuits between the two leagues. The circuit of one major league can be changed to include a city in the circuit of another major league provided that three-fourths of the clubs in that league approve and the following other conditions are met. The relocating team's park can be no closer than five air miles from the affected team's park. The relocating club must pay $100,000 to the club already located in the city. In the event that the city has a population of 2.4 million or more, the permission of the affected league or its constituent member clubs is not required, but the other conditions stated above must be met.

The major leagues stipulate the conditions under which an existing minor league can be reclassified to major league status and a procedure for creating an entirely new major league. For reclassification the minor league must have eight teams, acceptable bona fides as to the financial stability and moral character of the owners, have an aggregate of 15 million population in the eight cities, have stadia with a minimum seating capacity of 25,000, prove average paid attendance of 3.5 million over the previous three years, offer a balanced schedule of 154 games, adopt major league salary minimums, become part of the Major League Agreement and the Basic Agreement collective bargaining contract, and join the Players' Pension Plan or adopt a comparable plan. The requirements are similar for the creation of a new major league except for an important additional stipulation. No club in such a league can be located in a city whose population is less than the smallest city in the present major leagues. This stipulation in effect rules out the amicable creation of a new major league.

The major leagues are not as charitable with the territory of the minor leagues as the minor leagues are with major league territory. The minor leagues have agreed not to locate within five miles of a major league city without consent. The major leagues have agreed not to play exhibition games (except during spring training) or championship games in a minor league city without consent and not to locate in their territory without paying compensation. If compensation cannot be agreed upon, a seven-member arbitration panel, made up of three major-league members and three minor-league members, is to be established by the commissioner. The decision of the neutral seventh member would be decisive, but he or she is to be appointed by the commissioner, if the six other members cannot agree upon a choice.

Division of Gate Receipts and Broadcast Rights

Each league has a formula for dividing the gate receipts between the home team and the visitor. Originally, in the National League there was sufficient concern about inequality of market size to yield agreement on a near equal split of the gate. The visitor got 50 percent of the base admission price but nothing of the revenues from the more expensive seats. At that time this meant that the visitor received about 27.5 cents per admission. As teams added more expensive seating, the visitor's share declined. In 1892, visiting teams in the National League were getting 40 percent of the gate receipts. By 1929, the share had shrunk to 21 percent. By 1950, it was down to 14 percent.[11] The visitor's share has eroded even further as ticket prices have gone up. In the American League, the gate split is 80–20.

Elaborate safeguards to avoid cheating on gate receipts have been established. There is a requirement for the counting and reporting of attendance. Admissions are determined with the use of self-registering turnstiles, to which the agent of the visiting club has access. At the close of the seventh inning the counters of the turnstiles are removed and delivered to the agent of the visiting club. The agent has the right to request a count of the ticket stubs, if desired.

Historically, broadcast rights have been locally negotiated. These local broadcast rights vary greatly among the teams. Additionally, a national television contract is negotiated with the revenues evenly divided among the clubs. In 1957, these national broadcast rights were a small portion of broadcast revenues. By 1984, the value of national broadcast rights exceeded the value of local broadcast rights.[12]

Control of Playing and Scoring Rules

Rules are necessary to establish a winner. Baseball's playing rules have been often changed. In earlier times, the playing rules were constantly in flux, and there was even considerable tinkering with scoring rules. As the sport matured, these changes occurred less frequently.

Major league games are played according to the Official Baseball Rules as adopted in New York on 21 December 1949, and amended thereafter by the Playing Rules Committee. This committee consists of nine members, three of whom represent the American League, three from the National League, and three from the National Association. Any playing rule may be revised, repealed, or adopted by a two-thirds vote. By a vote of not less than seven members, an "experimental rule" may be authorized provided that three-fourths of the clubs in the league favor the rule. Not more than one of these experimental rulings can be in effect at one time.

The Official Scoring Rules Committee is a seven-member subcommittee of the Playing Rules Committee. Two of the members are appointed by the commissioner, one is appointed by the president of the National Association, one is the chairman of the Playing Rules Committee, and the other three members are the public relations directors of the National League, the American League, and the National Association. The Scoring Rules Committee determines which performance measures will be included in the official statistical records of organized baseball.

Changes in the playing and scoring rules may affect the absolute quality of play in baseball, alter competitive balance among the teams, change offense relative to defense, and affect team finances, as will be seen. The certification of the lively ball for major league play in 1920 increased hitting performance compared to pitching performance and ushered in the era of the homerun hero. It is often difficult to say whether any given rule change has enhanced the game. However, one cannot but recognize that part of the motivation for rule changes is financial. Surely, the vesting of authority for changes in playing rules in the hands of franchise owners cannot be justified on the basis of preeminent qualification. More frequently than not, these owners have been no more than sports dilettantes. The Players Association has made very modest gains in weakening owner autonomy over playing rule changes; to the extent that a rule change will affect player benefits, the clubs agree to notify the Players Association. Fans, of course, are not consulted.

Team Roster Limits

In the major leagues the player limit is 25 players from opening day until midnight, 31 August, when the limit increases to 40 players. In practice, the actual limit has been 24 players since 1984, by mutual agreement with the Players Association. Major league clubs have 40 players on their "protected" roster. For the minor leagues, in Class AAA clubs, no more than 38 players can be under contract, and this number must be reduced to 23 players on Opening Day. Twenty days before the close of the season, 25 players may be on the roster. For Class AA teams 37 players can be controlled until opening day, and then the roster must be reduced to 22 players. In Class A a maximum of 30 players can be controlled, with a reduction to 25 on the day of the season opener. Any team with a Rookie classification may carry 30 active players.

While roster size has been stable in baseball in modern times, team rosters were, as we have seen, considerably smaller in the early years of the sport. There are twice as many players on a team today as in the early 1870s, and most of this increase has gone into the pitching staff.

The justification for a player limit is that in its absence teams would be of unequal playing strengths. In the early 1900s, there was considerable variation in roster size among clubs. The first rule on player limits in 1912 ended this source of variation. In practice, however, access to playing talent is not constrained by roster size. Although there are restrictions, major leagues have access to minor league rosters, and there are mechanisms for transferring the players from team to team.

The larger roster today permits the fielding of a much wider array of specialized playing skills than the rosters of the 1870s and 1880s permitted. Such specialization has improved player performance and added to the quality of the games. By implication even larger rosters would permit greater specialization, but at increased cost. Roster limits serve to reduce team salary costs.

Player status affects the player limit rule. Rule 2 of the Major League Rules stipulates that the clubs "shall not have title to more than forty (40) player contracts, . . . including the contracts of players on the Active List, under reservation, and on optional assignment to other clubs but excluding the contracts of players on the Voluntary Retired, Disqualified, Restricted, Ineligible and Military Lists. . . ."[13]

Players who have received orders to report for military service are placed on the military list, and the player is not counted on the player list. Upon return from active duty, the player must be tendered a contract. The contract of a player on the military list cannot be assigned to a club of lower classification.

Players unable to render services to a club because of a specific injury or ailment may be placed on one of several disabled lists. In applying, the club must submit a "Standard Form of Diagnosis," completed by the club physician. No more than three of the club's players at any one time can appear on the regular disabled list, where they must remain for a minimum of twenty-one calendar days. Players may not be placed on the regular disabled list earlier than fifteen days before Opening Day. No more than two players, of which no more than one may be a pitcher, may appear on the supplemental disabled list. The minimum period of inactivity is fifteen days. Only one player at any one time may appear on the special disabled list and that player must remain inactive for 30 days. Appearance on this list occurs when clubs have reached the limits under the regular disabled and supplemental lists and have a player whose estimated disability is more than 21 but less than 60 days. Any number of players may be placed on the emergency disabled list, where they must stay for a minimum of 60 days. Players placed on this list after 1 August are required to be on the list until the end of the season.

The club physician must file another standard form of diagnosis when the player is eligible for reinstatement and then every fifteen days thereafter if the player is not reactivated. Players on the disabled list count on the 40-man protected roster but not in the 25-player limit. Disabled players cannot be assigned to the minor leagues, except for injury rehabilitation. Clearly, these rules on disability are designed to prevent clubs from adding more players to their rosters by a dishonest rendering of the players' physical condition.

Clubs may suspend players for insubordination or misconduct, fine the player, deduct the fine from his salary, and may suspend the player for up to 30 days. During suspension, the player is ineligible. A player not in physical condition may be suspended until he is in condition to play. Players on the suspended list count in the player limit.

A player who fails to report to his club within ten days of the season opener is placed on the restricted list and is not eligible to play until reinstated. A player who violates his contract or his player reservation agreement is placed on the disqualified list and is ineligible to play unless reinstated. A player or other person found guilty of misconduct or convicted of a crime involving moral turpitude may be placed on the ineligible list. Such a player may not be considered for reinstatement for at least one year. No player may have contact with a player who is on the ineligible list. A player who desires to retire from baseball may apply to the commissioner, who at his discretion may grant the status of "voluntarily retired" to the player. Players on the restricted, disqualified, voluntarily retired, or ineligible lists cannot be tendered contracts and are excluded from the player limit.

Restrictions Among Teams in the Players' Market

Turnstiles click for winners. Winning requires talent, which is expensive. The largest single expense on a team is player salaries. Owners have sought to reduce the cost of talent by imposing constraints on themselves which restrict competition for that talent. These restrictions include the reserve clause, drafting rights for new and established players, and the mechanisms of transfer and assignment of players. The owners maintain that the elaborate framework governing player transactions exists to promote competitive balance on the playing field. Economists are unconvinced of this argument, contending rather that these restrictions exist primarily because of the way they affect the division of revenues between the owners and the players.[14]

The Amateur Free Agent Draft

All players enter organized baseball through the amateur free agent draft. The Major League Rules call for a selection meeting to take place in early June (currently, 1–3 June). Clubs are free to contract with players who are U.S. residents and have not been previously signed. Such players must meet certain eligibility criteria. All major league clubs have working agreements with the minor leagues, so that all drafted players are linked to a major league club. The major league clubs, Class AAA clubs, and Class AA clubs may select only one player at the meeting. There is no limit on the selections of a Class A club. Thus, nearly all amateurs enter the game through the rookie leagues. The priority of selection is from the major league clubs down to the Class A clubs. Within each league selection rights are in reverse order of finish from last season. Once selected, the player is placed on the club's negotiation list. That club has exclusive contract rights with the player. If the amateur does not sign, he becomes eligible for reentry into the next amateur free agent draft.

Eligibility of Amateurs

While clubs are free to talk to high school and college students about opportunities, they are forbidden from inducing such students to leave school to play professional ball. During the summer, students may be invited for tryouts. During the school year, high school students may be invited for tryouts only if the principal of the school agrees. No college player tryouts are allowed during the school year. NCAA restrictions notwithstanding, organized baseball is empowered to extend, liberalize, and improve summer amateur baseball programs for college-age players.

Once their eligibility for participation in school athletics ends, high school players can be signed. High school dropouts are eligible, if they have remained out of school for a year. A foreign student is eligible if he is sixteen now but will be seventeen at the end of the playing season or 1 September, whichever date is later.

There are fewer restrictions on the signing of college players. A player may not be signed during his four-year college eligibility period, or if he is a freshman, or if he is an upperclassman and a member of the varsity baseball squad. However, this restriction does not apply if the player is age 21 and between school years, if he is in his junior year and between school years, if he has completed his eligibility for intercollegiate baseball, if he has flunked out of college, or, if he has withdrawn from college and has stayed out for at least 120 days.

Restrictions on signing college athletes in football and basketball are more stringent than those in baseball. The colleges are the minor leagues of pro football and basketball, and thus these sports have a self-interest in maintaining the integrity and vitality of college ball. Some amateurs are ready for professional competition prior to the completion of college eligibility, but to pluck these players from the college ranks would weaken the competitive level of play. In the long run, such activities would damage the supply of talent to pro football and basketball. Because school generally is not in session in the summer, high school and college baseball programs in most parts of the country do not offer sufficient training opportunities for amateur players. The major leagues are therefore required to invest in player development through the minor leagues. Thus, the restrictions in baseball on signing high school and college amateurs have less to do with nurturing amateur baseball programs than with constraining owners from inducing youngsters to leave school, an activity that might generate unfavorable public reaction.

In keeping with the increase among the general population in the length of schooling after World War II, more players now are entering baseball after completing college. Pressure for the expansion of the major leagues and the great financial opportunities for the television broadcast of home games on pay TV threaten minor league baseball. Undoubtedly, major league baseball will remain dependent on college-trained players in the future, since college players advance more rapidly than those who go directly to the minors. Whether baseball training at the college level is a good substitute for minor league training of similar duration, however, is an open question.

The Uniform Players' Contract

To play professional baseball all players must sign a version of the Uniform Players' Contract. "To preserve morale and to produce the similarity of conditions necessary to keen competition, the contracts between all clubs and their players in the Major Leagues shall be in a single form. No club shall make a contract different from the uniform contract or a contract containing a non-reserve clause . . ."[15] Further, the contracts may not contain a bonus clause for playing, pitching, or batting skills, or a bonus contingent on club standing.

The Uniform Players' Contract contains a number of restrictive covenants which makes it unique as an employment contract. In signing his first players' contract the athlete "agrees to render skilled services as a baseball player during the year . . . including the club's training season, the club's exhibition games, the club's playing season, and the World Series . . . or any other official series in which the club may participate . . ." for a certain sum. If the player does not play out the entire season, he will be entitled to a salary proportional to the number of days of his actual employment.

Each contract contains a renewal clause. The player is free to terminate his contract with the club and seek a contract with another club only if "the Club shall default in the payments to the Player" or "fail to perform . . . (its) . . . other obligation(s) . . . and fail to remedy such . . . within ten (10) days after the receipt by the Club of written notice of such default." However, the club may terminate the contract, if the player (1) fails to demonstrate good citizenship and sportsmanship, keep himself in first class physical condition, or fails to obey the club's training rules; (2) fails to exhibit sufficient skill; or, (3) fails, refuses, or neglects to render other services stipulated in the contract.

The renewal or reserve clause was a matter of bitter dispute between management and the players in 1975. Prior to 1976, players were bound indefinitely to their clubs. As a result of the Messersmith arbitration decision, players were declared eligible for free agency after playing one year without a contract. The Basic Agreement between the owners and players stipulates conditions and procedures for free agency, binding salary arbitration, and player trading, which we will discuss shortly.

Playing Incentives in the Regime of Players' Contracts

Prior to the establishment of the system of club reservation rights, players annually negotiated their contracts to play baseball. In some cases players jumped contracts in mid-season. In many instances they negotiated contracts with other clubs for the following season before their current contracts expired. The incentive to play well was the promise of a better contract in the then highly competitive players' labor market.

With the system of player reservation, the player negotiated his salary and played with the club holding those rights, but he was not free to negotiate a contract with another club. In theory clubs could retain players in the game by paying them some small amount above their next best occupational alternative. In the past, as today, those alternative opportunities yielded incomes which were a fraction of potential earnings from baseball. But, small pay differentials in baseball would result in poor playing performance, since little economic loss would arise if the player was released from the club. The salary of a journeyman major league player, or even of a rookie, is a multiple of that of a minor league player. The pay of a star player is 15 or 20 times or more than that of a rookie, although the performance differentials are not as large between journeymen and veteran players. Is this perhaps evidence of owner altruism? Are these sums necessary to keep the players in the game? Certainly not! The extreme wage differentials are an incentive to players to perform to the best of their ability, signalling to them that exceptional performance will yield exceptional rewards.

When players enter baseball their abilities are largely untested and their prospects uncertain. If they are talented and demonstrate their skills in a convincing fashion, they may be sent up to the big leagues. Playing baseball is a risky occupation; in effect, many are called, but few are chosen. Only about 100 of the 3,500 rookie players entering baseball each year will eventually make it up to the majors. Thus, hard work at peak ability yields about a 3 percent chance of winning a major league uniform.

Until 1976, the incentive to perform was regulated by the wide pay differentials between star, veteran, and novice players. Veteran free agency brought with it the practice of signing players to long-term contracts, often guaranteed whether they played or not. The owners offered these terms to their better players to deter them from switching to other clubs. Nevertheless, these contracts severed the connection between pay and performance. Since he would be paid anyway, a player's incentive to perform at his best was reduced: his production and playing time fell and his injuries became more incapacitating— much to the chagrin of the team's owner. Incentive clauses (e.g., hitting or pitching production, Most Valuable Player or All-Star status, staying off the injured reserve, etc.) were negotiated with these players in an effort to restore some linkage between pay and performance. But these incentive clauses were a bitter pill for the owners to swallow: paying a million-dollar player an extra sum to play at a level that justified the salary in the first place seems absurd.

Around 1982, the owners sought to control their appetite for free agent players. Owner collusion in the free agent market led to a significant decline in the incidence of long-term contracts, a reduction in the length of the contracts, and a sharp curtailing of performance bonuses. Management justifies this return to the pre-1976 era of annual contracts as an attempt to induce greater playing effort among veterans.

The Player Draft

On or about 20 October, the major league clubs in reverse order of standing may select minor league players for major league status. All players on the reserve lists of National Association clubs are eligible for the draft. Clubs may continue to select players until their player limit is reached. The compensation for player selection rights is $25,000, if the selecting club is a major league club, $12,000 if a Class AAA club, and $4,000 if a Class AA club.

Once the player has been upgraded to major league status he may not be freely returned to the minors. No assignment of a player contract to a National Association club may occur without the granting of waivers by other major league clubs. If all of the major league clubs waive claims on the player contract, he may be assigned, and the assigned club pays 50 percent of the original price paid for the selection. The major league club is responsible for any difference between the player's contracted major league salary and the monthly salary rate in the player's National Association Uniform Player Contract.

Major League Waivers

A waiver is a permission granted by one club for the assignment of a player contract to another club. Waivers are granted for specified periods of time during which a club has the opportunity to accept the assignment of the contract. Waiver requests are taken from club officials by league presidents who notify all of the other major league clubs of the request. Clubs have 72 hours to claim a player. If no claims are made prior to the deadline, the waiver of the requesting club is secured. If the requesting club withdraws its waiver request, waivers on that player may not be requested by the same club for thirty days. In the event that more than one club claims a player on whom waivers have been requested and the waiver is not withdrawn by the requesting club, the club with the lowest standing obtains the assignment. If claiming clubs are in different leagues, preference always is to a club in the same league. If the player was selected in the preceding player draft, consideration is 50 percent of the original selection price. The waiver price on all other player contracts is negotiable, but is at least $20,000.

Player Trades and Sales

A club is free to assign a player contract to another club and that player is contractually bound to serve the new club. Players must report for the new assignment. "The death or permanent incapacitation of a player following assignment of his contract, or his failure to report to the assignee club, shall not void the assignment, unless the agreement provides otherwise."[16] If the player is a veteran with five complete years with a single club, his consent is required for the trade. Similarly, if the player has ten years in the majors, his contract is not assignable without his consent.

For each major league club, up to 16 players (the 25th through the 40th on its roster) may be conditionally assigned under optional agreements to minor league clubs.[17] These players cannot be optionally assigned to a club of lower classification than that from which they entered the major leagues, and these optional assignments can occur only for three seasons. The major league club has the right to recall the player, which must be exercised on or before 1 October.

The Legal Status of Collusive Agreements in Baseball

The Sherman Antitrust Act of 1890 contains two interrelated clauses which, within a broad context, seem applicable to organized baseball.

Section 1. Every contract, combination in the form of a trust or otherwise, or conspiracy, in restraint of trade or commerce among the several states, or with foreign nations, is hereby declared illegal. Every person who shall make any such contract or engage in such combination or conspiracy, shall be deemed guilty of a misdemeanor. . . .

Section 2. Every person who shall monopolize, or attempt to monopolize, or combine or conspire with any other person or persons, to monopolize any part of the trade or commerce among the several states, or with foreign nations, shall be deemed guilty of a misdemeanor. . . .

There are three areas of operation of the leagues that appear to be subject to the antitrust law: the regulation of membership within the league, the methods of transacting with players, and the collective negotiation of national television broadcast rights.

The Legal Status of Leagues

The first test of the applicability of the antitrust act to professional sports came in 1922 in the case of *Federal Baseball v. National League*. The plaintiff was an owner of a team in the eight-member Federal League that attempted to compete with the established American and National Leagues from 1914 to 1915. The National League sought to destroy the Federal League by buying up some of the clubs and inducing others to abandon the league. The plaintiff sought relief under the Sherman Act, charging the National League with illegal business practices and an attempt to monopolize baseball. Justice Holmes, who delivered the court's unanimous opinion, argued that baseball was not subject to the antitrust statutes, because it was not commerce. This decision, despite a widespread belief in the legal community of its error, has been reaffirmed several times [*Gardella v. Chandler* (1949), *Toolson v. New York Yankees* (1953), and *Flood v. Kuhn* (1972)].

Other professional sports have not fared as well in the courts. Since *The Washington Professional Basketball Corporation, Inc. v. The National Basketball Association, et. al.* (1956) and *Radovich v. National Football League, et. al.* (1957), professional sports have been held subject to the antitrust statutes. In the *Washington Professional Basketball* case, an attempt was made to purchase the defunct Baltimore Bullets, but the NBA blocked the acquisition. The Court held that this action was an illegal conspiracy by the NBA under the Sherman Act. In *Radovich*, the central issue was the legal right of the league to blacklist a player. The Court ruled that the business practices of football were subject to the antitrust act. The rule established in *Federal Baseball* was held to be specifically limited to the business of organized baseball. More recently, in *Robertson v. National Basketball Association* (1970), the Court held that there is no longer any question that the Sherman Act applies to the commercial activities of professional team sports other than baseball.

The last club challenge to league governance was Charles O. Finley's suit against Bowie Kuhn in 1976. Finley had a talented team in Oakland during the early 1970s with little community support. The team had won five divisional titles, three American League pennants, and three World Championships from 1971 to 1975. In 1976, Finley began liquidating his talented players. Finley traded Reggie Jackson and Ken Holtzman to Baltimore for Don Baylor, Mike Torrez, and Paul Mitchell on 2 April 1976. On 15 June, the final day of the baseball season on which interclub player transactions are allowed, Finley agreed to sell outfielder Joe Rudi and relief pitcher Rollie Fingers to the Red Sox for $1 million each and starting pitcher Vida Blue to the Yankees for $1.5 million. On 18 June Commissioner Kuhn disapproved the sales as "inconsistent with the best interests of Baseball, the integrity of the game and the maintenance of public confidence in it."[18] On 25 June, Finley sued Kuhn for $10 million, charging that Kuhn had overextended his authority and that his actions constituted a conspiracy in restraint of trade. Kuhn filed a motion for summary judgment, which was heard and granted.

Legal Challenges to Baseball's Reserve Clause

The same 1922 Supreme Court decision that removed the baseball monopoly from the broad umbrella of the Sherman Act also supported baseball's reserve clause. Despite the widespread belief that Holmes and the other Justices had erred, the Court has consistently declined to reverse its decision.

There have been three major legal challenges to the reserve clause since 1922. In 1949, the District Court agreed to hear arguments in *Gardella v. Chandler* concerning the blacklisting of a player who earlier had jumped to the Mexican League. However, prior to trial, the suspension was lifted and Gardella and organized baseball settled out of court. In 1953, the Supreme Court heard arguments concerning the reserve clause in a similar case, *Toolson v. New York Yankees*. The Court reaffirmed *Federal Baseball* by arguing not that the reserve clause was legal but rather that as Congress had done nothing to reverse the Federal League decision, it must have intended for baseball to be exempt.

THE CURT FLOOD CASE

The last legal challenge to the reserve clause was brought by Curt Flood over his transfer to Philadelphia. Following a contract dispute in 1969, after Flood had played twelve seasons at St. Louis, Bing Devine, general manager of the Cardinals, sent Flood notice of his outright assignment to Philadelphia. While in St. Louis, Flood had established a photography shop and thus the move to Philadelphia would have been costly for him. Flood could either accept the transfer, get out of baseball, or seek injunctive relief in the courts. The last alternative was not attractive in light of past legal history and the legal fees that would be involved. The Major League Baseball Players Association ultimately agreed to underwrite the legal costs, but this meant that the case would be theirs to argue, not Flood's.

The plaintiffs argued that the reserve clause was a collusive agreement among the teams designed to suppress player salaries. Flood's salary figures beginning at $4,000 in 1956 in Cincinnati and ending at $90,000 in 1969 in St. Louis were entered in testimony. Robert Nathan, a Washington economic consultant, asserted that the reserve clause depressed player salaries but failed to establish the magnitude of the loss to players in general and to Flood in particular. The defendants offered evidence on how well baseball player salaries compared to other professional workers. The failure of Flood's attorneys to establish damages was critical, for no judgment in the plaintiff's behalf could ever be made in the absence of evidence of damage. Undoubtedly, this is the main issue on which Flood lost the case.

The second charge leveled by Flood was that the reserve clause was similar to involuntary servitude. Since most ballplayers sign their first contract at age 17 or 18, they are, in essence, being sold into slavery by their parents. The contract was for a lifetime and they had to accept complete dominion over their careers by management or quit baseball. The defendants simply claimed that the reserve clause was not involuntary servitude, since players had all other occupations besides organized baseball open to them. The plaintiffs probably lost on this issue by insisting on calling the problem a violation of the constitutional prohibition against slavery. Rather than focussing on the unreasonable control that management had exercised over the players, the plaintiffs made emotional appeals which in the end were unconvincing.

The third issue raised was that blacklisting was used as a weapon to enforce illegal labor practices. It was charged that the clubs exercised considerable control over the lives of the players in violation of the Wagner Act, a 1935 law that established the ground rules for collective bargaining. Jim Brosnan testified on interference and blacklisting by the owners concerning his off-season, nonbaseball employment in writing, personal appearances and other activities. The defendants argued that since they had substantial investments in developing players, they had a right to protect their investment by controlling off-season activities, which might lead to injuries. Furthermore, the public image of baseball was important to the economic viability of the franchises and, therefore, to protect their investments they had a right to restrict players from making statements in conflict with that image. While the plaintiffs appeared to have made a stronger argument on this issue, it was not germane to the Flood case. Flood never showed, or even claimed that he was a victim of unfair restrictions.

Next, the plaintiffs tried to establish that in-season trading was costly to the players by (1) disrupting their personal lives (the 72-hour reporting rule), (2) causing a loss of nonbaseball income through severance of connections made by the player in the home city, and (3) increasing residence costs. The defendants did not argue specifically against the points raised by the plaintiffs but were content to argue that trades were necessary to equalize playing strengths. Flood stipulated that he was not seeking damages resulting from his trade based on the loss of his income from the photography store in St. Louis. Therefore, the testimony introduced by the plaintiffs was really not relevant to the case.

Finally, the plaintiffs argued that the reserve clause had a particularly bad effect on second string or fringe ball players. Often, it was argued, a team had so much depth in a particular position that players who would be regulars on other teams are destined to sit on the bench. The reserve clause allows teams to maintain custody of these players, thereby making interteam competition more unequal. Jackie Robinson and Jim Brosnan named several players who were in this category. In response, the defendants claimed that all of the players named by Robinson and Brosnan had gotten their chance. The plaintiffs won on this issue but missed the opportunity to pursue the point forcefully. None of the fringe players testified, nor was the salary history of such players introduced into evidence and compared with that of players who had been regulars. Furthermore, the issue was not relevant to the Flood case, since Flood was a regular at St. Louis (although at Cincinnati he was platooned and probably would have ended up a second stringer behind Vada Pinson had he not been traded).

Since Flood never proved damages, his chances of winning were marginal from the beginning. Flood was represented by Arthur Goldberg, a distinguished jurist. Most of the trial was handled by Jay Topkis, who knew a great deal about the antitrust aspects of baseball. But Goldberg was inept in his opening and closing arguments; moreover, little evidence was introduced and numerous issues not germane to the Flood case were presented. The course of attack by the plaintiffs actually would have served Jim Brosnan better had he brought the suit. In return for shouldering the trial costs, Flood allowed the Players Association to wage a broadened attack on the reserve clause rather then pursue personal damages for Flood. In adopting such a broad stratagem with little evidence to support the broadened charges, the outcome was inevitable. Had Flood's attorneys argued Flood's case, the outcome might have been different. Perhaps Bill Veeck was right when he said the players made a mistake in pinning their case on Flood, a high salaried, controversial star. He suggested the players should have chosen as their standard bearer a Class AAA player with ten years in the ranks and not a dime in the pension fund.

The majority opinion in the five to three decision handed down by the Supreme Court in *Flood v. Kuhn* in 1972 was written by Justice Blackmun. He found baseball to be a business and the exemption of the reserve clause from the antitrust law an aberration. However, he also found it was an aberration that had lasted five decades and was entitled to the benefit of *stare decisis,* the legal principle which favors the preservation of previous decisions. Chief Justice Burger recognized the error of the exemption, but thought that the affairs of too many people rested on that error to justify reversal. In dissenting, Justice Douglas, with Justice Brennan concurring, found that the owners were guilty of a proclivity for predatory practices and that the equities of the law rested with the victims of the reserve clause.

The Legal Status of League Broadcast Rights

In 1983, the major leagues negotiated a six-year contract with ABC-TV and NBC-TV for television broadcast rights worth $1.2 billion to the teams. In 1987, the teams received a total of $190 million for the television rights from the two networks and $6.5 million from CBS-Radio for the radio rights. Nielsen ratings for the regular season games are in the range of 6.3–6.4, which represents 20 to 21 percent of the households watching television. Play-off and World Series ratings are much higher.[19]

The clubs negotiate collectively with the television networks. Thus, leagues of baseball teams face a tight oligopoly of television networks to divide up the broadcast market for baseball games. Clearly, this type of arrangement has anticompetitive implications, which has not escaped the attention of the U.S. Justice Department. As early as 1946, the major league rule that prohibits a club from broadcasting into another's home territory was seen to raise antitrust issues. In 1950, the rule was modified to allow blackouts only in minor league territories or where the major league home team was broadcasting an away game back to its home territory. In 1952, Liberty Broadcasting System sued baseball for attempting to monopolize the broadcasting of games.[20] After the Justice Department successfully attacked certain collusive broadcast practices,

Congress in 1961 passed the Sports Television Act (amended in 1966), which extends the antitrust exemption to the broadcasting of all professional team sports. Thus, the collusive negotiation of broadcast rights now is perfectly legal.

Players' Association Attempts to Restrict League Autonomy

Early Players' Associations in Baseball

There were a number of early, unsuccessful attempts by players to speak to owners with a collective voice. The baseball business was very risky in the early years of the sport. Owners of course sought policies which would hold down costs, particularly as regards player salaries, which were the largest cost of a team. For example, between 1876 and 1879, player salaries represented 64.4 percent of the team costs of the Boston Red Sox.[21] Owners sought a rule which would inhibit them from competing among themselves for playing talent in ways that would escalate player salary costs. In Buffalo, on 29 September 1879, they agreed to a reserve of five players on each squad, who could not be approached by other owners. In 1883, the reserve roster was extended to eleven and then four years later to fourteen players. In 1887, the reserve clause was written expressly into the player's contract.

The reserve rule had its intended effect. Player salary costs on the Boston Nationals fell by 20 percent between 1878 and 1880.[22] Baseball became profitable during the 1880s as attendance rose and costs were controlled. Yet further measures to cut salary costs were sought. At Saratoga, in 1885, the Limit Agreement was struck under which the owners agreed not to pay a player more than $2,000 (about $24,000 at today's prices) for the season.

The players revolted. On 22 October 1885, nine players on the Giants formed the Brotherhood of Professional Base Ball Players, with John Montgomery Ward as their president. By 1886, unionism spread to other teams. Ward's "monumental achievement," however, was getting the owners to incorporate the reserve clause specifically into the players' contracts, having come to accept the owners' view that the reserve clause was necessary to the financial stability of baseball.

The owners, however, were still not satisfied that they had done enough to control salary costs. In 1888, they advanced the Brush Classification Plan, under which players were to be classified according to skill and paid by skill category (much like union pay scales). The players were less than enthusiastic about the idea. Ward negotiated with Al Spalding, who represented the National League, to get the plan rescinded, got nowhere, and the threat of a players' strike emerged.

Ward had alternatives, however, since there was financing available for the start of a new league to compete with the National League. With this financing, Ward created the Players League in November of 1889.

The Players League was organized as a cooperative. Revenues were pooled and shared. Players were on three-year contracts and could be dismissed only by the majority vote of the team.[23] The National League strategy was to get players to jump contracts and schedule games for head-to-head competition with the Players League. Accordingly, both leagues bled financially during 1890, and ultimately the Players League bled to death. The player reservation system continued.

Bitterness continued among the players over the abuses that arose from the reserve clause. Players were traded and sold at will and fined for a myriad of offenses. In June 1900, the Protective Association of Professional Baseball Players was formed. This association was ineffective, but fortunately for the players, the American League–National League "war" broke out. Interleague competition greatly reduced the effects of the player reservation system. Players now had alternatives and salaries soared. Lee Allen estimated that some 111 players on American League teams were former reserved players from the National League.[24] Meanwhile, interest in player unionism faded.

The interleague bidding for playing talent had escalated salaries to such a degree that after the Major League Agreement was signed *The Sporting News* called for an across-the-board one-third reduction in salaries.[25] Players watched their gains erode, and as the erosion continued some players became contract holdouts. The most famous holdout was Ty Cobb in 1912. As a five-time batting champion Cobb demanded $15,000 (about $165,000 in 1987 prices), as opposed to the $9,000 he had been receiving since 1909. Cobb did not show up on Opening Day and was suspended. Eventually, Cobb signed for $11,332.55, paid a $50 fine, and suffered a reprimand.[26]

Discontent of the sort that led to Cobb's actions seethed among the players. The third players' union, the Base Ball Players' Fraternity, was formed in 1912. The Fraternity attracted wide player support, but never formulated a plan of action. The formation of the Federal League, which competed for fans and players with the American and National Leagues during 1914 and 1915, made the union unnecessary. Some 221 players jumped contracts to the Federal League.[27] Player salaries nearly doubled. But the Federal League collapsed soon thereafter (bringing about the famous antitrust suit against baseball), and the Fraternity faded away by 1918.

League peace and the player reservation system brought prosperity to baseball after World War I. It has been estimated that gross revenues after World War II were eighty times those of 1883, but player salaries were only seven times as great. While player costs were two-thirds of a club's budget in 1876, by 1946 they were less than a fourth.[28] It was in 1946 that Robert Murphy, a Harvard-trained lawyer, founded the American Baseball Guild to challenge the reserve clause and to promote income security for players after their playing careers.

Murphy presented the Pittsburgh Pirates with a set of demands on 7 June 1946. He claimed to represent the majority of players on six teams.[29] The owners refused to recognize the Guild as a collective bargaining agent. The Guild petitioned the Labor Relations Board of Pennsylvania for certification. An election was held in Pittsburgh, and the Guild lost 15 to 3.[30] Murphy's inept efforts actually brought benefits to the players, but for reasons having not much to do with player unionism. The 1946 season was a strain on the owners, as the winds of change were blowing from at least two directions. The Mexican League was succeeding in getting some players to jump contracts, and, at home, there was growing agitation to end the color ban in baseball. For the owners, disposing of the union issue was prudent. After Murphy's fiasco, they instituted a pension plan, modified the waiver rule, and granted a weekly expense allowance during spring training, which to this day is known as "Murphy money." However, the reserve clause remained inviolate.

The Major League Baseball Players Association

In 1954, the players voted to form the Major League Baseball Players Association. Bob Feller was the first president. Feller saw no future for collective bargaining in baseball. He thought that the players were too individualistic and that essentially they were hostile to the idea of unionism. As a result, until 1966, the Players Association was content to negotiate over Murphy money, moving expenses, minimum salaries, and clubhouse conditions. Then, Marvin Miller took office.

Miller had a long association with the United Steelworkers, with its tradition of negotiated pay scales. He shrewdly eschewed this traditional approach and focused on collective concerns among the players. Their major concerns were the inadequacy of the pension program, the minimum starting salary for rookie players, and the lack of a formal grievance procedure for handling player-management disputes.

In the first Basic Agreement of 1967, Miller succeeded in raising the minimum salary from $7,000 to $10,000, the maximum salary cut in the event of a failure to reach an agreement on salary terms was reduced from 25 to 20 percent, spring training meal allowances increased from $8 to $12 a day, and Murphy money was increased from $25 to

$40 a week. The owner contribution to the pension fund was raised from $2.5 to $4.1 million per year.[31] Finally, a formal grievance procedure was instituted, but the baseball commissioner had the final word.

The major achievement in the 1969 Basic Agreement was an increase in the owner contribution to the pension fund to $5.45 million. A player with five years in the ranks could retire at age 50 on $300 a month.[32] Additional features of the agreement were increases in severance pay, salary minimums, player play-off shares and Murphy money.

Of greater long-term importance were the agreements to changes in the grievance procedure and in the clubs' posture toward the Players Association as a recognized collective bargaining agent. The clubs agreed to a grievance procedure that would automatically send to the commissioner all matters relating to the integrity of the game with the commissioner's decision final and nonappealable, but submit for arbitration all disputes over the Basic Agreement to a three-man panel— one representing the players, one the owners, and one appointed by the other two arbitrators. Furthermore, the owners agreed that any changes in the agreement had to be negotiated, that the Players Association was recognized as the players' principal bargaining agent, and that players could be professionally represented in their contract negotiations with the clubs. In August 1969, the Players Association proposed formal negotiation of the reserve clause and called for free agent status for players after three years, a reduction in the number of reserved players, salary arbitration, and a prohibition against trades unless approved by the players in question. These proposals were rejected out of hand. In the 1970–72 Basic Agreement, however, the clubs accepted the reserve clause as a mandatory collective bargaining subject.

The owners took a hard line on the pension fund and medical benefits in the 1972 negotiations. In response, the players nearly unanimously voted for a spring strike, which began on 1 April 1972. The players wanted the contribution to the pension fund raised $1.56 million; the owners refused. In the end 86 games went unplayed, the owners raised the contributions, and the players absorbed a salary loss.

Final-Offer Salary Arbitration

The 1973–75 Basic Agreement contained a grievance procedure, but not a great deal of progress had been made in player-club dispute resolution. Miller got the contribution to the players' pension fund increased modestly and the salary minimum raised to $16,000 for the 1975 season. Owners accepted a restriction of not unilaterally trading veterans with ten years of experience, the last five of which were with the same club. They also agreed not to unilaterally assign veterans with five or more years in the majors to the minor leagues.

A sigh of relief was heard from the owners when the decision in *Flood vs. Kuhn* was handed down. The victory offered assurance that the reserve clause was to be enshrined as a feature of the labor market for ballplayers. The owners, in a gesture of magnanimity, decided that the players should have an opportunity to have salary grievances heard by a neutral party. Barely a month after the 1973–75 Basic Agreement went into effect, the owners proposed salary arbitration. An agreement was reached toward the end of February 1973, and the procedure was accepted for the 1974 season.

Until 1987, the agreement provided that any club or player with between two and six years of service in the major leagues who had not reached a salary agreement could submit the dispute to arbitration. The period for eligible players to submit salary disputes to arbitration currently is 5 to 15 January. The arbitrator is constrained to choosing between the player's demand and the owner's offer. The Players Association and the Player Relations Committee jointly selects the professional arbitrators. The criteria employed by the arbitrator in reaching a decision are the player's contribution to the club in the prior season, the length and consistency of his performance, the history of his past salary, comparative baseball player salaries (except for players with five or more years of service who are now restricted to comparisons with players' contracts whose service does not exceed one year beyond that player's annual service group), the existence of any injuries, and the recent standing and attendance of the club. The arbitrator may not take into consideration the financial position of the player or the club, press comments or testimonials, previous player or club offers, or the salaries in other sports or occupations. The agreement requires that the clubs provide the Players Association with the previous season salaries for all players on the roster as of 31 August.[33] The availability of player salary data classified by length of service and player performance gives the arbitrator the financial criteria upon which to evaluate the competing claims.

The owners insisted on final offer arbitration because they did not trust arbitrators. To an arbitrator in dispute resolution fairness generally means splitting the difference. Players could make exorbitant salary demands and "evenhandedness" would then bankrupt the clubs. By forcing the arbitrator to choose between the club's offer and the player's demand, the owners bet that the players would be more reasonable. In 1974, out of 500 eligible players, 54 filed for arbitration.

Prior to a hearing, 25 settled with their clubs. Of the twenty-eight cases resolved, the owners won 15 and the players won thirteen.[34] On average, about 100 players file for arbitration each year. Most of these players settle with their clubs prior to arbitration. The availability of an arbitration alternative puts upward pressure on salaries. Since the probability of winning through arbitration is about one-half, owners are willing to grant salary increases at least up to the expected salary increase of the player through arbitration.

In 1987, the minimum service requirement was raised to three years by mutual agreement with the Players Association. The concession by the players is a significant one. In 1986, those players with two years of service on average won salaries of $309,604. Their 1985 salaries averaged $213,189. In 1987, the salary of two-year veterans dropped by 38 percent to $191,703.[35]

The Seitz Decision and Free Agency

Jim "Catfish" Hunter became baseball's first free agent through arbitration, but the decision had no implications for the reserve clause. Hunter's 1974 contract with Oakland was for $50,000 in cash and $50,000 in a tax-free annuity. Oakland owner Charles Finley reneged on the agreement, paying Hunter all cash. Hunter filed a grievance, charging that Finley's action constituted a contract default. On the basis of paragraph 7(a) of the Uniform Players' Contract, Hunter had the right to terminate the agreement and play for whomever he pleased. In December 1974 arbitrator Peter Seitz ruled in Hunter's favor. Subsequently, Hunter signed with the Yankees for $2.5 million over five years.

In 1975, Andy Messersmith demanded and failed to get a no-trade guarantee with the Dodgers. He played the season without a signed contract and, at the end of the season, declared he was a free agent. For their part, of course, the Dodgers claimed he was still bound to the team under the conditions of the reserve clause. The Players Association filed a grievance on behalf of Messersmith and Dave McNally of Montreal, whose circumstances were similar to Messersmith's claiming that the interpretation of the period of renewal in paragraph 10(a) of the Uniform Players' Contract was a legitimate contract dispute. The pitchers interpreted the clause as a one-year contract with a one-year club option. The clubs interpreted the clause as a perpetual renewal. On 23 December 1975, arbitrator Peter Seitz ruled in favor of Messersmith and McNally. The decision had the effect of granting free agency to any player who played one year without signing a contract.[36] The owners appealed to the courts but lost.[37]

Player Reservation under the Basic Agreement

The ruling alarmed the owners, who predicted that hundreds of players would take advantage of their new rights and that a bidding war of monumental proportions would ensue. In fact, a total of 35 players went unsigned.[38] The owners sought out Marvin Miller with much trepidation. Miller might have taken the position that the Messersmith rule would govern all future player-club contracts, but in fact the Players Association backed off this view and negotiated a six-year rule for free agency.

Under Article XVIII of the 1976 and the 1980 Basic Agreements, the clubs had the right to reserve up to 40 player contracts. Free agency was granted to players after six or more years of major league service. All players who became free agents during this period were subject to a free agent reentry draft. The clubs selected the veteran free agents in inverse order of finish. On their side, the free agents were restricted as to the number of clubs with which they could negotiate. Under the "Memorandum of Settlement" (the 1984 collective bargaining agreement) between the clubs and the Players Association, beginning with the 1985 season players with six years of service were free to negotiate with any team they chose.

The Players' Strike of 1981

Between 1976 and 1979, 150 players became free agents.[39] Since the option of free agency was available, owners sought to keep the players off the market by granting them long-term contracts at considerably increased salaries. Average player salaries rose from $51,500 in 1976 to $113,558 in 1979.[40] The stars negotiated salaries that were judged astronomical at the time. Reggie Jackson signed a five-year $2.66 million contract with the Yankees in 1976. Pete Rose signed a four-year $3.2 million contract with Philadelphia in 1978. In 1979, Nolan Ryan signed for $3.5 million for three years with Houston. The owners complained bitterly, but paid.

Compensation for players lost through free agency was the key to ending this salary escalation. The owners sought to change the formula in the Basic Agreement. They demanded that a professional player and an amateur draft choice be the compensation for a lost free agent. Under their proposal, fifteen to eighteen players on the roster would be protected and any one of the rest might be selected as compensation. The players would have none of this. They held out for no change in the compensation formula and demanded a reduction to four years for free agency status.

To demonstrate their commitment to the existing compensation arrangement of free agency the players struck for a week during the 1980 exhibition season. A strike deadline of 22 May 1980 was set, if the owners persisted. A strike was avoided when both sides decided to postpone the issue for a year. A joint management–Players Association study committee was established to look at the compensation formula. In the event that no compromise could be reached, it was agreed that the owners would implement their proposal.

There was no progress. The owners announced their intention to implement their plan, and the players then struck on 12 June 1981. The owners, having in the meantime purchased strike insurance, had no incentive to settle the dispute with the players and thought that the financial strain would soon bring the players to their senses. On 8 August, the day the owners' insurance ran out, the strike was settled in the players' favor. Some 714 games had been canceled. The owners remained bitter about not being able to raise the compensation terms to a level that would restrain them from bidding for free agents. This failure undoubtedly led them subsequently to collude in the market for free agents.

Club Collusion on Free Agents

Testifying before Congress in 1982, Marvin Miller expressed deep concern that the clubs were colluding to prevent the operation of a free market for free agents. The owners had agreed in Article XVIII (H) of the Basic Agreement that "Players shall not act in concert with other Players and Clubs shall not act in concert with other Clubs."

Some 62 players filed for free agency in 1985, among them Rod Carew, Bobby Grich, Don Sutton, Carlton Fisk, Joe and Phil Niekro, Tommy John, Al Oliver and Kirk Gibson. No club pursued them unless the players' own clubs expressly relinquished interest in them. Kirk Gibson led Detroit to the 1984 World Championship and finished the 1984 season with 29 home runs, 30 stolen bases, 97 RBIs (Runs Batted In), and a .287 batting average. He was the prize among the 1985 crop. No club made him an offer. Gibson re-signed with Detroit.

On 3 February 1986, the Players Association filed a grievance that charged the clubs with colluding to boycott the free agents with the intent of destroying free agency. Thomas T. Roberts, who had arbitrated salary disputes in baseball since 1974, was selected to hear the case. The owners fired him when he ruled in another matter that the clubs could not unilaterally insert a drug-testing requirement into the players' contract. He was reinstated by another arbitrator, who ruled the dismissal illegal. On 21 September 1987, Roberts ruled that the clubs had colluded to suppress free agency and that this clearly violated Article XVIII (H) of the Basic Agreement.

Roberts concluded that the free agency market in 1985–86 was observably different in character than the market in 1984. Then, sixteen out of twenty-six clubs signed free agents. In the 1985–86 reentry draft twenty-nine free agents re-signed with their former clubs. Only one of the twenty-nine (Carlton Fisk) received a bona fide offer from a team other than his former team. "The clubs showed no interest in the available free agents at any price until such time as their former club declared the player no longer fit into their plans." [41]

Roberts pointed to a series of management meetings. In Itasca, Illinois, on 27 September 1985, the commissioner chaired a meeting on a report about the cost of the player development system. On 22 October 1985, Lee MacPhail, the retiring director of the Player Relations Committee, circulated a memorandum condemning long-term contracts for ballplayers. MacPhail called for self-discipline in player acquisition and for financial prudence. Commissioner Ueberroth expressed support for the MacPhail memorandum, and an informal poll of the owners revealed an intent to avoid long-term contracts. At the General Managers' Meeting at Tarpon Springs, Florida on 6 November 1985, Ueberroth reportedly told the owners that "it is not smart to sign long-term contracts." At the annual major league meeting in San Diego on 11 December 1985, the list of free agents was distributed and the owners agreed to abstain from the free agency market during the winter until an available free agent was released by his former club. Such action constituted a violation of Article XVIII (H) of the Basic Agreement. [42]

Roberts encouraged the owners and the players to negotiate remedies, but common ground between them was not found. Several remedies were suggested, including a so-called "free-look" or "second-look" free agency for the 1985 free agents, the award of damages to the free agents, and the award of damages to all veteran players. On 21 December 1987, Roberts ordered that seven of the 1985 free agents be given a chance as free agents once again. Of the 62 players who were free agents then, only 14 were under contract with the clubs. Of these players, 7 were ruled ineligible for the benefit, because they had become free agents after the 1985 season. The players who were offered the opportunity had until 1 March 1988 to negotiate with a new team without relinquishing their existing contracts. Only Kirk Gibson changed teams. Gibson turned in his $1.3 million contract at Detroit for a three-year $4.5 million contract with the Dodgers, a relatively small pay differential of 15 percent resulting from club collusion.

Carlton Fisk, Donnie Moore, Butch Wynegar, Joe Niekro, Juan Beni-
quez, and Tom Brookens all decided to remain with their clubs.

Further grievances were filed by the Players Association on behalf
of the 1986 and the 1987 free agents. Among this crop of free agents
were the so-called Elite Eight—Andre Dawson, Tim Raines, Lance
Parrish, Bob Horner, Ron Guidry, Rich Gedman, Bob Boone, and
Doyle Alexander. None of these players received offers from other
teams. On 1 May 1987, Raines, who had won the National League batting title and hit .334 in 1986 with 70 stolen bases, re-signed with the
Expos. Raines sat out spring training, got off the bus on 2 May at Shea
Stadium, walked to the plate and tripled on the first swing of the bat.
Andre Dawson refused to return to Montreal. He offered Cubs' president Dallas Green a signed, blank contract to play for him. Green filled
in a $500,000 base salary, with an additional $150,000 if Dawson stayed
off the disabled list before the All-Star Game, and $50,000 if he made
the All-Star team.[43] Dawson had a league-leading season at Chicago,
while working for half his former salary. Dawson hit .287, with 49
home runs and 137 RBIs. His home runs, RBIs, and game-winning
RBIs led the league. He was voted the Most Valuable Player in the
National League. Still, the Cubs finished 18.5 games behind St. Louis,
which, according to *The Sporting News*, "again shows that the flesh
market is no sure cure for franchises working on a 42-year rebuilding
plan."[44] Bob Horner signed with Yakult of the Japan Central League for
$2.25 million over three years, and was known as "Mr. Hom-ah."[45]

Roberts scheduled hearings for the last of January 1988 to acquire
information to arbitrate the monetary damages to the whole group of
1985 free agents. The Players Association requested a formal ban on
further collusive practices in the free agent market, the voiding of the
contracts of all 1985 players still under contract with the clubs, player-
specific damages for the free agents, player-specific damages for 98
players who filed for salary arbitration in 1985, general damages to all
other players who signed contracts in 1985, and general and punitive
damages against the clubs. The Players Association further commissioned a study of the loss of salaries in 1986 and 1987 due to owner
collusion in the free agent market. The consultants concluded that collusion had lowered aggregate player salaries between $20 and $30 million in 1986 and between $50 and $60 million in 1987.[46]

In August 1988 arbitrator George Nicolau ruled in favor of the
seventy-nine players who were free agents in 1986. It is unlikely that
Roberts or Nicolau will award financial damages on a scale envisioned
by the players. By their calculations damages to the players from collusion on free agents in 1985–86 was about $75 million.[47] A punitive fine

against the owners is possible. But the imposition of a $10 million fine, which would be extraordinary, would amount only to $385,000 per club, which is what has been saved in a one-year salary increase from one free agent.

There is no prospect of solution to the dispute over the organization of the market for player services until the current labor-management agreement expires on 31 December 1989. Some sportswriters saw in the signing of Jack Clark by the Yankees a signal that club collusion over free agents had ended. But Clark only received a 15 percent pay increase from New York, and Jack Morris, Dave Righetti, Dave Smith, Mike Witt, and Gary Gaetti re-signed with their clubs. Because of the labor exemption, under the antitrust law the players have no opportunity to seek a court remedy. A way around the labor exemption is to dissolve the Players Association and form 26 separate club players' associations. But dissolution of the Players Association is unlikely. Rather, the dispute is so contentious that another players' strike or an owners lockout could well occur after the expiration of the current collective bargaining contract.

Both the players' union and the owners have adopted strategies consistent with a strike or lockout scenario. Beginning in 1987 the union began to earmark a large portion of player licensing revenues into a strike fund. It is expected that the union will have $35 to $50 million in the strike fund by Opening Day of the 1990 season. For the players, the optimal time for a strike is toward the end of the 1990 season. By August the players have received 80 percent of their seasonal income, while the owners have received only about 20 percent.

The owners have structured a national television contract that heavily weights broadcast revenues from league play-offs and the World Series. To deny the players income during a labor dispute and to make it more likely that such a dispute would occur earlier in the season rather than later, the owners have introduced so-called "lockout clauses" into a number of the players' contracts. At the 7 December 1988 winter meeting in Atlanta, the owners were encouraged to introduce these clauses into the players' contracts as a means of shifting the financial burden of the dispute on the players and as a means of dividing the strength of the players' union.

Two types of lockout clauses have appeared in players' contracts: the so-called "defensive" language (the "Gibson" clause) and the so-called "neutral" language (the "Ripken" clause). It appears that under the defensive language of the clause the only way that the affected players will not be paid is if the lockout is a response to a players' strike. If the owners lock out the players in anticipation of a strike, such players would be paid during the lockout period. The players obviously prefer this lockout language. Under the "neutral" language the question of player pay is left to arbitration. Since player pay is suspended during a lockout, the players dislike this language. Moreover, some players have agreed to a lockout clause that treats a lockout like a strike. Thus, players like Willie Randolph, Jim Clancy, Bret Saberhagen, Lee Smith, Dave Smith, Mike Boddicker, and others would receive no income during a lockout. Clearly, these strategies promote the possibility of a disruption of the 1990 baseball season.

3

League Operating Rules and the Level of Team Performance

The league operating rules have been forged with the intent of improving the quality of play. In this chapter I discuss the effect of these rules on the *absolute* quality of play. By absolute quality of play, I mean the level of player and team performance narrowly measured with performance statistics. Absolute quality of play is an ephemeral concept. It is difficult to measure in team sports. Few fans would dispute that the absolute quality of play is higher in the major leagues than in the minor leagues or in amateur baseball. The contests may be as close and exciting and the game statistics equivalent, but there are dimensions of expertise, precision, and aesthetics in major league play not found in the other circuits in baseball. However, trends in the absolute quality of play are difficult to interpret, because in baseball, as in all team sports, there are both offensive and defensive components of the game. For example, a periodic or sustained rise or fall in the batting average is not an independent measure of the evolution of hitting ability, partly because it depends on changes in the quality of pitching and in the playing rules. While difficult to measure, the concept is clear. The absolute quality of a team is related directly to the absolute quality of the players on the team. From a theoretical perspective, the effect of league operating rules on the absolute level of performance can be evaluated.

Expected Effects of League Operating Rules on the Absolute Quality of Play

Several developments in baseball have a potentially significant impact on the absolute quality of play. First, baseball players have been able to benefit from the experience of previous generations of athletes and baseball players, thereby improving current performance. Second, several league operating rules can be expected to affect performance. Among these are investment in player training, the number of teams in baseball, the player roster limit, and the playing rules. Several other rules discussed in chapter 2 have no impact on the absolute quality of play but do affect *relative* team playing strengths. The effect of these rules on the balance of competition on the playing field will be discussed in chapter 4.

The Supply of Athletic Quality

There is little doubt that the performance of today's athletes is superior to that of past athletes. There are at least three reasons for this. First, the athletes of today are superior physically. In part, this is due to increases in size, strength, and agility induced by changes in diet over the last 50 years or so, but there have also been striking advances in the conditioning methods advocated by sports medicine and kinesiology. A second factor is the cumulative experience of previous generations of athletes. The longer a sport exists, the more is learned about how to compete successfully in it. Holding physical characteristics, training regimes, equipment, etc., constant, we can observe an increase in athletic performance over time that can be explained simply as a consequence of learning. The strategy of competing is easily observed, quickly learned and refined. To a substantial degree, athletes run faster and jump and throw farther today because they are heirs to the experi-

Table 3.1   Growth in Athletic Performance as Measured in the Olympics

Event	Initial Year	Record	Record in 1984	Percentage Change	
				Total	Average
Running Events					
100 Meters	1896	12.0	10.0	−16.7	−0.88
200 Meters	1900	22.2	19.8	−10.8	−0.60
400 Meters	1896	54.2	44.3	−18.2	−0.96
800 Meters	1896	2:11.0	1:43.0	−19.8	−1.04
1,500 Meters	1896	4:33.2	3:32.5	−22.2	−1.17
5,000 Meters	1912	14:36.6	13:05.6	−10.5	−0.70
10,000 Meters	1912	31:20.8	27:47.5	−11.3	−0.75
Marathon	1896	2h58:50.0	2h09:21.0	−27.6	−1.45
Jumping Events					
High Jump	1896	5′11¼″	7′8½″	29.8	1.57
Broad Jump	1896	20′9¾″	28′0¼″	34.6	1.82
Throwing Events					
Shot Put	1896	36′9¾″	69′9″	89.5	4.71
Discus	1896	95′7½″	218′6″	128.5	6.76
Javelin	1908	178′7½″	284′8″	59.4	3.71
Hammer	1900	167′4″	256′2″	53.1	2.95

Source: The World Almanac and Book of Facts 1986 (New York: Newspaper Enterprise Association, Inc., 1985), 795–98.

ence of earlier generations of competitors. A third factor that accounts for today's superior athletic performance is improvements in equipment. For example, advancement in glove design has resulted in more effective fielding, while batting helmets and catchers' gear have reduced injuries.

As evidence that athletes are superior today, consider the magnitude of change in some of the men's track and field events in the Olympic games from 1896 to 1984, as set forth in table 3.1. Every event shows a distinct improvement over the score from the initial year.

While the Olympics is the premier athletic event, the progress of athletes could be documented through consideration of the records of any set of athletic events. Running times, distances jumped or thrown are continuously changing in AAU, NCAA, collegiate, and high school track, field, and other athletic events. Professional team sports have been beneficiaries of this athletic progress. The players that are recruited by the teams are stronger, more agile, faster, and better conditioned than they were in the past. As no small example of this fact, recall that a number of players recruited into the National Football League have been Olympic Gold Medal winners. Thus, the increase in general athletic ability leads one to believe that the supply of quality athletes has increased in professional team sports, including baseball.

Performance Profiles in Baseball

The performance profile is a way of describing the absolute quality of players. It can be drawn for both individual players and for teams. For example, we know that veteran players are superior to novice players for at least two reasons. First, the skills of veteran players have been tested by competition. Many first-year players will be returned to the minor leagues, and thus the fact that a veteran has survived competition for his job by new entrants into the game implies that he is a better player. Second, competitive play is learned. No matter how talented the player, experience in the game improves performance. Presumably, the gains from experience are largest early in the player's career. On the other hand, the physical condition and the reflexes of players diminish with age.

In many occupations job productivity rises in the beginning years, levels off, and then declines. Earnings may follow a similar pattern when workers are classified by years of experience. Such a path in productivity occurs because of the pattern of firm and worker investment in job training and because of "learning by doing."[1]

Both players and teams make training investments, which improve performance. During spring training and in the regular season the coaching staff works with the players to correct mistakes and improve technique. Pitchers expand their portfolios of pitches, learn the weaknesses of hitters that they will face, and so on. Hitters are offered advice on their stance, position in the batter's box, the characteristics of their swing, and so on. Additionally, successful players may pass on tips to other players which improve their performance. The players invest their time in practicing technique. Players sacrifice alternative income and leisure by engaging in a physical conditioning regime during the off-season and in practicing.

The evolution of the batting average of a representative major league player is shown in figure 3.1. The hitting performance profile is based on the career hitting of the regular starting players on the rosters of National League teams in 1986. There were 96 players with a total of 564 years of playing experience. The representative major leaguer completed his first season as a regular player with a batting average of .267. The batting average rises at a diminishing rate for several seasons and reaches a peak between the sixth and seventh year. Thereafter, the batting average declines.[2] Performance profiles of all the major league outfielders on teams in 1971 reveal a similar pattern.[3] Performance follows a similar pattern in other dimensions of baseball such as pitching and fielding.

The quality of play on a team of veterans (say an average of 8 or 9 years of playing experience) is likely to be higher than on a team of journeymen players (about an average of 5 years of experience). This is

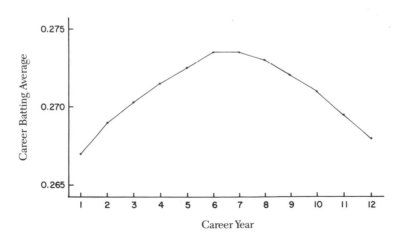

Figure 3.1 Career Batting Profile of an Average Regular Starting National League Player, 1986 Season

especially true if the veterans have been playing together for some time. Part of the reason that the 1986 New York Mets were so successful was that they were a veteran team. The 13 regular players on the roster averaged nine years of experience. On the other hand, the players on the last place Pittsburgh Pirates averaged 5 years of experience. By comparison with other teams in the league, individual performance on the Pirates was good, but the inexperienced team was not able to translate performance into victories. Pittsburgh had a team batting average of .250, a team ERA (Earned Run Average) of 3.90, and a win record of .395. Second place Philadelphia had a team batting average of .253, a team ERA of 3.85, and a win record of .534.

Investments in Training Players

Players enter the major leagues from the farm teams. The quality of the players promoted depends partly on the investments the major leagues make in the farm teams. In general, these investments have been falling. In 1952, there were 364 minor league teams in organized baseball from Class AAA to Class D. Of these teams, 195 were owned or controlled by the majors. There were 70 teams in Class A and above, of which 57 were owned or controlled by major league teams.[4] In 1987, there were 145 minor league teams from Class AAA to rookie Class A. The majors owned only 4 teams in Class AA and Class AAA leagues.[5] This reduction in the minor leagues means that only about one-third as many ballplayers can be trained today as could be trained three decades ago. Furthermore, in 1952 there were 16 major league teams drawing from a stock of about 9,000 minor league players. Since players average about seven years in the majors, the implied replacement rate was about 60–75 players per year. With the expansion to 26 teams, the annual replacement rate is now about 90–120 players. However, the stock from which the majors may now draw talent has shrunk to about 3,500 players. Of these minor league players only about 600 are on Class AAA teams, the normal source of supply of trained playing talent. Thus, with an increased demand for talent and a reduced supply, the absolute quality of the playing talent has suffered. Simply put, there is insufficient seasoning of playing talent in the minor leagues before promotion to the major league circuit.

In light of the reduction in the number of teams in the minor leagues it is possible that the absolute quality of play in the minors has risen. If this proposition were true, the major leagues would benefit from having the smaller quantity of quality minor leaguers trained in competition with other quality players. However, while entry into the majors is based on the ranking of the player's talent relative to others in the minors, entry into the minor leagues is based much more on player potential than on performance. Turnover rates are high even in the major leagues. There is simply no way of knowing whether a high school star will prove to be major league material. New entrants into the sport need to undergo a period of development in the minor leagues before their playing talents become known with greater certainty. All one need recall to understand this point is the fading of so many high-bonus players. Such bonuses were paid in anticipation of achievements by these players which were never realized. Since there is so much uncertainty about the potential of unseasoned players, the larger the stock of players undergoing training, the greater will be the number of quality players that emerge as candidates for the major leagues. Reducing investments in the minor leagues by reducing the number of high-quality players contributes to a lowering of the absolute quality of play in the major leagues.

There is some evidence that the quality of players promoted to the major leagues has declined in recent times. In the 1985 season there were 73 rookie players and 18 of them started the Opening Day games. For the 1986 season 67 rookies appeared on the Opening Day rosters and 17 of them were starters. In 1988, 50 Minor League players were promoted to the majors, but only 9 were starters.[6]

Of course, the reasons for the decimation of the minor leagues are well understood. Expansion of the major leagues and televised games seriously undermined attendance at minor league games. While the public benefits of expansion and televised games undoubtedly exceed the costs of the reduced scope of the minor leagues, the magnitude of the cutback need not have been so large. Recognizing that expansion was to occur, the owners could have taken steps to insure an adequate source of playing talent by increasing investments in the minor leagues. The impact of television could have been reduced by increasing subsidies to the farm teams. The organizational structure of baseball has stood as a barrier to raising the absolute quality of play. Because each major league team controls barely a few minor league teams through outright ownership or through affiliation agreements, each team has only a narrow interest in the status of the minor leagues. Suppose each major league controlled several minor leagues. Investments in the minors would be pooled among the major league teams and each team could have drawing rights to all of the players on the minor league teams, distributed in reverse order of finish. Such an arrangement might put minor league baseball on a sounder financial footing, which is required if potential major league talent is to be seasoned.

A second aspect of training investment is the length of the preseason training period. All of the leagues set maximum preseason training periods. The rationale for this rule is to equalize playing strengths by preventing some teams from investing in longer training periods. However, the length of the preseason training schedule will affect the quality of regular season play. In general, the longer the preseason training period, the higher the quality of play. Spring training in baseball generally starts about 1 March. Since training takes place in warm climates, there is no reason (beyond the expense involved) why training schedules could not begin at an earlier date, say 1 January. Furthermore, individual conditioning of players during the off-season is left to their own initiative. The competition from upcoming players for starting positions is a powerful incentive for veteran ballplayers to stay in shape. But a year-round regimen of training and conditioning of rostered players would tend to increase the quality of play.

Number of Teams and Roster Size

League rules insure that the home team has the only game in town. Even in the case of cities with two teams or with multiple professional team sports, home games are scheduled to minimize competition. If the leagues did not restrict team entry, what would be expected to happen to the level of playing ability? In figure 3.2, a hypothetical distribution of playing ability has been drawn. The distribution is a common one that suggests that most people have average or slightly below or above average playing skills, while only a small fraction is truly superior or inept. Teams, which select players from a group ranked by skill, attempt to choose the best first and the less skilled last. Considerable resources are devoted to the discovery and development of talent. The American League employs about 330 scouts and the National League

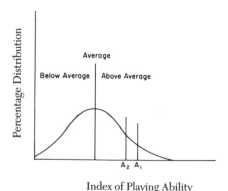

Index of Playing Ability

Figure 3.2   Hypothetical Distribution of Playing Ability

about 420.[7] Some 3,500 players are in training in the minor leagues. Given a roster of a certain size, the number of players needed to fill the roster is determined by the number of teams. With a roster size of 25 players and 16 teams, 400 players will be selected from the total available supply. The skill level of the 400th player will be the minimum required to be selected for a major league team, and this is represented by point A_1 in the figure. If the number of teams is expanded and the roster size held constant, teams will have to dig further down in the ability distribution, say to A_2, and the average level of playing skill within the league will fall. There may be steps that can be taken to offset this decline, such as expanding the available supply of highly talented players, perhaps through increased investment in scouting and in farm teams. But in the absence of such investment in player development, increasing the number of teams lowers the absolute level of team quality.

The effect on the absolute quality of play of a change in the player limit with the number of teams held constant is not as conclusive. Over some range of the roster size, player additions improve quality through the gains arising from specialization. These gains may be greater than the losses that arise from the lowering of average quality of playing talent. A 9-man team of truly great players may not compete effectively against a 25-man team of just good players. Larger rosters permit specialization in pitching (rotation, relief pitching) and hitting (platooning). The optimal size of a roster is not obvious in baseball. Since the market for baseball is hardly competitive, we cannot take the 25-man limit as optimal for achieving the highest absolute level of performance.

Playing Rules

Changes in the playing rules can clearly affect offensive and defensive performance. For example, the 1893 rule that increased the distance between the pitcher's mound and home plate by more than ten feet caused hitting performance to rise and pitching performance to decline. Most rule changes are of this nature. They alter offense relative to defense and, hence, alter scoring. Empirical evidence on the effect of changes in the playing rules on performance statistics will be presented below.

In modern times rule changes have been infrequent. Since 1947, there have been six rule changes of consequence. In 1950, 1963, and 1969, the strike zone was changed (the effect of the change in the strike zone for the 1988 season cannot be calculated yet). In 1959, minimum fence distances were established for fields constructed after 1 June 1958. In 1969, the pitcher's mound was lowered to ten inches above the base lines and home plate. In 1973, the Designated Hitter rule was adopted experimentally in the American League, an innovation that was rejected by the National League.

While the playing rules have important consequences with respect to performance, the rules themselves are arbitrary. Baseball has been played with the pitcher's mound at a distance of 45 feet and with a nine-ball, three-strike rule. Within fairly broad limits, nothing is sacrosanct in the playing rules.

During the 1960s and for part of the 1970s attendance in baseball stagnated. Owners became pessimistic as professional football began to overshadow baseball as the "national pastime." In 1960, average regular season attendance at baseball games was 1.24 million; by 1970, this had slipped to 1.20 million.[8] Suggestions for speeding up the game (e.g., three balls and two strikes, seven-inning games) were made and ultimately rejected as too radical. The decline in offensive performance was noted with concern.[9] However, in the last half of the 1970s attendance began to rise. By 1980, average team attendance was 1.65 million.[10] Furthermore, broadcast revenues were rising rapidly, up from $1.7 million per team in 1971 to $3.1 million in 1980.[11] The decade of the 1980s has witnessed something of a renaissance of fan interest. In 1987, attendance reached a record 52 million (2 million per team), up from 47.5 million in 1986.[12] Broadcast revenues were $350 million ($13.5 million per team).[13]

The organizational structure in baseball precludes frequent rule changes. Because various teams will have specialized in hitting or pitching as a strategy for winning, they will necessarily have a vested interest in protecting those imbalances in the rules which they have exploited to their advantage. Thus, a team with strong hitting and weak pitching treats a rule which favors hitting as a property right to be protected. The team will attempt to block any rule change that weakens the role of hitting even if it is for the general good of baseball. Since changes in the playing rules require a two-thirds vote of the Rules Committee, whose members are appointed by the league presidents who themselves serve at the sufferance of the owners, playing rule changes are an owner prerogative. Nothing in the leagues is changed unless three-fourths of the owners want the change. A minority of owners can block any playing rule change that is not in their interest.

Player Performance in Baseball since 1876

League average hitting, pitching, and fielding statistics have not remained constant over the history of the game but have risen or fallen at various times. These changes are not random, but occur for the reasons previously discussed, e.g., technical developments or changes in the playing rules. Let us now examine the historical evolution of player performance, paying particular attention to the way in which it has been affected by changes in rules and equipment.

Offensive Performance

THE BATTING AVERAGE

The evolution of hitting as measured by the batting average is illustrated in figure 3.3. Three distinct periods in hitting are revealed. From 1876 to 1919, the batting average was very volatile. No trend is apparent. From 1920 to 1968, the batting average declines, more or less continuously. In general, from the 1969 season on, the batting average rises.

The instability of playing and scoring rules largely is responsible for the instability of the batting average from 1876 to 1919. In 1879, as we have noted, a batter was allowed nine balls and three strikes. Changes in the number of balls and strikes occurred frequently during the 1880s. It was not until 1889 that the four-ball–three-strike rule was applied. In 1880, the pitcher's mound was 45 feet from home plate. While the eight balls and three strikes rule then in force helped the batter, a fast ball has great velocity when thrown from 45 feet. The .245 batting average that year thus comes as no surprise. In 1881, the mound was

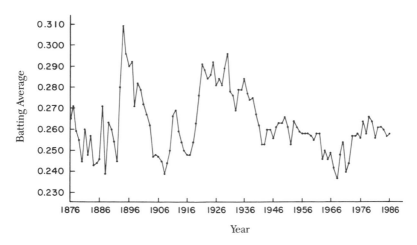

Figure 3.3   Batting Average in Major League Baseball, 1876–1986
Source: The Baseball Encyclopedia.

moved back to 50 feet, and the batting average rose to .260. The pitcher's mound was moved a final time in 1893 to its present 60 feet and 6 inches. The batting average shot up 35 points to .280. The following season, the batting average reached .309. In 1894, Hugh Duffy, the Boston center fielder, turned in the top-ranked all-time single season batting average of .438.

While the cork center ball, which came into use in 1909, had some effect on hitting, it was the rubber center ball that produced a large jump in the batting average. The rubber center ball, known as the lively ball, represented a significant advance in design, since when hit it traveled much faster and farther than the ball used before. When it was introduced, in 1920, the batting average rose 15 points over the prior season. In 1921, the batting average stood at .291. Except for 1925 and 1930, the batting average never reached the .290 mark again.

The spectacular rise in the batting average following the introduction of the lively ball was followed by a near half century of decline, as changes in playing rules and in pitching techniques reduced the hitting statistics. The batting average fell nearly one point per season from 1920 to 1968, when it reached its historic low of .237. Pete Rose's .335 batting average at Cincinnati and Carl Yastrzemski's .301 average at Boston look much more outstanding when we recognize that league averages that year were .243 and .230, respectively.

In 1887, the strike zone was defined as the area between the top of the hitter's shoulder and the bottom of the knee. In 1950, the strike zone was narrowed to the area from the batter's arm pits to the top of his knee. In 1963, the strike zone was widened to the area defined by the 1887 rule. In 1969, the strike zone was returned to the area defined by the 1950 rule. Beginning with the 1988 season, the strike zone extends from "an upper limit of the midpoint between the top of the shoulders and the top of the uniform pants to a lower limit of the top of the knees." [14] This narrowing of the strike zone from 1950 to 1962, widening from 1963 to 1968, and subsequent narrowing from 1969 to 1987 on had important effects on modern batting averages, as is easily verified by examining figure 3.3. From 1950 to 1962, the narrowed strike zone yielded a batting average for the period of .259. From 1963 to 1968, the period of the widened strike zone, the average batting average was .245. From 1969 to 1986, the average batting average was .257. Fans are seeing a lot more hitting today mainly because of a narrowed strike zone.

THE SLUGGING AVERAGE AND HOME RUNS PER GAME

Of course, the slugging average is naturally higher than the batting average. [15] Over baseball's history the slugging average has been .368

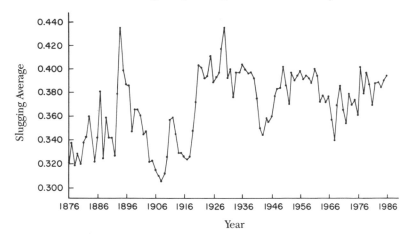

Figure 3.4   Slugging Average in Major League Baseball, 1876–1986
Source: The Baseball Encyclopedia.

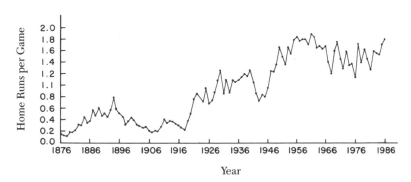

Figure 3.5   Home Runs per Game (Both Teams) in Major League Baseball, 1876–1986
Source: The Baseball Encyclopedia.

compared to a batting average of .263. The path of the slugging average more or less follows the path of the batting average (see figure 3.4). While there is no discernible trend in the measure from 1876 to 1919, the appearance of the lively ball in 1920 raised the slugging average 24 points over the 1919 season and 31 points over the 1920 season. The peak slugging average in the lively ball era has been .435 in the 1930 season. In that year, Babe Ruth at .732 and Lou Gehrig at .721 contributed to the Yankees near record .488 team slugging average.[16] In spite of their performance, the Yankees finished in third place. Slugging averages declined after the 1930 season, as pitchers adjusted to the lively ball. From 1920 to 1968, the average decline in the slugging average was about one-half of a point per year. By 1968, the slugging average had sagged to .340. Slugging averages began to rise after the strike zone was narrowed in 1969 and are pushing the .400 mark now.

The 1987 season brought a record number of home runs. Figure 3.5 shows the number of home runs per game and reveals a much higher incidence of home runs in modern baseball. Today, a fan sees on average close to two home runs hit in each game. In 1876, a fan would have to go to six or seven games to see one home run. When the lively ball was introduced in 1920 and pitched to Babe Ruth by quality pitchers like Jim Bagby (31 wins and 12 losses) of Cleveland, or Eddie Cicotte (21 and 10) of Chicago, or Urban Schocker (20 and 10) of St. Louis, or any of the other lesser American League hurlers, he hit it over the fence 54 times.

STOLEN BASES PER GAME

The lively ball changed managerial strategy and, I think, made managing a baseball team easier. Prior to 1920, a manager had to take more risks to score runs: hit and run, stolen bases, etc. After the lively ball came into play, a manager could wait for a Babe Ruth or a Lou Gehrig or a Rogers Hornsby or a Hack Wilson to hit the ball out of the park. Stolen bases plummeted, as can be seen clearly in figure 3.6. At the turn of the century, a fan would see about three stolen bases per game. By 1919, the number had fallen to about two. Partly, this drop in stolen bases was due to the introduction of better, padded gloves into the game. However, the introduction of the lively ball caused a precipitous drop of one-half of a stolen base per game in 1920 alone, and the decline continued through 1950, when a stolen base occurred about every other game.

Figure 3.6   Stolen Bases per Game (Both Teams) in Major League Baseball, 1898–1986
Source: The Baseball Encyclopedia.

Perhaps because hitting was on the decline during the 1950s and the 1960s, there was renewed interest in stolen bases and base running as ways to increase scoring. Speed became an additional criterion in scouting potential major leaguers. Stolen bases per game began to increase slowly, but steadily, after 1950. By 1972, a fan would see about one stolen base a game. By 1982, when Ricky Henderson stole 130 bases for Oakland, fans were seeing about two stolen bases a game.[17] Base running is becoming an important feature of the game, much as it was during Ty Cobb's time.

Defensive Performance

PITCHING

In general, any technological or playing rule change in the game that favors hitting will at the same time disfavor pitching, and vice versa. Thus, the ERA rose one full point between 1920 and 1922. Errors per game fell with the introduction of new glove designs (up to a point), and batting averages also fell as more efficient gloves turned what would have been hits into outs.

The Earned Run Average. The most popular measure of pitching performance is the earned run average. ERAs in baseball have been rising in recent times. The 1983 Cy Young award winner, LaMarr Hoyt of Chicago, pitched a 24 and 10 season with a 3.66 ERA. In contrast, the 1966 Cy Young winner, Sandy Koufax of the Dodgers, won 27 games with a 1.73 ERA.[18] The evolution of pitcher performance as measured by the ERA is seen in figure 3.7.

From 1876 until 1894 earned run averages generally rose. As has

Figure 3.7   Earned-run Average in Major League Baseball, 1876–1986
Source: The Baseball Encyclopedia.

Figure 3.8   Relief Pitchers per Game (Both Teams) in Major League Baseball, 1876–1968

Source: The Baseball Encyclopedia.

been mentioned, playing rule changes were frequent in this period. Reducing the number of balls necessary for a walk favored the hitters, as did increasing the distance from the mound to the plate. The movement of the mound in 1893 to 60 feet and 6 inches was responsible for a rise in the ERA to 4.66 from 3.28, followed by a further rise to 5.32, the maximum average ERA ever recorded. Pitchers were experiencing great difficulty in retiring batters in 1894. The decline in the ERA until 1908 occurred partly because of scoring rule changes, which were unfavorable to hitters.[19]

The switch from the wood center to the cork center ball increased the ERA, but the big increase came with the introduction of the lively ball. During the 1920s and the 1930s, ERAs above 4.00 were the rule, not the exception. Thereafter, the ERA declined until 1968.

During the era of the declining ERA, managers adopted the strategy of using relief pitchers more frequently. Figure 3.8 documents this growth in relief pitcher usage from 1876 to 1968. Prior to the late 1880s a relief pitcher appeared in one in ten games. Frequently teams had only one pitcher on the roster. By 1920, on average five pitchers were on a team roster, partly because more games were being played. By the 1939 season eight-man pitching rosters were becoming common. Today, a ten-man pitching roster is common.

The availability of relief pitchers permitted managers to rotate starting pitchers in an orderly fashion and to pitch them intensively for five to seven innings with relief, rather than pace them for a full game. This defensive response to the lively ball contributed to an erosion in the batting average and in scoring. On the other hand, the rise in relief pitching does not seem to have had as much of an impact on long-ball hitting. While the slugging average declined over the period, its rate of decline was one-half of that of the batting average. Moreover, home run production more than doubled. The declining trend in the ERA was reversed in 1968, with the widening of the strike zone.

Strikeouts, Bases on Balls, and the Strikeout-to-Walk Ratio. Alternative measures of pitcher performance are strikeout and walk frequencies and strikeouts relative to walks. Examination of the graphs on strikeouts per nine innings and walks per nine innings (figures 3.9 and 3.10) reveal an upward trend in both over the entire period. In 1876, a fan witnessed one strikeout per game and a little more than a walk every other game. The strikeout-to-walk ratio, in 1876, was 1.75. By

Figure 3.9   Strikeouts per Nine Innings in Major League Baseball, 1876–1986
Source: The Baseball Encyclopedia.

Figure 3.10   Bases on Balls per Nine Innings in Major League Baseball, 1876–1986
Source: The Baseball Encyclopedia.

Figure 3.11   Strikeout-to-walk Ratio in Major League Baseball, 1876–1986
Source: Calculated from data in *The Baseball Encyclopedia.*

1967, the fan was seeing about six strikeouts to a little over three walks per game. Strikeouts declined until 1982, and then began to rise again, but it is too soon to tell whether the upward trend will be sustained (see figure 3.11). The strikeout-to-walk ratio in 1986 is pretty close to the 1876 level.

FIELDING

Fielding Averages and Errors per Game. Two measures of fielding performance are available from 1876: errors per game and the fielding average. Double plays are also examined here, although they measure a somewhat different dimension of the game.

Fielding averages have been rising and errors per game falling over the entire period. This remains true today. The reduction in errors is extreme; from 12 per game in 1876 to about 5 per game in 1900, and then declining more slowly after that. The early rapid decline was due partly to changes in scoring rules and partly to improvements in glove design. According to the rules in effect in 1883, an error was charged to the pitcher for a base on balls, a wild pitch, a hit batter, or a balk. This is not quite as bizarre as it seems, since it took seven balls for a walk. But, the rule must have added greatly to the number of designated errors per game. If walks counted as errors today, the error statistic would be appalling. In the 1986 season there were a total of 3,450 errors in major league baseball, which resulted in an error rate of 1.64 per game. At the same time, there were 14,227 bases on balls, which, if counted as errors, would increase the error rate to 8.39 per game!

In the 1887 season, the 1883 scoring rule was rescinded, as was the rule charging the catcher with an error on a passed ball. Errors per

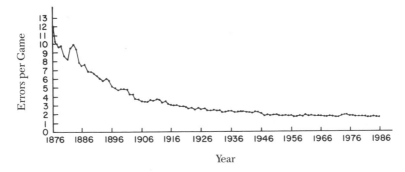

Figure 3.12   Errors per Game (Both Teams) in Major League Baseball, 1876–1986
Source: The Baseball Encyclopedia.

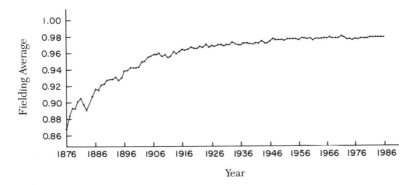

Figure 3.13   Fielding Average in Major League Baseball, 1876–1986
Source: The Baseball Encyclopedia.

game were 7.66 in the 1887 season. In the 1888 season, the 1883 rule was reinstated. In the 1889 season, the scoring rule was changed back again. Tinkering with scoring rule changes, with numbers of balls and strikes, and with the pitching distance from home plate continued in the 1890s. Furthermore, glove design changed significantly during this period. Barehanded baseball was the only kind of baseball played until well after the Civil War. In the 1877 season fingerless gloves were introduced, and these remained popular until 1886. A radical improvement in glove design was marked by the appearance of the padded, 10-ounce glove that was in use from 1890 to 1920.[20] Fingers and padding in gloves surely were a major factor in the decline in errors per game from 6.66 to 2.83 over the period. A similar improvement in fielding averages is revealed in figure 3.13. In the 1876 season, the fielding average was 86.6 percent. By 1920, the fielding percentage was 96.6, which is only 1.3 percentage points lower than it is today.

After 1920, errors continued to decline and fielding averages to rise. The Bill Doak glove of 1920 introduced webbing into glove design, allowing the built-in pocket. The Mort Cooper oversized glove of 1942 was popular among pitchers, but it was the Marty Marion "Mister Shortstop" glove with a thick heel and light finger padding that became popular among infielders. The three-fingered "Playmaker" glove introduced by Rawling Sporting Goods was popular during the 1948 season. The Mickey Mantle glove with a "V" anchored web and an adjustable wrist strap appeared in the 1954 season. The six-finger Trapeze glove, a revolutionary design, appeared in 1960. All that was required was that the player get the glove on the ball—the glove more or less took care of the rest. While each of these design changes, and, subsequent changes, contributed to the decline in errors after World War II, there was not much more that a glove could do to help the fielder. In the 1947 season, there were less than two errors per game anyway. Fingers, a little padding, and string webbing had cut the error rate. Computer design, fancy stitching, and artificial turf reduced the error rate to 1.64 by the 1986 season.

Double Plays. Double plays have ranged from one to two per game over the history of baseball (see figure 3.14). From 1876 to the mid-1890s there was a rise in double plays, but after the 1894 season they drifted down, reaching an all-time low in 1908. From 1908 until 1919 double plays increased. Measured over the period 1920 to 1986,

Figure 3.14   Double Plays per Game (Both Teams) in Major League Baseball, 1876–1986

Source: The Baseball Encyclopedia.

there has been no trend in double plays. The double play measure is somewhat more complex as a performance measure than the others. Several factors act on it simultaneously. The effect of any single change is somewhat obscured. Nevertheless, some rule changes clearly do appear to affect the statistic. The strike zone favored the pitcher during the 1950s and the 1960s, and double plays declined. If there are fewer hits, there will be fewer opportunities for double plays, other factors held constant. The wider strike zone in 1969 and thereafter encouraged greater hitting and the incidence of double plays increased.

The Effect of Rule Changes on Hitting and Pitching Performance

The rule changes that have been introduced into baseball would be expected to affect batting and pitching performance statistics. In table 3.2, the rule changes that seem most significant to me are listed, along with the expected effect on the performance measure and the actual effect on batting and earned run averages. Any rule change that affects batting averages affects ERAs in the same direction. A rule change that was expected to increase or decrease the respective performance statistic is designated with a plus (+) or a minus (−) sign.

The measured effect of the rule change is confined to the year of the rule change. Accordingly, the magnitude of change will be understated. Sometimes it takes several seasons for the effect of a rule change on performance to be fully realized. Since there is no way of knowing a priori the time frame, the analysis is confined to a single year change. Examination of figures 3.3 and 3.7, which graph the batting average and the ERA, will help in judging the effect of a particular rule change over time. The analysis is restricted to the effects on the batting average and the ERA. Obviously, other performance measures are affected by rule changes. The reader may examine table 3.2 and the other graphs of performance data to assess the impact of rule changes on these other performance measures.

Reductions in the number of pitched balls that constitute a walk would be expected to work against the hitter, since the total number of pitches available for hitting are then reduced. In actuality, each reduction in total balls between 1880 and 1889 reduced batting averages from 10 to 14 points. The rule changes of 1886 and 1887 favored the hitter. In 1886, the number of balls allowed for a walk was raised to seven. In 1887, the number of strikes necessary for a strikeout was raised to four. That year several other changes in the rules were also recorded. The batter was no longer allowed to call for a high or a low

Table 3.2   The Effect of Playing Rule Changes on Performance and Scoring

Playing Rule Change	Year	Pre-dicted Effect	Actual Effect		
			BA	ERA	RPG
Balls for a walk reduced to 8	1880	−	−.010	−0.13	−0.53
Pitcher's mound moved to 50′	1881	+	.015	0.40	0.39
Balls for a walk reduced to 7	1882	−	−.012	0.05	0.25
Balls for a walk reduced to 6	1884	−	−.014	−0.13	−0.27
Balls for a walk increased to 7	1886	+	.002	0.35	0.36
Strikeout changed to 4 strikes	1887	+	.025	0.79	0.89
Strikeout changed to 3 strikes	1888	−	−.032	−1.22	−1.60
Balls for a walk reduced to 4	1889	−	.024	0.98	1.17
Pitcher's mound moved to 60′6″	1893	+	.035	1.38	1.45
Lively ball introduced into play	1920	+	.013	0.39	0.46
Strike zone narrowed	1950	+	.003	0.24	0.25
Strike zone widened	1963	−	−.012	−0.50	−0.54
Strike zone narrowed	1969	+	.011	0.64	0.66
Designated Hitter in American League	1973	+	.013	0.48	0.68

pitch, as previously had been his privilege, and the strike zone was widened to the area between the top of the shoulder and the bottom of the knee. Also, a base on balls was granted after five balls and a walk counted as a hit. All in all these changes favored hitters. Another rule change that favored hitters was the movement of the pitcher's mound from 45 feet to 50 feet.

The rule changes of 1888 and 1889 favored the pitchers. In 1888, a strikeout was registered after three strikes, and in 1889 four balls constituted a walk. Thus, it was not until 1889 that the 4-ball–3-strike rule that characterizes the game today came into being. The rule change of 1893, which moved the pitcher's mound to its current distance from the batter's box, in my judgment, constituted one of the two most important playing rule changes in baseball history. While the previous move from 45 to 50 feet probably did not slow the ball down significantly for the hitter, the increase to 60 feet and 6 inches certainly did so. The batting average rose 35 points in 1893. In 1894, it rose another 29 points to .309, an all-time high. The second important change, as we have seen, was the introduction of the lively ball in the 1920 season. The batting average increased 13 points in 1920 and 15 points in 1921. Of course, the effect on the slugging average was even greater. It rose 55 points between 1919 and 1921. In 1950, the strike zone was narrowed and the batting average rose as a result. In 1963, the strike zone was widened and the batting average fell 12 points. Note in figure 3.3 the precipitous decline in the batting average from 1963 to 1968. In

1968, it reached an historical low of .237. In 1969, the strike zone was narrowed to that defined in the 1950 rule, and the batting average rose 11 points. The batting average rose from .244 to .257 in 1973 with the introduction of the Designated Hitter (DH) rule into American League Baseball.[21] In the American League the batting average rose 20 points in 1973.

Taking into consideration all of these rule changes, the overall effects on hitting and pitching can be calculated. Rule changes that favored hitters added an average of 14 to 15 points to the batting averages and .59 points to the ERAs of the pitchers. Rule changes that favored pitchers reduced batting averages about 16 points and lowered ERAs about .39 points. Thus, the rule changes have significant effects on player statistics.

The modern rule changes affecting the strike zone merit further discussion. These changes have had an impact for several seasons after they were introduced. The graphs in figures 3.15 and 3.16 show the batting average and the ERA from 1947–1987. The mean batting average over the period was .256. From 1950–62, the strike zone had been narrowed. For 11 of the 13 years the batting average was above .256. From 1963–68, the strike zone was widened and the batting average was below .256. In 1969, the strike zone was narrowed and the rule remained in effect until 1988. Also, in 1969 the leagues expanded. The addition of less talented players to the rosters lowered the average quality of play. Nevertheless, the batting average remained below .256

Figure 3.15   Batting Average in Major League Baseball, 1947–1987
Source: The Baseball Encyclopedia.

Figure 3.16   Earned-run Average in Major League Baseball, 1947–1987
Source: The Baseball Encyclopedia.

from 1969 through 1972. In 1973, the American League adopted the DH rule. A regular batter substituting for a pitcher in the hitting lineup would be expected to raise the team average by one-ninth times the difference between the DH and pitcher batting averages. After 1973, the batting average generally was at or above .256.

Of course, the rule changes have opposite effects on pitching performance. Over the entire period the mean ERA was 3.79. Except for 1952, the ERA was above the mean from 1950 through 1962, when the narrow strike zone rule was in effect. The widened strike zone improved pitcher performance statistics during 1963–68. ERAs have been rising since the strike zone was narrowed again in 1969.

The Designated Hitter Rule in the American League

Until 1973, both leagues adopted the same rule changes. In 1973, however, the American League introduced the Designated Hitter rule into play but the National League did not accept it. After the 1972 season, therefore, the performance statistics of the two leagues need to be examined separately.

As seen in figures 3.17 and 3.18, from 1947 through 1972 batting averages were higher in the National League in 18 of the 26 years (69 percent of the time) and ERAs were lower in 15 (58 percent) of the years. Since the DH rule, batting averages and ERAs in the American League have been above those of the National League. Perhaps the effect of the DH rule on the interleague performance difference can be

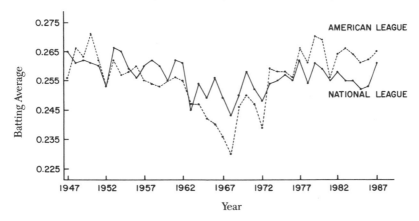

Figure 3.17 Batting Averages in the American and National Leagues, 1947–1987
Source: The Baseball Encyclopedia.

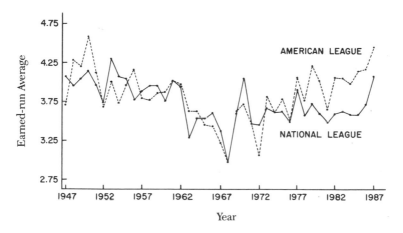

Figure 3.18 Earned-run Averages in the American and National Leagues, 1947–1987
Source: The Baseball Encyclopedia.

seen a little more clearly in figures 3.19 and 3.20. In figure 3.19, the American League batting average is divided by that of the National League. A value of 1.00 means interleague parity. A value less than 1.00 means that the American League batting average is less than that of the National League. A value greater than 1.00 means that the American League batting average exceeds that of the National League.

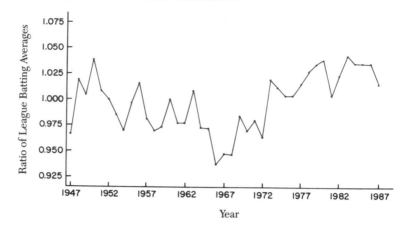

Figure 3.19   Ratio of American League Batting Average to National League Batting Average, 1947–1987

Source: Calculated from data in *The Baseball Encyclopedia.*

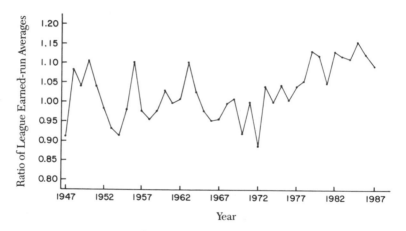

Figure 3.20   Ratio of American League Earned-run Average to National League Earned-run Average, 1947–1987

Source: Calculated from data in *The Baseball Encyclopedia.*

A similar interpretation is intended for the comparison of the leagues' ERAs in figure 3.20.

From 1947 through 1972 the mean batting average in the National League was .257 compared to .252 in the American League. From 1973 through 1987 the mean value of the American League batting average was .262 compared to .256 in the National League. Thus, between periods the mean batting average in the American League rose by ten points and the mean in the National League fell by one point, creating an inter-period, inter-league differential of eleven points in the batting average. The designated hitter ought to bat at least as well as the player roster, while pitchers are poor hitters. There is a differential of about 100 points between player and pitcher hitting. The DH rule should and has added about 10 to 12 points in the American League batting average.

Prior to the DH rule, ERAs were higher in the National League, but the difference was small (3.79 versus 3.77). Since the rule, the ERA in the American League has been substantially higher (3.96 versus 3.66). ERAs have been strongly rising since 1985. In 1985, the ERA was 3.59 in the National League and 4.15 in the American League. In 1987, the ERA rose to 4.08 in the National League and 4.46 in the American League, the highest since the early 1950s.

Offense has increased in the American League as a result of the DH rule. Naturally, the games are higher scoring. Compared to 1947–72, as mentioned, the batting average over the period 1973–87 is ten points higher in the American League compared to the National League, while the ERA is about .33 points higher.[22] Of course, some would disagree that the DH rule is the sole source of the performance differential that separates the two leagues. If that is true, the effect of the DH rule is overstated in these calculations.

The Effect of Rule Changes on Scoring

The output of one team in competition with another is a victory or a loss. Games are won when one team scores more runs than the opponent. Thus, producing the most runs and minimizing the opponent's runs is the intermediate step from which team standings are determined. Scoring depends on the quality of player inputs and on the playing rules. It is commonly believed that fans prefer higher scoring contests to lower scoring ones, all else being equal. Higher scoring games are filled with more action, and are by nature more exciting. Rule changes that favor hitting, in general, will increase scoring. Conversely, rule changes favorable to pitching produce lower scoring games.

The Effect of Hitting, Pitching, and Fielding Performance on Scoring

The historical pattern of scoring in baseball is illustrated in figure 3.21. Broadly, scoring has declined. Measured since 1876, scoring has fallen .14 runs per decade. Since 1947, it has fallen .10 runs per decade. This

Figure 3.21   Runs per Game in Major League Baseball, 1876–1986
Source: The Baseball Encyclopedia.

pattern is reminiscent of the pattern in some of the other performance measures already analyzed. In particular, compare the evolution of runs per game with that of the batting average (figure 3.3) and the ERA (figure 3.7). Clearly, they are related.

The effects of the various measures of player performance on scoring are given in table 3.3. Increases in batting and in slugging averages increase scoring. Measured over the entire period a 10-point increase in the batting average yields a .33 point increase in runs per game. Alternatively, runs scored per game increase by one run for a 30-point increase in the batting average. The effect in the post-1947 period is about the same. Slugging average changes naturally produce smaller changes in scoring. Mainly, this is so because the slugging average has a higher mean than the batting average (.368 versus .263) and the distribution of hits (singles versus extra base) is not particularly sensitive to changes in the playing rules. Over baseball's recorded history, a 125-point increase in the slugging average produced a 1-run increase in scoring. Since 1947, a 50-point rise produces a 1-run increase in scoring.

Improvements in pitching performance reduce scoring. Measured over the entire period, a 1.6-point decline in the ERA is associated with a 1-run decline in scoring. Since 1947, there is an approximate one-to-one relationship between changes in the ERA and in scoring. Similarly, the increased sensitivity of scoring to pitching performance is revealed by the strikeout-to-walk statistic. Part of the increased impact of pitching is due to the greater utilization of relief pitching. In the post-1947 era an extra relief pitcher per game is associated with about a .6 decline in runs scored per game.

Errors increase scoring opportunities. Figures 3.12 and 3.13 reveal

Table 3.3   Gross Effect of Performance Measures on Runs per Game

	Effect on Runs per Game	
Performance Measure	1876–1986	1947–1986
Offensive Measures		
Batting Average	33.2	39.0
Slugging Average	8.0	19.0
Defensive Measures		
Earned Run Average	0.61	1.12
Strikeout-to-Walk Ratio	−0.35	−0.74
Relief Pitchers per Game	−0.40	−0.62
Fielding Average	−18.91	−151.45
Errors per Game	−0.52	1.92

the tremendous improvement in fielding. This fielding improvement has reduced scoring. Since 1876, a 5-point improvement in the fielding average reduced scoring by about one run. In modern baseball, fielding averages change very slowly. A 1-point improvement in the fielding average is a grand accomplishment. Such a change would reduce scoring by 1.5 runs per game. Similarly a large effect on scoring occurs with reductions in errors. A 1-error-per-game increase results in nearly two extra runs per game. Errors are very costly in modern baseball.

A problem with the above discussion is that the effect of each of the measures on scoring has been analyzed without taking into account the fact that all of the measures are changing together. Thus, the effect of any one of the measures on scoring is overstated. To overcome this limitation I picked two performance measures and statistically analyzed their relationship to scoring over the period 1947–86. The following equation was obtained:[23]

$$\text{Runs Scored} = 4.1 + 30.6 \times \text{Batting Average} - .25 \times \text{Strikeout-to-Walk Ratio.}$$

The intercept (4.1) has been set as the average number of runs scored per game over the period. Each 1-point increase in the batting average yields a .03-point increase in runs scored per game. Each 1-point increase in the strikeout-to-walk ratio is associated with a .25-point decrease in runs scored.

Over the period 1947–68, when runs scored were declining, the batting average was declining and the strikeout-to-walk ratio was rising. The batting average declined 24 points between 1947 and 1968, which accounted for a .73-point reduction in the number of runs scored per game (30.6 × −.024 = −.73 Runs Scored). Over that same period, the strikeout-to-walk ratio rose 1.097 points, which accounted for a .27-point decline in scoring ($-.25 \times 1.097 = -.27$ Runs Scored). The total reduction predicted by the equation above is 1.0 runs per game ($-.73 + -.27$). In reality, that was the decline over the period (from 4.42 runs per game to 3.42).

Since 1968, scoring has increased. The batting average has been rising and the strikeout-to-walk ratio has been declining. The batting average rose 31 points, which is estimated to have added .95 points to scoring. The strikeout-to-walk ratio has declined .352 points, for an estimated .09-point increase in runs per game. The predicted increase in scoring from the combined effects of pitching and hitting changes is 1.04 points. In reality, runs scored per game have increased by 1.77 points since 1968. The discrepancy between the actual and the predicted runs per game for the post-1968 period is due to the effect that the DH rule had on scoring in the American League. Generally, then, the estimated relationship between hitting and pitching performance on scoring predicts the actual changes fairly well.

The Effect of Changes in Playing Rules on Scoring

Since playing rules affect performance and performance affects scoring, each rule change will tend to increase or decrease runs scored per game. Return again to table 3.2. Each of the eight rule changes that favored hitting over the period on average added .64 runs per game. The rule changes with the largest effects were those of 1893 and 1920. Between 1892 and 1894 runs scored per game rose from 3.28 to 5.32 runs. Between 1919 and 1921 runs per game increased from 3.88 to 4.88 runs. The modern changes on the strike zone and the DH rule have had a substantial impact. The wider strike zone of 1963 accelerated the decline in scoring. By 1968, the last year of the rule, runs per game were down to 3.42, a 60-year low. The narrowed strike zone of 1969 contributed to an upward drift in scoring. In the National League, where scoring has not been affected by the DH rule (see below), scoring has risen from 3.44 runs in 1968 to 4.51 in 1987.

Rule changes that favored pitching reduced scoring. As the number of balls allowed the batter declined, scoring declined. The 1888 rule of three strikes for an out produced a very large decline in scoring. The widened strike zone of 1963 reduced scoring about one-half of a run per game.

THE DESIGNATED HITTER AND SCORING IN THE
AMERICAN LEAGUE

The DH rule increased hitting relative to pitching in the American League. A natural result of the rule has been increased run production.

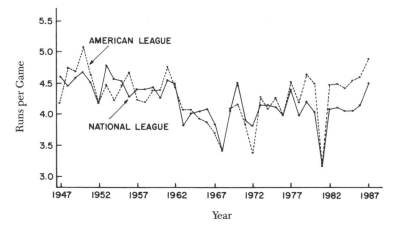

Figure 3.22   Runs per Game in the American and National Leagues, 1947–1987
Source: The Baseball Encyclopedia.

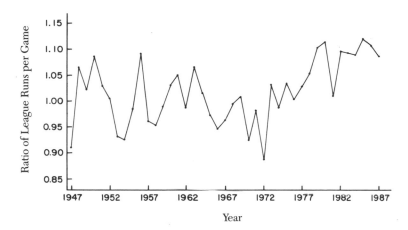

Figure 3.23   Ratio of American League Runs per Game to National League Runs per Game, 1947–1987
Source: Calculated from data in *The Baseball Encyclopedia.*

In figure 3.22, the runs per game for both leagues are graphed. In figure 3.23, the American League runs per game has been divided by that of the National League. Prior to 1973, the difference in scoring between the two leagues was insignificant. More runs per game were scored in the American League in 11 of the 26 years and more in the National League in 15 of 26 years. With the exception of 1974, the American League has outscored the National League since the DH rule went into effect. The gap in scoring between the leagues has been as large as one-half of a run. Since 1981, the year of the long players' strike, the American League has averaged 4.6 runs per game, while the National League has averaged 4.2 runs. Increased scoring in the American League has helped to draw fans to the parks. (See figure 5.1, which documents the closing gap in attendance in the American League compared to the National League after the DH rule went into effect.)

4

League Operating Rules and the Distribution of Team Playing Strengths

In addition to the aesthetic satisfaction of watching games of a certain absolute level of quality, fans also are concerned about the relative quality of team play. It matters to fans how their favorite teams finish compared to the other teams in the league. If the relative playing strengths of teams were so unequal that team A was always victorious over teams B,C,D, . . . in the league, and team B always beat teams C,D, . . . , but always lost to team A, and so on, the outcome of the contests would be known in advance and watching them would be a colossal bore. If such win records existed within a league, a condition of absolute inequality of play would prevail and the relative quality of play would be at its lowest. Uncertainty of outcome is a necessary feature of competitive team sports, and this uncertainty is largely determined by the relative playing strengths of the teams. The more equal the playing strengths of the teams within a league, the more competitive are the contests and the more uncertain is the outcome of the game. The relative quality of play within a league is highest when the win records are equal among the teams. However, it is important to distinguish between a distribution of playing strengths that leads to mathematical equality of play (all teams having .500 records) and a distribution of skills that results in statistical equality of play (all teams having records in the long run that deviate to only some small degree from .500). In this discussion, we will use the concept of equalization of playing strengths in the statistical sense, whereby some teams win and some teams lose, but by small margins and the winners and losers change from year to year.

The relative playing strength of a team depends on the financial strength of the team and its owner. The principal source of revenues for a team is from the sale of its games at baseball parks or over the airwaves. The main cost for a team is for the player roster. In chapter 2, we discussed several agreements among the clubs that seek to restrict competition in the markets in which baseball operates. The major restrictive practices of baseball are (1) the division of geographical markets and territorial rights; (2) the cartelization of national television broadcast rights with network television; (3) the sale of expansion teams; and (4) the control of the market for players through drafting and player reservation. These restrictions have very important implications for the distribution of team playing strengths (win percentages) within the leagues.

Expected Effects of League Operating Rules on the Relative Quality of Play

Control of Entry and Territorial Rights

By restricting expansion and assigning exclusive territorial rights, the teams within a league obtain valuable monopoly rights to supply games to local markets. The value of these rights naturally depends on the size of the market and on the degree of competition from other professional sports.

Consider the value of the rights of a hypothetical team described in figure 4.1. The attendance at the games depends largely on the size of the population of the city in which the team plays, the win record of the team, and on its ticket prices. All else equal, big city franchises outdraw small city clubs, and winning teams outdraw losing teams. Also, low ticket prices draw more fans than high ticket prices. Once assigned to a particular geographical market, teams cannot change territories without league permission. Hence, choice of market size is largely beyond the control of the team, once the league is formed. Within the control of the team are its quality and ticket prices.

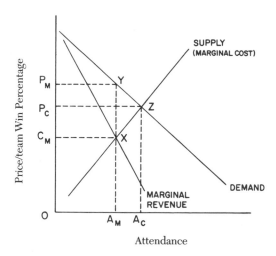

Figure 4.1   Price, Attendance, and Profits for a Hypothetical Team with an Exclusive Territory

The nominal price of a product contains much of the information necessary to make consumer choices. There is, however, much more to price than the nominal cost of the product or service. The price of attending a ball game is not just the ticket price. That expenditure may only be a small fraction of the total outlay and of the cost of foregoing other activities (the opportunity cost). Furthermore, a $5.00 ticket to watch a championship quality game is more valuable than a $5.00 ticket to watch a bush league performance. There is a quality price that affects the decision to attend games. To make the analytics simple, in figure 4.1 ticket price is divided by win percentage, a measure of team quality. The law of demand is as valid when quality price (as opposed to nominal price) is considered. Suppose the team in question is a .500 club and two nominal ticket prices are considered: $10 and $5. The respective prices per unit of quality are 2 and 1 cent per percentage point in the win record (e.g., $10/500 = 2 cents). We would expect fewer fans to attend the games of a .500 club at $10 than at $5 ticket prices. Alternatively, consider a $5 ticket price for a .400, .500, or .600 club. The respective quality prices are 1.25 cents, 1.0 cents, and 0.83 cents. At a $5 ticket price more fans will attend the games of a .600 club than a .400 club. The demand curve in the diagram asserts an inverse relationship between ticket price per unit of quality and attendance.

Next to the demand curve in the diagram is a more steeply sloped line labeled "Marginal Revenue." The demand curve or average revenue relates attendance to price. Marginal revenue is the relationship between change in total revenue (price times attendance) and change in attendance. Given fan demand, as expressed in the demand curve, the team can sell more tickets only by lowering the price of all of the tickets. For example, suppose that a team with a certain quality level would draw a million fans at a $5 ticket price. If the team charged $4, 1.5 million fans would come to the park. The total revenues are $5 million and $6 million, respectively. The increase in revenue is $1 million for the $1 reduction in ticket price and the increase in attendance is 500,000. The marginal revenue is the change in revenue divided by the change in attendance, or $2. Marginal revenue is less than average revenue or price.

The supply curve or marginal cost curve is also drawn on the diagram. The cost of fielding a team of a certain quality includes the obvious direct costs (player salaries, game costs, etc.) and the less obvious indirect or opportunity costs. It is important to incorporate foregone opportunities as a cost of providing baseball games to the fans. Opportunity costs are those profits or returns that could have been earned in the next best alternative business endeavor but were foregone in the interest of owning a franchise. Thus, opportunity costs are foregone profits. A normal return from owning a baseball team is sufficient revenues to recover costs, including opportunity costs. Revenues above that amount are not necessary and constitute an excess return or an economic rent. The supply curve is upward sloping to reflect the fact that costs rise at an increasing rate for proportional increases in win percentages. Because the supply of playing talent is limited, costs more than double for a doubling of team quality.

Axiomatically, profits are at a maximum when output is set where marginal revenue equals marginal cost. In figure 4.1, the team would charge price OP_M and OA_M fans would attend the games during the season. At price OP_M team revenues are the rectangle OP_MYA_M. Team costs are the rectangle OC_MXA_M. Team monopoly profits (recall that normal profits are included in the cost curve as opportunity costs) are revenues minus costs, or the rectangle C_MP_MYX.[1]

The implications of the analysis are that fans pay higher ticket prices, fewer fans attend games, and teams earn larger profits than in the absence of exclusive territorial rights. Given freedom of entry and of franchise movement, ticket prices per unit of quality would be set at a level just sufficient not to make it attractive for a competing team to enter the local market. In the diagram, price P_C is sufficient for the team to recover its direct and its opportunity costs. At that price OA_C fans attend the team's games. With freedom of franchise movement, prices above P_C would induce entry into the local market; prices below P_C in the long run would induce team withdrawal from the market.

While higher ticket prices and lower attendance are important welfare implications of the league restrictions on entry and territorial rights, the implication on the distribution of team playing strengths within a division or league is of greater importance to fans. The effect of the league rule of territorial exclusivity on relative team quality is shown analytically in figure 4.2. The teams are assumed to have the same market characteristics except that they are located in territories whose populations are of different sizes. The demand curves are not drawn in the diagram to avoid clutter. Since the teams compete in the same market for players, their cost functions are assumed identical ($MC_1 = MC_2$). Team 2 is located in a big city; team 1 is located in a small city. The demand in the market for the games of team 2 is greater than the demand for that of team 1. Hence, *the marginal revenue of a win is greater in the big city market than in the market of the small city.* The profit-maximizing win record for team 2 is W_2 and for team 1 is W_1. If team 1 attempts to win more games than W_1, its marginal costs will be greater than its marginal revenue and its profits will shrink. At some win record above W_1 its profits will vanish entirely and the team

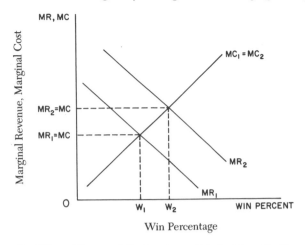

Figure 4.2   The Effect of Territorial Exclusivity on Relative Team Quality

will enter the zone of financial losses. The argument is analogous for team 2. A win record below W_2 lowers profit. Profit maximization yields a distribution of win percentages in a league determined by differences in the size of the markets for the teams' games.

Some may find this analysis too pessimistic and mechanical. After all, the pride of owners and those associated with the teams dictate a determination to be winners even if expenditures beyond those earned at the gate are required. Team owners are wealthy individuals whose desire for a championship may warrant personal financial sacrifice. And owners get more than mere money from backing a club—they get satisfaction. There is a ring of plausibility to these arguments. Tom Yawkey spent lavishly to bring a World Championship to Boston, without success. But some small city franchises have succeeded where Yawkey failed. Even if an altruistic motive in team ownership is assumed, market size constrains teams from sustaining win records beyond those warranted by fan demand. A wallet full of owner altruism in Atlanta, San Francisco, Kansas City, or Milwaukee will not produce a record that is sustainably better than that produced in New York or Los Angeles with team revenues alone. By restricting franchise movement the leagues have created the opportunity for big city dominance over the franchises located in the smaller markets.

GATE-SHARING ARRANGEMENTS

League rules divide the gate between the home and the visiting team. Overall the split is 85–15 in baseball. Gate division differs among leagues in professional sports. In basketball and hockey, the visitor receives nothing. In football, the division is 60–40. Obviously, the more equal the gate-sharing plan among the teams, the more equal the revenues. In turn, equality at the gate leads to equality on the playing field.

If gate revenue were the sole source of revenue in baseball, as it was before broadcasting, and the receipts were evenly divided, then playing strengths would be equalized no matter how different the size of the cities in which the teams were located (the effect of broadcast revenues on playing strengths is discussed below). In figure 4.2, let MR_1 and MR_2 be the marginal revenues for the small city and the big city teams under the 85–15 gate split. The corresponding records for the team are W_1 and W_2. A change to an even share in the gate split would redistribute revenues from the big city team to the small city team. Under a 50–50 gate split the marginal revenues of the two teams would be identical. Hence, the win percentages would tend toward equality.

The unequal gate-sharing arrangement in baseball contributes to inequality on the playing field. Big city teams have relatively little interest in subsidizing small city franchises. League voting rules give the big city franchises a minority blocking coalition. Some might view a scheme of socialization of revenue with disdain. A good case can be made that there is little financial incentive to win in the NFL. Any activity taken by a team basically yields 1/28th of the net gain to that team. The remainder goes to the other 27 teams. Of course, the award of a substantial prize to the world champion would overcome the disincentive of equal revenue division during the regular season. The net gate receipts for the 1987 World Series between Minnesota and St. Louis was over $10 million, a princely sum.[2] The 26 players on the Twins each got $85,581 for the Series, while 34 Cardinal players received $56,052 each.[3]

The Cartelization of Broadcast Revenues

Prior to 1950, broadcast revenues were a very small fraction of team revenues and they were exclusively marketed by the teams in their respective local markets. Beginning in the 1950s some of the broadcasts were packaged for the national television market and these revenues were evenly divided among the clubs. By 1960, only 25 percent of total broadcast fees came from national contracts.[4] The difference in the value of the local broadcast rights was enormous. Broadcast market size and the historical performance of the team determined the value of these rights. Differences in value remain today. For example, in 1987, the New York Yankees received $17.5 million from WPIX for local TV rights, while the Seattle Mariners got $2.2 million from KIRO broadcasting.[5] Broadcast fees now are approaching 40 percent of team revenues. The growth of broadcast revenues and the inequality in the size of the local rights increases revenue inequality in the leagues. On the other hand, the national broadcast contract, which is divided equally and is becoming a larger fraction of team revenues, is a source of revenue equalization. In 1987, the network contract with NBC-TV and ABC-TV and the radio contract with CBS constituted 44 percent of the $350 million rights payments to baseball. Baseball has cartelized its national broadcast rights and skillfully negotiated with the networks.

Clubs may bargain as a cartel with the networks because Congress exempted professional sports broadcasting from the antitrust statutes when it passed the Sports Broadcasting Act of 1961. As a consequence of this exemption the value of the rights fees paid to the teams rose and the number of games broadcast declined.[6]

The combined NBC/ABC contract for 1984–89 required fee payments of $1.125 billion over the six-year period and carefully limited and divided the market for broadcast games so that each network did not compete with the other. By limiting and segmenting the national television market, baseball maximized advertising revenue to the networks. Baseball and football games draw the largest young adult male audience and this audience is particularly valued by advertisers. Naturally, the clubs extract most of the benefits from these restrictions, since the networks must compete with one another and the clubs act as a block, which controls the sole source of supply.

The contract allocated the World Series to NBC in 1984, 1986, and 1988 and the League Championship Series and All-Star game for 1985, 1987, and 1989. ABC-TV had the alternate years for these games. During the regular season, NBC had the right to telecast 30 exclusive Saturday afternoon games (with an option on five additional afternoon telecasts) and two prime-time exclusive telecasts. During these telecasts local broadcasting by the teams was proscribed. ABC obtained the right to telecast 36 regular season games of which a maximum of 20 were exclusive prime-time telecasts. The balance were nonexclusive Sunday telecasts or non-Saturday afternoon broadcasts. For the prime-time telecasts no competing local club transmissions were allowed.[7]

Divisional play-off winners are not always the teams with the best performance over the season; indeed, the team with the lower win percentage wins the divisional play-off nearly as frequently as the league leader. But the arrangement makes financial sense. The value of these games from the sale of broadcast rights alone is significant. At the time of the negotiations with the networks, the League Championship Series (LCS) was a best-of-five play-off. The contract terms specified a $9 million reduction per year in which each of the LCS remained a five-game series. By expanding the LCS to a seven-game series in 1985, the teams collectively earned an extra $9 million per year in rights fees. Those extra four games (even if not played) brought broadcast revenues of $2.25 million each.[8]

Anticipating the growth of pay television, baseball reserved broadcasts not specifically granted to the networks. Each club's local pay television rights are reserved totally by the clubs, and baseball as a cartel reserves the right to sell to others national pay television rights to regular season games not competing with NBC or ABC exclusive broadcasts. However, in return for the national broadcast network contract, baseball agreed to withdraw from its national cable agreement with USA Network after the 1983 season.[9]

While local broadcast rights remain a very substantial source of revenue for the teams, satellite transmission and cable television have blurred the distinction between local and national television. In the process the value of exclusive local broadcast rights to on the road games potentially is reduced. The $500 million Yankee contract with Madison Square Garden cable network gives the latter rights to broadcast most of the club's home games beginning with the 1991 season. National cable TV stations like WTBS, WGN, and KTLA have enormous appetites for original sports programming. Since about 50–60 percent of households subscribe to cable, these cable broadcasts compete with those of the local team's away games. Further, pay sports channels are becoming a significant factor in the finances of several teams. In 1985, these teams were earning more than a million dollars from pay TV.[10] Some economists believe that pay TV in sports gradually will replace free TV; teams may even broadcast home games, sacrificing gate receipts for higher broadcast revenues.[11] Of course, in order to capture these enormous economic rents the local rights held by the teams have to be collectivized and marketed as a package, like the national rights. The 1990–93 national cable contract with ESPN, worth $400 million, gives the cable network free choice of 175 games each season. Revenues from the national cable contract are to be divided equally among the clubs. It appears that the trend towards increased broadcast revenues and their growing collectivization will tend to equalize revenues among the teams.

The Sale of New Franchises

In 1960, there were 16 teams in the majors. League expansions in 1961, 1962, 1969, and 1977 have brought the number of clubs to 26.

The leagues have expanded because it was in the interest of the existing teams. Baseball has always maintained the supply of cities served by the sport at a level that is lower than the number of cities demanding franchises. The threat by a franchise to move unless a new stadium is built at public expense or some other local concession is made has brought significant subsidies to the clubs. The San Francisco Giants have threatened to relocate after 1993 unless a new stadium is built to replace Candlestick Park.[12] If the number of potential locations for financially viable franchises is eight or more, the threat of the formation of a new league emerges. More than anything else, baseball has sought to prevent this from happening.

Expansion teams necessarily perform poorly on the field in the years immediately after they have been formed, and they may continue to do so for a substantial period. Adding teams of below-average quality always diminishes the relative quality of play within a league. Obviously, an expansion club with a .300 record will lose more frequently to a .600 ball club than to a .400 or a .500 team.

The prospects for further expansion in baseball are weaker today. The increased socialization of revenues makes the size of the indemnity payment prohibitive. To add a team in 1989 would reduce each club's national broadcast revenues by $350,000 per year. For all clubs, the loss is $9.1 million per year. Additionally, the poor competitive quality of the expansion club reduces gate revenues. Over a ten-year period several tens of millions of dollars would be lost collectively by the clubs. Second, while baseball strictly controls franchise relocation and has authority to do so by virtue of its antitrust exemption, the legal authority to block an unauthorized move is doubtful. Al Davis successfully moved the Oakland Raiders to Los Angeles without paying compensation. The NFL failed to block the move in the courts. The San Diego Clippers in the NBA unilaterally moved to Los Angeles. It is possible that expansion franchises in Washington, Miami, New Orleans, or Tampa unilaterally would move to the more populous markets. "Owners in lucrative markets may justifiably fear that today's expansion to a small city with no current team stands a good chance of creating tomorrow's new competitor in New York or Los Angeles."[13]

Restrictions in the Players Market

Because teams play in markets of different size and earn a large fraction of their revenues in local markets, players are worth more on big-city teams than on small-city teams. Consider highly talented players such as Tim Raines and Andre Dawson. Currently, these players might contribute an extra $3 million in revenues in New York or Los Angeles.

In Montreal, a smaller market, Raines and Dawson might be worth $1.5 million in extra revenues. Under current rules if they were free agents in a free market (i.e., absent any owner collusion) and subject to their locational preferences, Raines and Dawson would be offered contracts in the larger cities and would presumably each receive a $1.5 million increase over the salaries they would have received from Montreal. Prior to free agency, Montreal would have been carrying on its books an asset worth $3 million in New York or Los Angeles and $1.5 million in Montreal. With the reserve clause in effect, Montreal would then have sold Raines and Dawson to the larger market teams and pocketed the difference in value. Whether binding player reservation or free agency exists, the highly talented players eventually migrate to the larger markets. Thus, the distribution of playing talent is affected no differently by free agency than it is by player drafting and the reserve clause. All that is different is that Dawson and Raines get to keep the money in one case while Montreal does in the other.

That the allocation of resources is invariant to the initial assignment or subsequent reassignment of a property right is a renowned theorem due to Ronald Coase.[14] All that changes in the reassignment of the property right from teams (reserve clause) to players (free agency) is the distribution of wealth. By having to pay the players their competitive market value rather than a salary restricted by the reserve clause, teams suffered a loss of asset value that was transferred collectively to the players.

There are two arguments in the literature that do suggest that the player draft and the reserve clause affect the distribution of playing strengths. Simon Rottenberg first pointed to the income redistribution aspects of the draft and the system of player reservation.[15] Weaker teams obtain first choice of new playing talent, which can be trained and sold for cash to teams in larger markets. With free agency, income is redistributed from franchise owners to the players, but the subsidies to weaker clubs obtained through cash sales vanish. William Holahan then asked: What happens to competitive balance in the long run, if some of the marginal teams go out of business?[16] Obviously, the elimination of the weaker clubs will improve competitive balance, raise the average level of quality of play, and reduce the dispersion in quality among teams. The corollary of Holahan's argument is that the cash sale subsidy from large city to small city franchises that was a feature of the players' labor market prior to 1976 actually promoted greater inequality of play than does free agency.

A second argument is traced to the work of Michael Canes and has been reworked by George Daly and William J. Moore.[17] Fans are more attracted to uncertain contests than to more predictable contests. An increase in the quality of a poor club therefore raises the revenue for all clubs. But the club improving its quality cannot capture the gains external to it. Similarly, an increase in the quality of a good team reduces the revenues to the other clubs. More precisely, there exists a distribution of win percentages among the teams in a league that would maximize joint profits. Because the transaction costs are so high, such joint profit maximization is impossible. Each club ignores the external effect that its own win record has on other teams' revenues, since it has no property right in those external benefits. As a result, in the absence of any restrictions on player allocation, the distribution of playing strengths will be wider than socially desirable. The institutional mechanism of the player draft by inverse order of finish and the reserve clause become an inexpensive (low transaction cost) method of internalizing the externality.

A weakness of this characterization of organized baseball's intentions is that the sale of player contracts for cash historically has been a feature of the business. Equalization of playing strengths would have emerged naturally in baseball under reverse order drafting, player reservation, and a ban on the cash sale of player contracts. It is by no means obvious that equalization of team playing strengths is consistent with either joint club profit maximization or with profit maximization by individual clubs.[18] Nevertheless, the effect of the change in the ownership of the right to player services on playing equality within the leagues is a testable proposition. It has been more than ten years since player freedom of movement has been liberalized. We will examine the effect of this change on the distribution of team standings below.

Evidence of Changes in the Relative Quality of Play

The control of entry and territorial exclusivity, the division of attendance and broadcast revenues, and league expansion have effects on the distribution of playing strengths within a league. Theoretically, restrictions on player movement have no effect, but we will leave that issue aside until the next section. Here the larger question is examined: What is the historical evidence on relative team quality in major league baseball? Are playing strengths of teams within the leagues more or less equal today than in the past? Two measures of differences in team strengths will serve as evidence. Data is calculated on the number of pennants or league championships and on the distribution of team win percentages.

The Distribution of Championships

Of the several measures of team strength that shed light on the question of the relative quality of play, the most obvious is the distribution of league championships. Significant inequalities are present in both leagues, with one or two teams historically dominant.

In the American League from 1901 to 1987, of a possible 87 pennants among the original eight franchises, the most (33) are held by the New York Yankees and the least (3) by the Cleveland Indians (see table 4.1). If all of the teams were of equal strength during this period, then the winning of games would be determined by chance and the distri-

Table 4.1   Distribution of League Championships, 1901–1987

Team	Pennants 1901–87	Expected Pennants	Differ- ence	Pennants 1947–87	Expected Pennants	Differ- ence
American League						
Baltimore	7	9.8	−2.8	6	4.0	2.0
Boston	10	9.8	0.2	3	4.0	−1.0
California	0	2.3	−2.3	0	2.3	−2.3
Chicago	5	9.8	−4.8	1	4.0	−3.0.
Cleveland	3	9.8	−6.8	2	4.0	−2.0
Detroit	9	9.8	−0.8	2	4.0	−2.0
Kansas City	2	1.5	0.5	2	1.5	0.5
Milwaukee	1	1.5	−0.5	1	1.5	−0.5
Minnesota	5	9.8	−4.8	2	4.0	−2.0
New York	33	9.8	23.2	19	4.0	15.0
Oakland	12	9.8	2.2	3	4.0	−1.0
Seattle	0	0.8	−0.8	0	0.8	−0.8
Texas	0	2.3	−2.3	0	2.3	−2.3
Toronto	0	0.8	−0.8	0	0.8	−0.8
National League						
Atlanta	4	10.0	−6.0	2	4.2	−2.2
Chicago	10	10.0	0.0	0	4.2	−4.2
Cincinnati	8	10.0	−2.0	5	4.2	0.8
Houston	0	2.3	−2.3	0	2.3	−2.3
Los Angeles	17	10.0	7.0	15	4.2	10.8
Montreal	0	1.6	−1.6	0	1.6	−1.6
New York	3	2.3	0.7	3	2.3	0.7
Philadelphia	4	10.0	−6.0	3	4.2	−1.2
Pittsburgh	9	10.0	−1.0	3	4.2	−1.2
St. Louis	15	10.0	5.0	6	4.2	2.2
San Diego	1	1.6	−0.6	1	1.6	−0.6
San Francisco	16	10.0	6.0	3	4.2	−1.2

Source: Compiled from data in Joseph L. Reichler, editor, *The Baseball Encyclopedia*, Sixth edition (New York: Macmillan Publishing Company, 1985); *The 1986 Baseball Encyclopedia: An Update* (New York: Macmillan Publishing Company, 1986); and, *The 1987 Baseball Encyclopedia Update* (New York: Macmillan Publishing Company, 1987).

bution of pennants should be equal. That is, we would expect each of the original eight teams to have won 9.8 pennants, or about one a decade. Clearly, New York has won more than expected, while Baltimore, Chicago, Cleveland, Minnesota, and most of the expansion clubs have won fewer than expected. Boston, Detroit, Kansas City and Milwaukee have a number of pennant victories not statistically different than would be expected.

The distribution of championships over the same period in the National League is not as skewed. Los Angeles with 17 pennants, about 7 more than expected, and San Francisco with 16, lead the league. Philadelphia and Atlanta with 4 each have the fewest championships among the original eight franchises. Additionally, St. Louis has won more than expected, while Cincinnati and Houston have won fewer. The other teams have a number of pennants not significantly different from the expected number.

In the era 1947–87, inequality increased. The Yankees have fifteen more championships than expected. Relatively few pennants were left to be had by other American League teams, but what was left was equally divided, more or less. All of the original franchises, except New York, won fewer pennants than expected. The distribution of championships in the National League also became more unequal. During 1947–87, the Los Angeles Dodgers won 15 championships, and Cincinnati and St. Louis were credible contenders. With the exception of Atlanta, Chicago, and Houston all the remaining teams more or less won about as many pennants as expected. Overall, the distribution of pennants in the National League, while unequal, was less unequal than in the American League.

As a measure of quality, the league championship has become less reliable since 1969, when divisional play-offs were established to determine the champion. Before then, the league championship was earned over the course of an entire season of contests. The divisional play-off system, however, does not guarantee that the two clubs with the best seasonal records will compete in the World Series. Since 1969, the team with the lower win percentage has won the play-off 7 of 19 times in the National League and 9 of 19 times in the American League. As was pointed out, the play-offs are attractive from an economic perspective; but from a competitive perspective the concept of a league champion has lost some of its validity.

The Distribution of Win Percentages

A major limitation of using the number of championships amassed is that it is a binary measure (either you win or you do not). Also, the evolution over time of interteam playing strengths is obscured. The

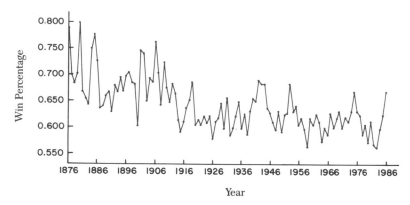

Figure 4.3   Percentage of Games Won by National League Champion Clubs, 1876–1986

Source: The Baseball Encyclopedia.

statistic does not indicate the margin by which teams were victorious. In fact, as is revealed in figure 4.3, the win percentage of the league champion has declined dramatically between 1876 and 1986. A cardinal measure of team performance that more adequately assesses the relative quality of play in baseball is thus needed, that is, one which takes into account the *distribution* of team win percentages. The most useful measure of this distribution is the standard deviation of team win percentages.

The concept of standard deviation is not understood widely by those who do not use statistical analysis. Since extensive use of the concept will be made, the statistic needs to be described. Suppose we have, as in table 4.2, a five-team league, consisting of teams A through E, that play each other an equal number of times. At the end of the season, team A has a record of .700, team B a record of .600, and so on. The average win percentage always must equal .500 (the mean), since each team's victory entails another team's loss. We want to know the statistical variation around the mean (.500) so that we can measure in a single number the distance from .500 that the teams collectively lie. To find this single measure, the mean is subtracted from the win percentage of each team and then the difference is squared, as in the table. When the squared differences are summed, the variance has been obtained. In our example, the variance in team win percentages is .10. The variance is a measure of dispersion, but it is inconvenient to interpret. When the variance is divided by the number of teams less one and the square root of that number taken, the standard deviation is obtained. In our example, the standard deviation is plus or minus .158.

Table 4.2   Example Calculation of the Standard Deviation of the Win
Percentages of a Hypothetical 5-Team League

Team	Win Percentage	Win Percentage Minus .500	Square of Result
A	.700	.200	.04
B	.600	.100	.01
C	.500	0	0
D	.400	−.100	.01
E	.300	−.200	.04
League Average[1]	.500	—	—
Variance[2]	—	—	.10
Standard Deviation[3]	.158	—	—

[1]The average is the sum of the team win percentages divided by the number of teams.
[2]The variance is the sum of the squared differences between the team win percentages and .500.
[3]The standard deviation is the square root of the variance after it has been divided by $n - 1$. In the example, since there are 5 teams, the variance is divided by 4. Thus, $.158 = \sqrt{.10/(5 - 1)}$.

Now, for the interpretation! At one standard deviation (+1.58 or −1.58), win percentages in the hypothetical league are distributed in the range of .342 to .658. One standard deviation applies to the distribution of win percentages of approximately two-thirds of the teams. That is, two-thirds of the teams in a league in a statistical sense are distributed within the win-percentage interval of .342 to .658. At two standard deviations (i.e., +.316 or −.316), 95 percent of the teams are distributed within the interval .184 to .816.

In figure 4.4, the standard deviation of the win percentages of National League teams is plotted from 1876 to 1987. Over the entire period, the average value of the standard deviation was about .100. Thus, on the average, win percentage records in the National League are distributed among the clubs in the range of .400 to .600. In the formative years, 1876–1900, both the average value of the standard deviation and its dispersion were higher. Team win percentages were in the range of .360–.640. The higher variance in the statistic reasonably can be attributed to the shorter schedules in these early years. From 1876–82, the number of games per season fluctuated from about 60 to 85. The pre-expansion 154-game schedule was established only in 1905. Since the number of games played in the early years was about one-half of those on today's schedule, we expect more volatility in the standings. The fewer number of games played between contestants, the more likely is the impact of random factors in the outcomes.

A second important observation about the standard deviation is that

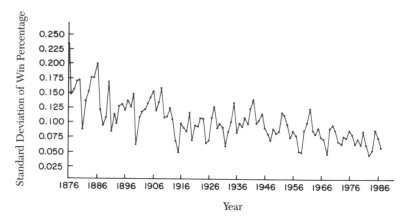

Figure 4.4   Standard Deviation of Win Percentage for National League Teams, 1876–1987

Source: Calculated from data in *The Baseball Encyclopedia.*

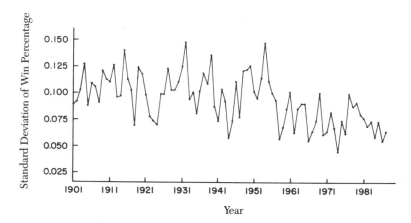

Figure 4.5   Standard Deviation of Win Percentage for American League Teams, 1901–1987

Source: Calculated from data in *The Baseball Encyclopedia.*

it is declining over time. The standard deviations in team win percentages in the National League declined at the rate of .0007 points per season. Team win percentages are now compactly distributed in the range of .430–.570 in contrast to the range of .360–.640 in the early years of the league.

Similarly, a negative trend in the standard deviation of the win percentage is found in the American League (see figure 4.5). Over the entire period, the average value was .090. In the early 1900s, the distribution of win percentages was in the range of .385–.615, similar to that in the National League. In recent years, the distribution has been about .430–.570, again similar to the National League.

Perhaps there is greater interest in the pattern of competition since 1947. The standard deviations of the win percentages from 1947 to 1987 for the National and American Leagues appear in figures 4.6 and 4.7,

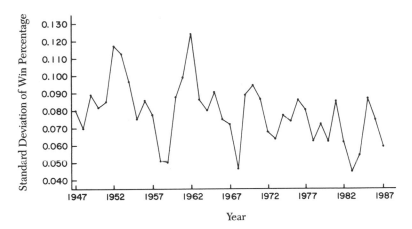

Figure 4.6　Standard Deviation of Win Percentage for National League Teams, 1947–1987

Source: Calculated from data in *The Baseball Encyclopedia.*

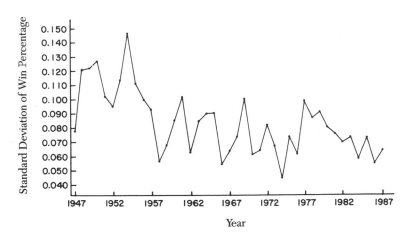

Figure 4.7　Standard Deviation of Win Percentage for American League Teams, 1947–1987

Source: Calculated from data in *The Baseball Encyclopedia.*

respectively. Before examining trends it is worth stopping to evaluate the effect of league expansion on playing quality. The expansion to ten teams in 1962 in the National League resulted in a large increase in the dispersion of club standings. The quality of play improved from 1963 to 1968 and then deteriorated in 1969 when the league expanded to 12 teams. Similar deteriorations in competitive playing strengths are revealed in figure 4.7 with the American League expansions in 1961, 1969, and 1977.

The relative quality of play has continued to improve in both leagues since World War II. The negative trend apparent in figures 4.6 and 4.7 is statistically significant. Interleague comparison of competitive playing strengths is facilitated by dividing the standard deviation of the win percentage of one league by the other league's standard deviation. The dispersion in club standings in the American League was divided by that in the National League standings and the result is graphically displayed in figure 4.8. Playing strengths were more equal in the National League during 1947–59 and 1977–83 and in the American League during 1968–76. However, there is no trend in the ratio. The two leagues' competitive playing strengths have been stable in comparison with each other throughout the modern era. However, competitive quality is somewhat greater in the National League.

Some significant conclusions now emerge. Over the history of the major leagues, relative team playing strengths have shown a tendency

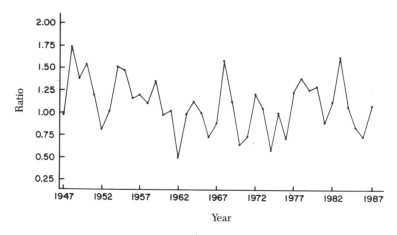

Figure 4.8   Ratio of Standard Deviations of the Win Percentages of the American to the National League, 1947–1987

Source: Calculated from data in *The Baseball Encyclopedia.*

to narrow, and this trend continues today. However, inequalities remain. To illustrate this point, if the trend in the standard deviation estimated for the period 1947–87 were to continue, statistical equality of play would not occur in the leagues for more than a century.

These findings need to be contrasted with the discussion on the distribution of league championships. Recall that the Yankees and the Dodgers grossly dominated their leagues in the post–1947 period. Inequality of playing strengths measured in this manner suggests continued inequality in both leagues in contrast to the findings regarding the distribution of win percentages. These findings are not inconsistent with one another. What it suggests is that while there are gross inequalities in the distribution of championships, the margin by which pennants are won is narrower today than in the past, and the margin separating the nonpennant clubs is narrowing.

Free Agency and Relative Club Quality

James Quirk and Mohamed El Hodiri first tested for the effect of size of city on the distribution of team standings using Spearman rank correlations, a test that measures the degree of statistical association between two variables, the values of which have been transformed to ranks in ascending or descending order.[19] They compared rank in the average win percentage of teams over the period 1900–1970 with rank in city population size. The Spearman rank correlations were positive but were not statistically significant. Correlations of rank of record and rank of city size from 1900 to 1952 in the National League and from 1903 to 1953 in the American League were higher than those of the longer period, but were still not statistically significant.[20] A correct conclusion from their test is that franchise location has no effect on team win percentages. However, the Quirk-El Hodiri test is flawed. The differences in population size among cities between 1900 and 1970 has narrowed substantially. This span of urban population history is simply too long to be meaningful. In light of the higher rank correlations for the earlier period of their study, an interpretation of their test is that big city dominance may have been a factor in major league baseball prior to World War II. Nevertheless, the positive correlations between city size and team record in the era of the reserve clause suggests that restrictions on player movement did not bring about competitiveness on the playing field.

The Effect of Free Agency on the Distribution of Playing Talent

Several studies have attempted to test for the effect of the 1976 change in the player reservation system on the distribution of club standings.

Most of these studies were premature. The research reported in this volume points to considerable instability in baseball data from year to year. Alleged effects need to be evaluated within an historical context. Often, changes in the framework of baseball take several seasons to work themselves out. An early study by Daly and Moore concluded that about two-thirds "of all free agents who were signed prior to January 1, 1980" moved from a smaller franchise market to a larger one.[21] There were 43 free agents whose movements were traced, and the source of the authors' data is the *New York Times,* 18 June 1978. We have already noted that 150 players became free agents prior to 1 January 1980.[22] Obviously, Daly and Moore examined the movement of the 1978 free agents. Their conclusion that the reserve clause was an effective constraint and that its removal adversely affected league balance is much too strong. The evidence from one season of free agents is inconclusive.

Christopher R. Drahozal calculated the mean size of the city in which 129 top quality free agents who signed contracts of five or more guaranteed years.[23] The free agents who moved were previously in cities with an average population of 2.75 million and relocated to cities whose average population was 2.72 million. The free agents who re-signed with their precontract clubs were in cities of a 3.04 million average size. No statistically significant differences in the average size of cities of movers and stayers was found.[24] Furthermore, he performed a Spearman rank correlation test on city size and team record for each league for the reserve clause period 1972–76 and the free agency period 1977–82. All of the rank correlations were positive and insignificantly small (.14 to .33). Thus, no relationship between city size and club win records was found.

Five more years of experience with free agency is available at this time. The period 1977–87 is sufficiently long to determine if anticompetitive playing effects are a consequence of veteran player free agency. In table 4.3, the relationship between franchise city size and win percentage is examined since league expansion. The win percentage in this case is cumulative wins divided by cumulative games from 1962 to 1987 in the National League and from 1961 to 1987 in the American League. Toronto and Seattle, which were expansion teams in 1977, are not included, since insufficient time has passed to calculate meaningfully their long-run competitiveness. The Spearman rank correlation is .09 in the National League and .41 in the American League. As a correlation coefficient of at least .55 is required for statistical significance, the hypothesis that franchise location is a significant determinant of playing strength over the 1961–87 period cannot be con-

Table 4.3   Win Percentage and Population Rankings and Correlations, 1961–1987

Team Location or Correlation	Population Rank	Win Percentage since 1961–62	Win Percentage Rank
National League			
Los Angeles	1	.547	2
Philadelphia	2	.510	6
New York	3	.454	11
Chicago	4	.474	10
Montreal	5	.481	8
St. Louis	6	.527	3
Houston	7	.481	7
Pittsburgh	8	.523	4
Atlanta	9	.474	9
San Diego	10	.437	12
San Francisco	11	.513	5
Cincinnati	12	.548	1
Rank Correlation 1962–87 0.09			
American League			
Detroit	1	.532	3
New York	2	.553	2
Chicago	3	.496	8
Boston	4	.521	5
Dallas/Fort Worth	5	.468	11
Baltimore	6	.565	1
Minneapolis	7	.503	7
Cleveland	8	.467	12
Oakland	9	.506	6
Anaheim	10	.485	9
Kansas City	11	.522	4
Milwaukee	12	.482	10
Rank Correlation 1961–87 0.41			

Note: City rank is adjusted for two-team cities. Team records are cumulative for games, since 1961 in the American League and 1962 in the National League. For Oakland the win percentage is calculated since 1968. Other records were calculated from the year in brackets as follows: Texas (1972), California (1965), Kansas City (1969), Milwaukee (1970), Montreal (1969), and San Diego (1969). Toronto and Seattle were created in the 1977 expansion and are ignored in the calculations.

firmed. In table 4.4, population rank and win percentage have been calculated for the pre–free agency (1961 or 1962 to 1976) and post–free agency (1977–87) periods. While the Spearman rank correlations are higher for the era of free agency, they are not statistically different from zero. *The hypothesis that free agency adversely affects league balance is therefore rejected.*

As a final test of the effect of free agency on the distribution of club standings, the standard deviations plotted in figures 4.6 and 4.7 were

Table 4.4   Win Percentage and Population Rankings and Correlations, before and after Free Agency

Location or Correlation	Pre–Free Agency, 1961–76			Post–Free Agency, 1977–87		
	Population Rank	Win Percentage	Rank	Population Rank	Win Percentage	Rank
National League						
Los Angeles	1	.555	2	1	.535	2
Philadelphia	2	.492	6	2	.537	1
New York	3	.440	10	3	.474	9
Chicago	4	.477	8	4	.469	11
Montreal	5	.430	11	5	.519	4
St. Louis	6	.529	5	7	.524	3
Pittsburgh	7	.542	3	8	.497	7
Houston	8	.457	9	6	.517	5
Atlanta	9	.488	7	9	.460	12
San Francisco	10	.535	4	11	.482	8
Cincinnati	11	.571	1	12	.515	6
San Diego	12	.393	12	10	.469	10
Rank Correlation						
1962–76 0.03						
1977–87 0.44						
American League						
Detroit	1	.525	5	1	.543	4
New York	2	.541	3	2	.570	1
Chicago	3	.497	8	3	.495	8
Boston	4	.507	6	5	.543	3
Dallas/Ft. Worth	5	.438	11	4	.483	9
Baltimore	6	.574	1	6	.551	2
Cleveland	7	.476	9	9	.455	12
Minneapolis	8	.529	4	7	.464	10
Oakland	9	.567	2	10	.455	11
Anaheim	10	.470	10	8	.501	7
Milwaukee	11	.429	12	12	.517	6
Kansas City	12	.498	7	11	.539	5
Rank Correlation						
1961–76 0.29						
1977–87 0.40						

Note: See note in table 4.3.

compared for the periods 1961–76 or 1962–76 with the period 1977–87. In the American League the average standard deviation rose from .073 in 1961–76 to .074 in 1977–87. The difference is not significant. In the National League the average standard deviation fell from .081 in 1962–76 to .068 in 1977–87. The drop in the dispersion of club standings is statistically significant. Recall that the American League expanded in 1977 and that expansion increases the dispersion in team standings. So if free agency has had any effect at all it has been a positive one: At least for the National League, competition on the playing field was keener during 1977–87 than during 1962–76.[25]

The Effect of the Narrowing of Market Size

During the lifetime of organized baseball, there has been substantial change in the distribution of the population of the United States. At the turn of the century, a significantly greater share of the total population was located in the urban centers of the Eastern coastal cities. Today, the U.S. population is more evenly distributed across the country. This trend in the diffusion of the population has had an impact on the variation in attendance across teams. The particular measure of variation utilized here is the *coefficient of variation*. The coefficient of variation is the standard deviation divided by the mean. This measure is employed because the mean contains a trend; i.e., league attendance has risen over the years. Failure to adjust for the growth of league attendance would bias the measure of the relative variation of attendance in an upward direction.

The coefficient of variation of team attendance for the two leagues exhibits a negative trend. The standard deviation of win percentages is statistically related to the coefficient of variation of team attendance. By statistical estimation we can determine that for every one-hundredth point reduction in the coefficient of variation of attendance in the American League, say from .500 to .499, the standard deviation of team win records fell one-thousandth of a point, say from .1000 to .0999. The coefficient of variation of attendance in the American League fell by more than half over the period. This was responsible for more than a .035 point drop in the standard deviation of club standings. In the National League, the effective reduction on the standard deviation of team win percentages is about half of that in the American League. Apparently, a narrowing of the size of the market in which teams compete has contributed to competitiveness on the playing field.

2
THE BUSINESS OF BASEBALL

5

The Fans' Demand for Winning

Over 52 million fans attended regular season major league games in 1987, spending $500 million on tickets, beer and food, and parking. More than 20 million went to minor league games. Many more fans heard games on the radio or saw them on television. Of course, baseball competes with other spectator sports for attention, as well as other leisure activities. In this chapter, two main questions are addressed. First, how viable is baseball financially? Is there sufficient demand for the games that the current size of the leagues is optimal? Second, what are the motivations of the owners? Do teams set ticket prices to cover costs or to maximize revenue? Or is there no relationship between team costs and ticket price?

The Growth of the Baseball Industry

Increases in the Supply of Team Contests

Only a small fraction of the population had the opportunity to see major league games in 1947. Historically, teams have located in major population centers, and prior to the development of the interstate highway system access to the city from the suburbs and beyond was inconvenient. Now, a much greater proportion of the population can physically attend games and almost everyone can see televised games, although not necessarily ones of their choosing. In 1947, each of 16 major league clubs in ten cities played a 154-game schedule. St. Louis was the westernmost on the circuits. Now, there are 26 teams playing a 162-game schedule in 24 cities, and there is some interest in the American League in expansion. The expansions thus far have brought a 70 percent increase in the supply of season contests and have added 12 cities to the league circuits.

While most people live in areas too small to support franchises, television has brought the game into almost everyone's home. But baseball was slow to realize the potential of television. In the 1940s and 1950s, televised games were rather modest undertakings by today's standards. The games were broadcast much like radio, only there was a picture. Now, games are elaborately packaged to fill certain market slots, and broadcasting represents 40 percent of team income. There is even some willingness to trade park attendance for pay-TV broadcast of home games. Because of the technological limitations on the broadcast of the full visual field of play, baseball is less suitable to the television medium than basketball or football. While the net benefits to baseball remain unclear, it is certain that broadcasts have made the game more accessible to fans.

Attendance Growth, 1947–87

A lot of people go to baseball games. The postwar course of average club attendance in the leagues is shown graphically in figure 5.1. On average, attendance has risen at the rate of 15,000 per year in the American League and 21,000 annually in the National League. Measured in percentage change, the growth rates have been 1.1 and 1.5 percent respectively in the American and National Leagues. National League clubs continue to outdraw American League teams. The gap was most noticeable in the late 1950s to the mid-1970s. But, the interleague attendance differential has shrunk. Less than 100,000 in attendance now separates the leagues. In 1987, seasonal attendance for teams in the National League averaged over 2 million fans per club, and the American League was not far behind.

Part of the growth in attendance is due to increased support from American business and from the season ticket purchases of avid fans. Roger Noll estimates that the number of separate individuals who at-

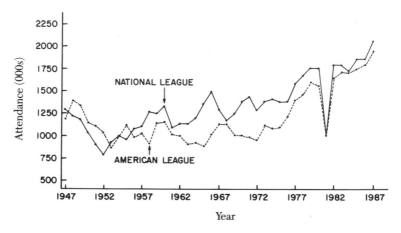

Figure 5.1   Average Club Attendance in the American and National Leagues, 1947–1987
Source: Collected from various editions of the *World Almanac* and *The Sporting News.*

Table 5.1   Major League Ticket Sales by Club and Category, 1984

Club	Attendance (000s)	Business (%)	Season (%)	Single Game (%)
National League				
Atlanta	1,725	34.2	21.5	59.3
Chicago	2,104	20.4	8.6	73.0
Cincinnati	1,278	53.9	61.0	31.8
Houston	1,230	55.1	55.0	29.4
Los Angeles	3,135	51.7	69.0	27.3
Montreal	1,607	53.2	56.7	29.5
New York	1,843	41.9	24.3	54.2
Philadelphia	2,063	61.5	30.8	23.8
Pittsburgh	774	51.9	41.0	39.0
St. Louis	2,037	48.2	34.3	49.3
San Diego	1,984	22.8	13.7	58.9
San Francisco	1,002	29.7	19.5	50.3
American League				
Baltimore	2,046	40.4	32.0	39.8
Boston	1,662	58.6	24.1	25.6
California	2,403	55.5	58.3	32.8
Chicago	2,137	41.2	31.1	39.3
Cleveland	734	44.4	16.9	54.0
Detroit	2,705	26.2	12.6	71.7
Kansas City	1,810	43.9	52.5	42.3
Milwaukee	1,609	35.7	27.1	60.4
Minnesota	1,598	45.3	11.3	53.3
New York	1,822	48.9	40.2	44.4
Oakland	1,353	31.9	16.6	62.1
Seattle	870	31.0	23.6	63.2
Texas	1,102	61.9	41.2	36.0
Toronto	2,110	50.5	34.5	46.0
Total	44,739[a]	42.9	33.8	46.5

[a]The total figure is accurate. The sum of individual figures differs from the total because of rounding.

Source: Ernst and Whinney, Report To Major League Baseball of 1 April 1985.

tend games during the season is roughly 10 to 20 percent of total attendance.[1] Thus, perhaps 200,000 to 400,000 individuals attended one or more league games in 1987. Less than half of all ticket sales in 1984 were private, single game tickets.[2] The source of attendance by team for 1984 is given in table 5.1. Business purchases ranged from a low of 20 percent or so in Chicago (Cubs), San Diego, and Detroit to more than half in Cincinnati, Houston, Los Angeles, Montreal, Pittsburgh, Boston, California, Texas, and Toronto. Moreover, businesses purchase more expensive tickets (luxury boxes, box seats, and reserved seats) and their purchases are less sensitive to ticket price changes and team standing.

Season ticket sales are sensitive to the previous season finish of the club. Certainly, the Chicago Cubs' .438 record in 1983 and Minnesota's .432 finish did not inspire fan enthusiasm for the 1984 season. Chicago turned in a .596 record in 1984 and sold a lot of single game tickets. But, previous finish is not a perfect predictor of season ticket sales. Detroit finished the 1983 season with a .568 record but had very poor season ticket and business sales.

Table 5.2 reveals wide differences in attendance among the clubs. In the 1969–74 period, average seasonal attendance in the American League was 1,027,417 plus or minus 242,873, for a coefficient of variation of 23.6 percent. In the National League the average attendance was 1,364,750 plus or minus 447,688, for a coefficient of variation of

Table 5.2   Average Seasonal Paid Attendance (000s), 1969–1986

Club	1969–74	1975–79	1980–84	1985–86
American League				
Baltimore	993	1,198	1,705	2,053
Boston	1,346	2,078	1,682	1,968
California	902	1,555	2,300	2,612
Chicago	924	1,015	1,597	1,547
Cleveland	716	773	848	1,064
Detroit	1,588	1,446	1,517	2,093
Kansas City	955	1,840	1,925	2,242
Milwaukee	832	1,372	1,744	1,308
Minnesota	987	895	923	1,439
New York	1,130	2,055	2,073	2,242
Oakland	1,133	637	1,306	1,325
Seattle	—	—	845	1,078
Texas	823	1,302	1,134	1,402
Toronto	—	—	1,494	2,462
National League				
Atlanta	1,013	780	1,444	1,369
Chicago	1,439	1,335	1,321	2,011
Cincinnati	1,681	2,471	1,382	1,764
Houston	1,319	1,176	1,548	1,459
Los Angeles	2,029	2,818	3,177	3,144
Montreal	1,223	1,304	1,998	1,316
New York	2,151	1,212	1,235	2,765
Philadelphia	1,228	2,490	2,172	1,882
Pittsburgh	1,245	1,187	1,042	869
St. Louis	1,588	1,493	1,773	2,555
San Diego	674	1,449	1,364	2,008
San Francisco	787	1,009	1,036	1,174

Sources: Collected from various *World Almanacs* and *The Sporting News.*

32.8 percent. Thus, at least in this period there was more variability in attendance among the clubs in the National League than in the American. The strongest drawing clubs in the American League during the 1970s were Boston, Detroit and New York. The weakest clubs were Cleveland, Minnesota, and Oakland. In the National League, the clubs with the best attendance during the 1970s were Los Angeles, Philadelphia, and Cincinnati. The teams with the poorest attendance records were Atlanta, San Diego, and San Francisco. The conventional wisdom in baseball is that 1.5 to 1.7 million in attendance currently is roughly the point at which operating revenues begin to exceed operating costs. In the 1985–86 period, attendance was in the interval of 1.25 to 2.3 million in the American League and 1.18 to 2.55 million in the National League. Six clubs in the American League averaged over 2 million fans. Cleveland and Seattle were the lowest drawing clubs. In the National League, Los Angeles dominated with over 3 million in attendance, but the Mets, St. Louis, Chicago, and San Diego drew over 2 million fans to the park. Pittsburgh did poorly at the gate, as did San Francisco.

Ticket Prices

Whatever other complaints fans may make of their teams, ticket prices should not be included. Obviously, ticket prices have gone up, but they have not increased at the rate of general prices. Nominal and real average ticket prices from 1920 to 1986 are given in table 5.3. From 1920 to 1970 ticket prices rose from $1.00 to $3.18, but real ticket

Table 5.3 Average Nominal and Real Ticket Prices, 1920–1986

Year	Average Ticket Price ($)	Real Ticket Price (1967 $)
1920	1.00	1.66
1939	1.20	2.88
1946	1.40	2.39
1950	1.60	2.22
1958	1.87	2.16
1960	2.05	2.31
1965	2.46	2.60
1970	3.18	2.73
1976	3.45	2.02
1980	4.53	1.84
1986	6.70	1.98

Sources: 1920–50, *Organized Baseball*, 98; 1958–70, calculations by Roger G. Noll based on Commerce Department data; 1976–86, *Amusement Business*, 1 August 1987.

prices (ticket price divided by the Consumer Price Index) were erratic and were within the range of $1.66 to $2.88. Ticket prices in 1986 were twice those of 1970, but still the increase was less than the rate of inflation. In real terms, during the 1980s ticket prices were as low as they were in 1920.

Prices vary considerably among the clubs (see table 5.4). Historically, prices have been marginally lower in the American League. In 1980, the average ticket price in the American League was $4.43 compared to $4.24 in the National League. In 1984, average ticket prices were more than $1.00 higher in the National League. The lowest ticket prices in the American League were at Toronto, Oakland, and Seattle. The highest prices were at Boston and New York. In the National League, Chicago and Montreal charged the least and Houston, Pittsburgh, and San Francisco the most for the games.

Table 5.4   Ticket Prices by Club, 1980–84

Club	Price 1980	Price/Win Percentage	Price 1984	Price/Win Percentage
American League	4.43	8.9	5.81	11.6
New York	5.99	9.4	6.70	12.5
Boston	5.10	9.8	6.67	12.6
Milwaukee	4.82	9.1	6.36	15.3
Detroit	4.74	9.1	6.03	9.4
Texas	4.62	9.8	6.24	14.6
Kansas City	4.50	7.5	5.62	10.8
Minnesota	4.40	9.2	5.33	10.7
Toronto	4.35	10.5	4.54	8.3
Cleveland	4.30	8.7	6.02	13.0
Chicago	4.30	9.8	6.06	13.3
Baltimore	4.10	6.6	5.58	10.6
Seattle	4.00	11.0	5.24	11.5
California	3.85	10.6	5.81	11.6
Oakland	3.00	5.9	5.14	10.8
National League	4.24	8.5	6.88	13.8
Montreal	5.00	8.5	5.99	12.4
St. Louis	4.75	10.4	6.72	12.9
Cincinnati	4.75	8.7	7.47	17.3
New York	4.55	11.0	6.52	11.7
Philadelphia	4.50	8.0	7.44	14.9
Chicago	4.48	11.3	5.64	9.5
Houston	4.34	7.6	7.99	16.2
Pittsburgh	4.05	7.9	7.92	17.1
Atlanta	4.05	8.1	6.65	13.5
Los Angeles	3.70	6.6	6.48	13.3
San Francisco	3.65	7.8	7.73	19.0
San Diego	3.05	6.8	6.05	10.7

Source: The Sporting News, 12 April 1980; Ernst and Whinney Report, 1 April 1985.

An alternative way of looking at ticket prices is to deflate them by team quality. The method of comparison is somewhat more cumbersome but makes price comparisons more meaningful. In the table, the average ticket prices for 1980 and 1984 are divided by the club's win percentage. By this method, the least expensive baseball in the American League in 1984 was in Toronto and Detroit. In Toronto, the fans paid 8.3 cents per point in the club's win percentage. In Detroit, the fans paid 9.4 cents. The Toronto fan benefited from low ticket prices ($4.54) and above-average quality (wins = .547). In Detroit, the fans paid above-average ticket prices ($6.03), but got well above-average baseball (wins = .642). At the other end of the price-quality spectrum in the American League were Milwaukee and Texas. Fans in both locations got above-average ticket prices ($6.36 and $6.24) and below-average quality (wins of .416 and .427, respectively). In the National League, fans paid dearly for games in Cincinnati, Pittsburgh, and Houston. The best price-quality ratio was at Chicago ($5.64 for a .594 win percentage) and San Diego ($6.05 for a .565 club record).

Broadcast Rights

Most fans see the games on television. Broadcast rights were worth $350 million in 1987—about $13.5 million per club. Part of these rights were packaged in a national contract with ABC-TV, NBC-TV, and CBS-Radio, negotiated by the Commissioner's Office, and worth $196.5 million. The contract covered Saturday and prime-time regular season games, the All-Star Game, League Championship games, and the World Series. Partly, these national rights are of great value, because TV audience ratings for baseball are high. From 1980 to 1986, baseball household audience shares averaged 11.1 percent. While lower than pro football (with an average share over the same period of 16.5 percent), the baseball audience share is larger than that of any other professional or collegiate sport.[3] Sponsors pay dearly for access to the young male audience who watch the games. In 1986, the top 25 network sports advertisers spent $767 million hawking their products.[4] Local rights, negotiated by each club and mainly covering road games, brought $153.4 million to the clubs collectively.

Television income has grown more rapidly than gate receipts. Prior to 1965, clubs earned less than $1 million from the sale of broadcast rights. The lion's share came from the sale of local rights (see table 5.5). The value of both the local and national television rights grew at the same rate through the 1970s. About 60 percent of the broadcast revenues came from the local market sales. In 1980, the value of the national broadcast rights rose dramatically, jumping from $23.3 to $41.6 million. In 1984, the value of these rights rose from $58 to $163 mil-

Table 5.5   Fees from the Sale of Broadcast Rights, 1946–1987 (figures in 000s)

Year	Local Rights	National Rights	Total Rights	Per Club
1946	838	—	—	52
1950	3,365	—	—	210
1955	6,123	—	7,308	383
1960	9,355	3,174	15,779	783
1965	15,970	5,950	25,670	1,096
1970	21,850	9,600	38,150	1,310
1972	23,085	18,000	41,185	1,716
1973	24,385	18,000	42,385	1,766
1974	25,245	18,000	43,245	1,802
1975	26,495	18,000	44,495	1,854
1976	26,885	23,250	50,820	2,118
1977	28,835	23,250	52,110	2,004
1978	29,235	23,250	52,510	2,020
1979	31,225	23,250	54,500	2,096
1980	38,650	41,575	80,275	3,088
1981	48,400	41,575	89,975	3,461
1982	64,950	53,400	118,350	4,552
1983	94,710	58,000	152,710	5,873
1984	105,400	163,000	267,950	10,306
1985	116,900	161,000	277,900	10,688
1986	139,450	181,000	320,450	12,325
1987	153,350	196,500	349,850	13,456

Sources: 1946–70, Ira Horowitz, "Sports Broadcasting," in Government and the Sports Business, ed. Roger G. Noll (Washington, D.C.: The Brookings Institution, 1974), 287; 1972–87, Broadcasting, annual March issues.

lion, and now, 56 percent of broadcast income arises from the national contract. Furthermore, the availability of extensive cable and pay-TV networks poses opportunities for the sale of broadcast rights. Some teams are taking advantage of these opportunities, now earning over $1 million from these sources. But, the potential has been barely exploited. Large fees might be obtained by selling these rights collectively in the manner of the network national broadcast contract. Collusively marketed, these rights would be worth a multiple of local broadcast rights on free television. But such a move is not costless. National cable television of course penetrates the formerly insular local broadcast markets. For this reason alone it is now more difficult to protect home attendance and local market broadcast rights. While selling the broadcast rights to home games is financially attractive, there are implications for attendance. Furthermore, many clubs are the creatures of other businesses, whose profits depend partly on the current autonomous arrangements in local broadcasting (Anheuser-Busch and the St. Louis Cardinals, Turner Broadcasting and the Atlanta Braves, etc.). A large number of the teams in baseball are either owned all or in part by broadcasters or affiliated with them to market their broadcast rights. Broadcast of the team's games is part of their programming.

There is wide variance in the value of local broadcast rights among the clubs. Local rights by team for 1987 are given in table 5.6. The Yankees sold their television rights to WPIX-TV, their radio rights to WABC, and their cable rights to Sports Channel for a total of $17.5 million. The Mets were close behind at $16.5 million. The Mets have a partnership arrangement with the broadcast originators and like the Yankees sell cable rights to Sports Channel. Local rights were also lucrative for Philadelphia ($9.5 million) and the Chicago White Sox ($9.3 million). Both clubs sell rights to local stations. Contrast the relatively modest fees which accrued to the Chicago Cubs ($4.3 million); however, this probably does not represent their actual market value.

Table 5.6   Local Broadcast Fees, Originators and Sponsors, 1987

Club	Fees	TV	Radio	Principal Sponsors
Baltimore	6.3	WMAR	WCBM	Stroh's, Subaru, Firestone
Boston	6.5	WSBK	WPLM	Busch, Polaroid, Nissan, Chevrolet
Cleveland	3.0	WUAB	WWWE	Busch, Community Mutual
Detroit	5.0	WDIV	WJR	Miller, McDonald's, Taco Bell
Milwaukee	3.6	WVTV	WTMJ	Pabst, Amoco, Pepsi, State Farm
Yankees	17.5	WPIX	WABC	Busch, Dodge, Toyota, Burger King
Toronto	7.8	CTV	CJCL	Labatts, Honda, Michelin
California	4.2	KTLA	KMPC	Chevron, Chevrolet, Busch
White Sox	9.3	WFLD	WMAQ	Miller, Nissan, Illinois State Lottery
Kansas City	3.1	WDAF	WIBW	Miller, Busch, Ford
Minnesota	4.0	KMSP	WCCO	Miller, Busch, Red Owl
Oakland	3.0	KPIX	KSFO	Busch, Unocal, Toyota
Seattle	2.2	KIRO	KIRO	Busch, GTE, AllState, Unocal
Texas	6.0	KTVT	WBAP	Busch, Nissan, Texaco, True Value
Cubs	4.3	WGN	WGN	Busch, Pepsi, Buick
Montreal	7.0	CBC	CFCF	Labatts, Coca Cola, Chrysler
Mets	16.5	WOR	WHN	Busch, Nissan, Manufacturers Hanover Trust
Phillies	9.5	WTAF	WCAV	(Not listed)
Pittsburgh	4.0	KDKA	KDKA	Busch, Giant Eagle, Chevrolet
St. Louis	5.1	KSDK	KMOX	Busch, Chevrolet, True Value
Atlanta	4.0	WTBS	WSB	Busch, Coca Cola, Delta, True Value
Cincinnati	6.8	WLWT	WLW	Busch, Ford, Long John Silver
Houston	3.6	KTXH	KTRH	Busch, Goody's, American Air
Los Angeles	5.0	KTTV	KABC	Miller, Nissan, Coca Cola
San Diego	4.2	KUSI	KFMB	Mitsubishi, Jack in the Box
San Francisco	2.9	KTVU	KNBR	Toyota, Pacific Bell

Source: Broadcasting, 2 March 1987.

WGN-TV and WGN (AM), the rights holder, are owned in common with the Cubs. A similar arrangement exists for the Atlanta Braves and WTBS. There are implications of this type of arrangement for the profitability of baseball franchises, which will be discussed in chapter 7. The Braves and the Cubs aside, the value of the local rights more or less is determined by the size of the broadcast market. The New York market is huge—a potential audience of perhaps 20 million. The Seattle, Kansas City, and Milwaukee markets are small. Some markets are shared (San Francisco and Oakland) and others overlap.

The young males who constitute the audience for baseball games are not a major market for deodorants or detergents. The sponsors of baseball games thus tend to be purveyors of cheap beer, inexpensive cars, and junk food. The most common ad is for Budweiser beer. Indeed, it has been claimed that August Busch bought a baseball team to peddle beer.[5] Since Budweiser is nationally marketed, ads appear in the broadcasts of most teams. The company spent $96.1 million in 1986 advertising on network sporting events.[6] Other breweries like Miller in the U.S. and Labatt in Canada purchase large blocks of commercial time. Tobacco used to rank second to beer as a source of sponsorship, but that ended in the early 1970s when the cigarette industry agreed to discontinue television advertising in the public interest. The sponsorship of clubs by petroleum, banking, insurance, and automobile (as well as brewing) firms has been a feature of the industry since the age of television.[7]

Ticket Price, Team Quality, and the Demand for Games

Does baseball obey the law of demand and do owners price the product rationally? To some readers the question may seem trivial, to others outrageous. The conjecture that motivates the question depends critically on whether baseball is viewed as a business or as a sport. The myth, more strongly held in the past, was that baseball is a sport whose participants are committed to winning at any price. Ticket prices were set more or less to defray expenses. The alternative view is that of small entrepreneurs coldly calculating the effect of every team initiative and response on the bottom line. This view also is mythical. Most club owners derive their income from other activities, and profit or loss from their clubs is not a preoccupation. A more accurate description of the motives of ownership of baseball clubs lies somewhere between these two caricatures.

The Determinants of Fan Attendance

The number of fans that click the turnstiles during a season ought to be related to several readily identifiable factors. Fans prefer winning clubs to losing teams and low ticket prices to high ones. More fans should attend games in large cities than in small ones. Factors other than these have been shown to affect attendance.[8] These factors include the number of star players on the team, per capita income, stadium age, various measures of the team's pennant hopes, and the proportion of the population in the urban area that is black. Some of these variables are analyzed here but appear to be less important than they were in the Noll study. A limitation to including more factors in the analysis is the paucity of data. The data used here consists of observations on 26 clubs during the 1984 season. Occam's Razor and the practical demands of statistical testing dictate that a demand model with a minimum number of variables be specified.

A naive demand function for baseball tickets relates quantity purchased to ticket price, the prices of related goods, income, and the size of the market. Where quality differences exist among the items, adjustment for the effect of each needs to be taken into account. In the demand models estimated below, two variables normally included in such an analysis are omitted—income and the number of substitutes. Their omission has no material effect on the other variables in the equations. In Noll's study of the demand for baseball in the 1970 and 1971 seasons, the effect of per capita income on club attendance was negative and statistically significant.[9] The result is paradoxical. Baseball may be a working man's sport, but it is not an inferior good. In various stages of the empirical analysis I included 1983 SMSA (Standard Metropolitan Statistical Area) per capita income, but the result never was statistically significant.[10] Also, Noll found that the greater the number of other professional teams, the lower the attendance in baseball. I found no such depressing effect on baseball attendance.[11] It may be that the seasons of competing professional sports overlap the baseball season insufficiently to have much of an impact. Or, the increase in the number of teams across cities and in the general popularity of team sports has reduced the variance in baseball attendance arising from the competition of these other sports.

Estimates of the demand for baseball tickets in the 1984 season appear in table 5.7. The dependent variable is season attendance. The independent variables are ticket price in 1984, the club's win percentage in the 1984 and the 1983 seasons, and the 1984 population of the

Table 5.7   Regressions of Season Attendance Correlated with Price, Team Standing, and Population, 1984

Variable	(1)	(2)	(3)
Intercept	−881.74*	8.43	1170.54
Ticket Price	−172.07	−0.61*	−0.092
1984 Win Percentage	84.74	1.28	0.78
1983 Win Percentage	2858.68	1.08	0.69*
1984 Population	0.18	0.22*	0.00009*
$\bar{R}^2$	.68	.51	.59
(N)	(26)	(26)	(26)

Note: In equation (1) all of the variables are arithmetic. In equation (2) all variables are in logarithms. In equation (3) all of the independent variables have been multiplied by 1984 Population.

All of the variables that are not statistically significant at the .95 percent level or better are noted with an asterisk.

Source: The data on attendance and ticket price are from tables 5.1 and 5.4. The data on the 1983 and 1984 club records is from The Baseball Encyclopedia. The data on 1984 Population is from the U.S. Bureau of the Census, Statistical Abstract of the United States: 1986 (106th edition) Washington, D.C., 1985.

city in which the franchise is located. Ticket price is total ticket receipts divided by total paid attendance, from records supplied by the Office of the Commissioner of Baseball. Thus, price reflects actual fan choices among available box seats, reserved seats, general admission, and bleachers. The club's win percentage in 1984 is a proxy for the team's quality during the season in which attendance is observed. Presumably, holding ticket price and the size of the market constant, the more games the team is winning the greater is fan interest. The club's record from the previous season is included for two reasons. In the beginning of the season attendance may be affected more by the club's previous finish than its current standing. As the season progresses more information about the club's prospects is available from its current standing than from the previous season's record. More importantly, season ticket sales are greatly affected by the previous season's standing, since that is the only information available to the fan at the time of purchase. Finally, population size in the franchise urban area in 1984 is employed as a measure of market size. The variable certainly is highly correlated with the team's market size, but it is by no means an exact surrogate. While expressways link the suburbs and outlying areas with the central city, urban traffic congestion differs as well as population density patterns. Census statistical designations are somewhat arbitrary and hardly tailored to our purpose. Nevertheless, there is no suitable alternative.

The demand equation was estimated in three functional forms. In equation (1) in table 5.7, all of the variables are in their original form, and hence the equation is what we call "linear." In equation (2), all of the variables have been transformed into logarithms. Relationships in the logarithmic form are employed when one is concerned with the relationship between percentage changes in the variables rather than absolute changes. In equation (3), a formulation suggested by Noll, the independent variables have been scaled (multiplied) by population size. The multiplicative specification represents the aggregation of individual demand functions. Also, the inclusion of the specification here permits comparison with Noll's results for the 1970 and 1971 seasons.

All of the independent variables are of the correct sign and are statistically significant at the 95 percent level or above in the linear demand function [equation (1)] in table 5.7. The estimate of the price effect is that each dollar increase in average ticket price reduced attendance by 172,000, holding team quality and market size constant. Converted to an elasticity at the mean ticket price ($6.31) and mean attendance (1,720.8), demand is inelastic at -0.63 [$= (6.31/1720.8) \times -172.07$]. If demand were truly inelastic at current prices (that is, if price did not matter much to a potential purchaser), clubs could raise revenues by raising ticket prices. Such a finding would offer some support for the notion that teams are run more as a sport than as a business. But, the error around the estimated coefficient is sufficiently large to include a value of the coefficient that is elastic. At one standard error, the estimated point elasticity of demand is -0.96. At two standard errors it is -1.29. Moreover, the price of the ticket is only a fraction of the total cost of attending a game. Opportunity costs aside, there are travel and parking costs as well as expenditures on beer, hot dogs, and souvenirs. If the ticket price were one-third of the fan's outlay the elasticity estimate is biased downward by a factor of 3. Thus, *there is no evidence that owners charge ticket prices any different from that which will maximize club revenues.* The demand function based on the linear equation is shown graphically in figure 5.2 for small, average, and large franchise cities.

Returning to table 5.7, holding ticket price and market size constant, more wins bring more fans to the park. Each one point increase in the 1984 record increased season attendance by 3,485 admissions. An additional game won (an increase of 6.2 points in the win percentage) brought in an additional 21,511 fans or $135,730 in ticket revenues, at the average ticket price. While the coefficient on the 1983 win percentage is a bit smaller, the effect is still quite large. The result is consistent with the high fraction of season ticket sales out of total attendance.

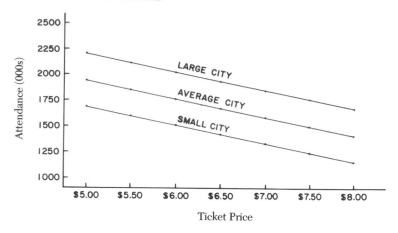

Figure 5.2   The Demand for Games: The Effect of Ticket Price on Attendance

Holding ticket price and team quality constant, an extra one million in population size is worth 180,000 fans or $1,135,800 in ticket revenues to a club. The effect of city size is seen graphically in figure 5.2.

Overall, the ticket price, team quality, and population variables are associated with 68 percent of the variance in attendance, which is comparable to Noll's results with a much larger number of independent variables. I have already pointed to the lack of statistical success of including per capita income and number of competing sports teams as regressors. I also experimented with the percentage of black population and championship status in the 1983 season, but these variables performed poorly.[12] Perhaps, the variable measuring the effect of star players on club attendance is the most interesting of those omitted from analysis. Noll found this variable to be a statistically significant source of attendance variation across teams. I believe that star players affect attendance, although measuring star status independently of performance is difficult. All-Star ballots may be a proxy, but there is a size-of-city effect as well as a performance effect in the measure. That is, a star player gets more votes playing in New York or Los Angeles than if he were playing in Kansas City or Milwaukee. Moreover, team performance is related to the number of star players in the sense that their superior performance produces more club victories.

Let us briefly review equations (2) and (3) in the table for comparison. In the log-linear format, the estimated price elasticity is −0.61 with a standard error of +/−0.41. Thus, the price elasticity of demand is within the interval −.020 to −1.02 and a unitary elasticity of demand cannot be rejected as an hypothesis. Where price is multiplied by population (equation number 3 in the table), the price elasticity of demand is −0.95. Adding the standard error to the coefficient includes unit elasticity in the interval. These results are consistent with the results for the linear demand equation. Ticket pricing is consistent with revenue maximization.

Quality Adjusted Ticket Price and Baseball Demand

The statistical significance of 1984 win percentage in the demand equations in table 5.7 supports the hypothesis that, holding ticket price and other factors constant, variations in team quality affect attendance. To a certain extent ticket price reflects team quality in baseball. Frequently, league champions raise ticket prices substantially in the following season. But, ticket prices are set prior to Opening Day and are based on expectations about what the market will bear for the club's expected performance during the season. While clubs may not perform as expected during the season, ticket prices are not adjusted to reflect the actual quality of the team. Thus, an interpretation of the coefficient of attendance on 1984 win percentage is that it adjusts ticket price for team quality.

A more direct approach to determining the demand for team quality is to adjust ticket price directly for team quality by dividing ticket price by win percentage. Ticket prices per unit of quality for teams in 1984 were given in table 5.4. Toronto at 8.3 cents was the lowest priced team, while San Francisco at 19.0 was the highest.

Table 5.8 presents the quality-price demand functions in the three functional forms previously discussed. Since ticket price is divided by 1984 win percentage, that variable no longer appears as a regressor. Other than these changes all else is the same as in the specifications in table 5.7. The demand function based on the linear specification and for the average size city is shown graphically in figure 5.3.

The quality adjusted ticket price variable is much stronger statis-

Table 5.8   Regressions of Season Attendance Correlated with Quality-Price, Team Standing, and Population, 1984

Variable	(1)	(2)	(3)
Intercept	974.90*	8.21	1512.73
Price/1984 Win Percentage	−101.91	−0.87	−0.04
1983 Win Percentage	3026.09	1.11	1.06
1984 Population	0.19	0.27	0.0002*
$\bar{R}^2$	.62	.51	.65
(N)	(26)	(26)	(26)

Note: See note in table 5.7.

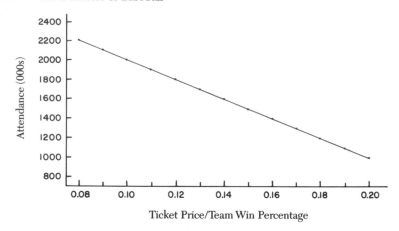

Figure 5.3   The Demand for Quality: The Effect on Attendance of Ticket Price per Win Percentage

tically. In the linear specification each one-cent increase in ticket price per point of club win percentage reduces attendance by 101,910, holding previous record and market size constant. At the mean quality-price (12.8 cents) and mean attendance, the point estimate of the elasticity of demand is −0.76. At one standard error the price elasticity is −0.97. In the log-linear format the own price elasticity is −0.87. At one standard error the elasticity is −1.13. In the multiplicative version of the model for the average-size city the price elasticity is −0.92. At one standard error, the elasticity is −1.14. Clearly, ticket pricing and level of team quality are set to maximize revenue among the clubs.

6

Team Revenue and Costs

In the previous chapter the great disparity in attendance and local broadcast rights among the clubs was documented. The ratio between the highest and the lowest attendance figures was about 3.6 to 1. With respect to local broadcast fees, the ratio was about 8 to 1. In chapter 4, the implication of this dispersion in team financial strength on the distribution of playing strengths among the clubs was discussed. The wide dispersion in attendance and in local broadcast fees within the leagues is an important concern, because of its implications for the financial health of some of the clubs and their ability to compete effectively on the playing field. In this chapter, the main factors affecting teams' revenues and costs are examined. Once these financial aspects of the clubs have been understood, we can take up the more controversial matter of club profitability.

Club Revenues in Baseball

Revenues arise mainly from three sources: (1) game receipts, (2) broadcast fees, and (3) concessions and parking revenues. About 80 to 85 percent of game receipts are net receipts from home games, with the remainder coming from shares from road games and from exhibition games. Of the broadcast fees, about 55 percent from the national contract and the remainder from the sale of local radio and TV rights and from cable and pay television. Of the local broadcast rights, 70 percent are from television. Concession revenues principally (70 percent) come from net receipts on beer, food, and novelty sales, but also from net restaurant and net advertising receipts. Additionally, some small revenue is earned from royalties and licensing fees and other miscellaneous sources.

The distribution of an average club's revenues by source and the growth of these revenues in recent years is given in table 6.1. In 1974, a typical club earned about $6.3 million, with better than 60 percent of its revenue arising from ticket sales. In the ten-year period, average club revenues rose at an annual rate of 13.5 percent to $20 million. The

Table 6.1   Operating Statements of an Average Baseball Team, 1974–1983 (all figures in 000s)

Item	1974	1977	1980	1983
Revenues	6,338	8,884	13,516	20,064
Game Receipts	3,871	5,555	7,797	10,370
Broadcast Fees	1,506	1,878	3,432	6,267
Concessions and Other	961	1,451	2,287	3,426
Costs	6,602	8,994	14,276	22,625
Team	1,998	3,182	6,071	10,665
Player Salaries	1,115	1,824	4,236	8,256
Player Development	914	1,029	1,546	2,180
Team Replacement	988	1,153	1,458	2,334
Stadium Operations	1,145	1,456	2,060	2,668
Sales	481	731	987	1,724
General and Administrative	914	1,280	1,786	2,449
Spring Training	108	104	265	414
Miscellaneous	53	59	102	192
Profit (Loss), Baseball Operations	(264)	(110)	(761)	(2,562)
Other Income (Expense)	(30)	(70)	(263)	(624)
Interest Income	88	47	254	199
Interest Expense	(161)	(164)	(352)	(776)
Other	44	47	(165)	(47)
Profit (Loss) before Taxes	(294)	(180)	(1,024)	(3,186)

Source: The data was provided to the author by Roger G. Noll.

greatest increase in revenues over the period was from the sale of broadcast rights.

Revenues by club for 1980, 1982, and 1984 are presented for the American League in table 6.2 and for the National League in table 6.3. Over the period, the average club earned $17.5 million in revenue. In the American League, the clubs with the largest revenues during this period were the Yankees, California, Detroit, and Kansas City. The weakest clubs financially were Seattle, Minnesota, Cleveland, Texas, and Oakland. In the National League, the Los Angeles Dodgers earned the largest revenues, followed by Philadelphia. Montreal and Houston ranked high, also. The weakest clubs were Pittsburgh, San Diego, Atlanta, San Francisco, and St. Louis. The average American League club had annual revenues of $16.4 million between 1980 and 1984, with a standard deviation of $5.4 million. The average National League team had revenues of $18.3 million, with a standard deviation of $5.7 million. Looked at another way, there were 5 clubs below $14 million in revenues in the American League and none in the National League.

The Main Factors Affecting Team Revenue

The factors that determine revenues are a subset of those already identified in the demand functions in the previous chapter. Club receipts basically are determined by the quality of the team and the size of the market. A simple linear total revenue function was estimated using the team total revenue data for 1984 contained in tables 6.2 and 6.3, and specifying the win percentage in 1984 and 1983 and the population size in 1984 as explanatory variables.[1] The reasoning for including the club record for 1983 in the determination of 1984 revenues is similar to the reasoning for its inclusion in the demand functions. Season ticket sales are determined mainly by prior finish. Local broadcast fees negotiated prior to the season may be partly affected by audience ratings from the previous season.

The estimated total revenue function appears in table 6.4. All of the independent variables are statistically significant at the 95 percent level or above. Each one million in population is worth $2.9 million in club revenues, holding the quality of the club constant. The relationship between population size and revenues for a .500 club is illustrated in figure 6.1. An average club in a city of one million would be expected to have earned a little over $18 million in 1984. The same club located in a population center of five million would have earned $30 million.

Each 1-point increase in a club's win percentage in 1984, holding the effect of its 1983 record and population size constant, added about $29,000 in revenue. The relationship between club quality and club revenue is illustrated in figure 6.2. A club located in an average size city and having had a .500 record in 1983 has predicted revenues of $23.4 million, if it turned in the same performance in 1984. If its record had slipped to .400, its revenues would have been $20.5 million. If its record had improved to .600, club revenues would have reached $26.3 million.

Of course, many other factors beside club quality and size of the market affect revenues. But these variables alone are associated with 75 percent of the variance in team revenues. Since there are so few observations available for analysis, the inclusion of more variables of lesser importance (e.g., age of stadium, fraction of night games, etc.) will not add at the margin that much more information to the study of club revenues.

Table 6.2   Summary Operating Statements of American League Teams, 1980–1984 (all figures in 000s)

	Baseball Averages	Balt	Bos	Cal	Chi	Clev
1980 Operations						
Revenues	12795	11581	16068	13147	9908	7549
Costs	11257	8983	11898	11821	8731	8171
Operating Profit (Loss)	1538	2598	4170	1326	1177	(622)
Other Income (Expense)	(2491)	(4978)	(5186)	(94)	(2546)	(2286)
Profit (Loss)	(953)	(2380)	(1016)	1232	(1369)	(2908)
1982 Operations						
Revenues	16224	13610	18106	21171	17235	9357
Costs	16322	12736	14353	21658	18867	12247
Operating Profit (Loss)	(98)	874	3753	(487)	(1632)	(2890)
Other Income (Expense)	(3934)	(2792)	(3651)	(635)	(6677)	(2767)
Profit (Loss)	(4033)	(1918)	102	(1122)	(8309)	(5657)
1984 Operations						
Revenues	23504	24658	22336	27272	27384	13918
Costs	21404	20092	17359	26029	23503	12951
Operating Profit (Loss)	2100	4556	4977	1243	3881	967
Other Income (Expense)	(4288)	(3742)	(4955)	(2789)	(4937)	(2413)
Profit (Loss)	(2188)	824	22	(1546)	(1056)	(1446)

Source: The data was provided to the author by Roger G. Noll.

Table 6.3   Summary Operating Statements of National League Teams, 1980–1984 (all figures in 000s)

	Baseball Averages	Atl	Chi	Cin	LA
1980 Operations					
Revenues	12795	8533	10236	15471	23415
Costs	11257	10207	10711	12389	16780
Operating Profit (Loss)	1538	(1674)	(475)	3082	6635
Other Income (Expense)	(2491)	(1766)	(1308)	(2307)	(4088)
Profit (Loss)	(953)	(3440)	(1783)	775	2547
1982 Operations					
Revenues	16224	14188	12933	14923	37340
Costs	16332	14145	16159	14582	22494
Operating Profit (Loss)	(98)	43	(3226)	341	14846
Other Income (Expense)	(3934)	(1643)	(7036)	(5245)	(5444)
Profit (Loss)	(4033)	(1600)	(10262)	(4904)	9402
1984 Operations					
Revenues	23504	20683	29783	20053	42018
Costs	21404	21368	23787	17880	28204
Operating Profit (Loss)	2100	(685)	5996	2173	13814
Other Income (Expense)	(4288)	(2241)	(7544)	(4838)	(7383)
Profit (Loss)	(2188)	(2926)	(1548)	(2665)	6431

Source: See table 6.2.

Det	KC	Mil	Minn	NY	Oak	Sea	Tex	Tor
13322	17742	12745	8325	26241	9327	5517	7899	10630
9030	12356	10499	7630	19818	8229	6996	8884	8973
4292	5386	2246	695	6423	1098	(1479)	(985)	(1657)
(2323)	(2906)	(1639)	(981)	(3395)	(2236)	(2172)	1950	(2333)
1969	2480	607	(286)	3028	(1138)	(3651)	(2935)	(676)
15682	17911	18144	9359	28245	13477	7961	10528	13377
12724	16729	16431	7959	25928	20346	9956	13661	10739
2958	1182	1713	1400	2317	(6869)	(1995)	(3133)	2638
(2423)	(2587)	(1889)	(1225)	(8629)	(6355)	(3092)	(5649)	(3499)
535	(1405)	(176)	145	(6312)	(13224)	(5087)	(8782)	(861)
30437	23382	20020	—	31717	16955	11807	19867	26319
19390	19465	19794	—	35942	25069	13585	17389	24945
11047	3917	226	—	(4225)	(8114)	(1778)	2478	1374
(3415)	(2843)	(2064)	—	(5165)	(7043)	(4321)	(6665)	(2193)
7632	1074	(1838)	—	(9390)	(15157)	(6099)	(4187)	(819)

Hou	Mont	NY	Phil	Pitt	SD	SF	St. L
16270	14401	10302	20434	13674	7780	—	9367
13329	12017	10971	17666	14090	9072	—	12177
2941	2384	(669)	2768	(416)	(1292)	—	(2810)
(3198)	(2944)	(4544)	(1325)	(2024)	(2714)	—	(1031)
(257)	(560)	(5213)	1443	(2440)	(4006)	—	(3841)
20824	19112	15328	21712	12468	12110	11996	14727
22296	22615	19077	22199	14929	12296	14739	14511
(1472)	(3503)	(3749)	(487)	(2461)	(186)	(2743)	216
(5201)	(2262)	(6023)	(7676)	(3407)	(1295)	(3775)	(1389)
(6673)	(5765)	(9772)	(8163)	(5868)	(1481)	(6518)	(1173)
—	22723	25358	29407	16314	23515	17674	20486
—	24050	22662	25084	19230	17584	19430	18899
—	(1327)	2696	4323	(2916)	5931	(1756)	1587
—	(3803)	(6478)	(6798)	(2913)	(3186)	(3708)	(1463)
—	(5130)	(3782)	(2475)	(5829)	2745	(5464)	124

Table 6.4   Total Revenue and Total Cost Functions, 1984

Variable	(1) Revenue	(2) Cost	(3) Cost
Intercept	−12,298*	−1,815*	4,814*
1984 Population	2.92	—	—
1984 Win Percentage	28,884	15,155*	—
1983 Win Percentage	26,070	31,160	33,058
$\bar{R}^2$	.75	.12	.13
(N)	(24)	(24)	(24)

Source: Data on total revenue and cost are from tables 6.2 and 6.3. The source of the data for the independent variables is noted in table 5.7.   *See note 2 on p. 200.

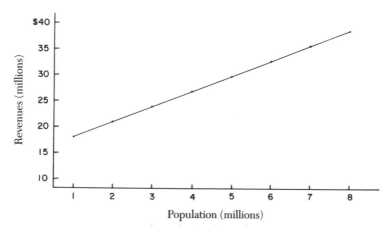

Figure 6.1   The Relationship between Population and Club Revenues for a .500 Club in the Major Leagues, 1984

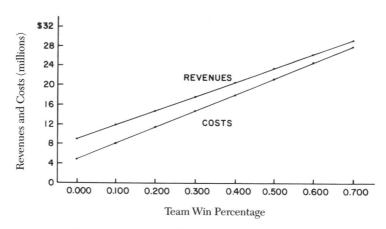

Figure 6.2   The Relationship between Club Quality and Club Revenues and Costs for the Major Leagues, 1984

Club Costs in Baseball

There are five major categories of *direct* cost associated with fielding a team: (1) team costs, (2) game costs, (3) player development and training costs, (4) sales and promotion costs, and (5) general and administrative expenses. Team costs consist mainly of player salaries and the salaries of the manager, coaches, trainers, and travel secretary. About 75 to 80 percent of team costs arise from these salaries. Additionally, transportation and other road trip costs, hotels and meals, and a variety of miscellany (e.g., bats and balls, photos, etc.) are included in this category. Game costs consist mainly of stadium rental fees, the salaries of the stadium personnel, field maintenance and facility repair, light, heat, and power costs, and security service. Player development and training costs consist of the salaries of minor league personnel, scouts and player development directors, farm club expenses, minor league player salaries and expenses, spring training, and Murphy and meal money. Sales and promotion costs are customarily salaries and commissions, publicity and advertising expenses. General and administrative expenses are the costs of the front office including the owner's salary, bonuses, and travel and entertainment expenses. There is much mischief in this category that we will discuss in detail in the next chapter. Finally, there are *indirect* or team replacement costs consisting of the amortization and depreciation of player contracts, the franchise, and other intangible assets. These will also be discussed later. Since they are not out-of-pocket expenses, they will not concern us in this chapter.

In 1974, a typical team had total expenses of $6.6 million (see table 6.1). Less than 17 percent of total costs were due to player and field staff salaries. By 1983, club expenses had grown to $22.6 million, a compound rate of increase of 14.7 percent. Under free agency, player salaries had risen to 36.5 percent of costs. Typically, each of the remaining cost items in the table other than spring training and miscellaneous expenditures account for 7 to 12 percent of expenses. Sales costs and general and administrative expenses rose the most over the period, while stadium operation costs increased the least.

Individual club costs for 1980–84 are given by league in tables 6.2 and 6.3. Average cost per team over the period was $16.3 million. Low-cost clubs in the American League were Minnesota, Seattle, and Cleveland. In the National League, the low-cost clubs were San Diego, Cincinnati, Atlanta, and St. Louis. Lowest cost in the National League was always greater than the costs at Minnesota, Seattle, and Cleveland. High-cost clubs in the American League were the Yankees,

California, Oakland, and Kansas City. In the National League the high-cost teams were Los Angeles, Philadelphia, and Montreal. Generally, the low-cost clubs are also low-revenue clubs and the high-cost clubs have high revenues. But, there are exceptions to this generalization (e.g., Oakland).

Team Salary Costs

A principal source of the difference in cost among the clubs is the quality and, hence, the pay of the players. The correlation between cost and revenue is due partly to the fact that both are governed by team quality. While the range in costs between clubs will be about 50 to 150 percent, depending on the year and the league, the range in player roster costs is much greater. In table 6.5, average player salaries by club for some years between 1978 and 1987 are presented. The deter-

Table 6.5   Average Player Salaries (000s) by Club, 1978–1987 (selected years) and Club Record, 1977–1987

Club	1978	1980	1985	1987	Win Percentage
Yankees	188.9	242.9	546.4	535.6	.570
Philadelphia	159.0	221.3	399.7	448.9	.537
Pittsburgh	127.9	199.2	392.3	160.6	.497
California	141.8	191.0	433.8	440.5	.501
Boston	147.8	184.7	386.6	499.0	.543
Los Angeles	135.9	183.1	424.3	408.8	.535
Houston	70.6	176.7	366.3	437.6	.517
St. Louis	89.3	173.5	386.5	397.9	.524
Cincinnati	132.8	162.7	336.8	325.3	.515
Cubs	96.2	160.2	413.8	494.9	.469
Milwaukee	92.0	159.1	430.8	303.9	.517
Montreal	105.6	158.2	315.3	301.0	.519
Texas	121.2	148.8	257.6	234.5	.483
San Francisco	106.3	148.3	320.4	392.4	.482
Atlanta	69.7	148.0	541.0	490.9	.460
San Diego	106.8	139.0	400.5	359.4	.469
Cleveland	77.0	127.5	219.9	282.7	.455
Mets	86.2	126.5	389.4	543.9	.474
Baltimore	82.9	116.2	438.3	485.8	.551
Kansas City	106.5	100.5	368.5	525.9	.539
Detroit	61.0	87.0	406.8	518.7	.543
Seattle	58.5	82.2	169.7	214.9	.416
Minnesota	51.3	80.5	258.0	494.0	.464
White Sox	81.3	72.4	348.5	321.1	.495
Toronto	63.6	67.2	386.0	479.3	.468
Oakland	49.3	55.0	352.0	423.7	.455

Sources: 1978–80, "Moneyball," Across the Board, September 1981, 16; The Sporting News, 16 December 1985; New York Times, 8 November 1987.

minants of salaries will be examined in chapter 8. Here our interest is in the effect of salaries on club cost.

In 1978, 1980, and 1985, the New York Yankees had the highest paid players in baseball, and arguably the best. The Yankees had a .570 record between 1977 and 1987, the best win percentage in baseball. In 1987, the Mets had the highest salaried players. Previously, the Mets were in the lower half of the salary and win percentage distribution. The club improved by the mid-1980s. Overall the Mets finished .474, but were much improved toward the end of the period. Clubs like Oakland, Seattle, and Cleveland have been low paying and low quality. Clearly, average player pay and average club record are linked.

Team Quality and Total Cost

Some of the costs that are identified in table 6.1 are fixed and some are variable. Player salaries and the salaries of the manager and coaches, player development costs, and spring training expenses affect team quality and, hence, output (the win percentage). Depreciation, stadium operation costs, sales and general administrative expenses do not affect the win record, and, hence, are treated as fixed costs. While some variability in these fixed costs is observed among clubs, particularly in the general and administrative expenses category, and tend to be higher for winning clubs, it is believed that this factor is explained by club attempts to disguise profits as costs. We will take this matter up later.

While revenue greatly is affected by current club quality, cost is more associated with *ex ante* or planned quality than *ex post* or realized quality. Teams commit resources prior to the season on the basis of expected quality during the season. Thus, the current quality of the team and its current total cost may not be closely correlated. Moreover, the disparity between planned and realized performance may be sufficiently large to weaken any correlation between measures of planned quality and observed costs.

With these caveats in mind simple linear total cost functions were estimated for 1984 with 1983 and 1984 win percentages as explanatory variables. The regression results are presented in table 6.4. The coefficient of total cost on 1984 win percentage is statistically insignificant. On the other hand, the win percentage in the 1983 season is a statistically significant predictor of total cost in 1984.[2] Overall, the percentage of the variance associated with team quality is small compared to the factors associated with team revenue. The total cost function based on equation (3) in the table is illustrated graphically in figure 6.2. There is sufficient statistical error in the estimates of both revenue and cost that the observed relationship should not be taken at face value. However, what can be concluded is that *both club revenues and costs are positively related to team quality and that they tend to increase at about the same rate.*

Profit "Gloom and Doom" in the Baseball Industry

Whining about the lack of profit from owning a baseball club has been a sacred tradition among owners from time immemorial. According to owner Harry Wright's *Note and Account Books*, Boston had losses of $3,346.90 in 1879 and $3,247.96 in 1880 on club receipts of $22,273.23 and $22,712.52, respectively. The club's net worth fell from a high of $3,261.07 in 1875 to $177.74 in 1880.[3] The source of the financial instability of baseball was traced to the high salaries of players and was a justification for the reserve clause. During the halcyon days after World War II owners like Phil Wrigley claimed a "bare living" from the game: "Averaging it out for 30 years, it has been in the black. I think it has averaged about 5 percent on investment over a 30-year period."[4] In recent years, the sports pages have been peppered with accounts of club financial losses and complaints that player salaries are too high. There is a monumental paradox here. Why does the value of the franchise rise in the face of perennial financial losses? Since the 1950s and 1960s, average franchise values have increased by an order of magnitude. The New York Mets were an expansion team in 1962 and cost the investors $3.75 million. In 1980, the Mets were sold for $26 million.[5] In 1986, the club was sold for $100 million.[6] This paradox will be resolved in the next chapter, but for now we report recent trends on the bottom line, taking major league baseball's accounting statements at face value.

According to the operating statements for the average club in table 6.1, between 1974 and 1983 expense exceeded revenue from baseball operations every year, with the losses growing. By 1983, the average club lost $2.6 million on revenues of $20.1 million. Moreover, there is income and expense exogenous to baseball operations, mainly arising from interest income or payments on loans and from amortization. When these items are included, club losses averaged $3.2 million.

Obviously, not all clubs lose money. Profits from baseball operations and overall profit by club for 1980–84 appear in tables 6.2 and 6.3. In any given year, between one-third and two-thirds of the clubs reported losses from baseball operations. Profit from all sources was negative for as few as 9 of 14 American League clubs in 1980 to as many as 11 of 12 National League clubs in 1982. Apparently, a necessary but not a suffi-

Table 6.6   Projected Revenues, Costs, and Profits for an Average Club, 1984–1988 (all figures in 000s)

Item	1984	1985	1986	1987	1988
Revenues	23,885	25,808	27,269	29,769	31,769
Costs	25,461	28,038	30,885	34,115	37,731
Operating Loss	(1,577)	(2,231)	(3,615)	(4,346)	(5,962)
Other New Expenses	(654)	(692)	(731)	(808)	(885)
Overall Loss	(2,231)	(2,923)	(4,346)	(5,154)	(6,846)

Source: Report prepared for major league owners by Ernst and Whinney, 1984.

cient condition for profitability is that the club be located in a large city and have a winning season. The Los Angeles Dodgers are profitable. Detroit usually is profitable. And Kansas City, or Minnesota, or San Diego, etc., will operate in the black, if they play championship-caliber ball.

After the 1983 season, the major league owners commissioned a "gloom and doom" financial forecast from the accounting firm of Ernst and Whinney. The consultants forecast revenues, expenses, and profits (losses) for the period 1984–88. The financial projections are reported in table 6.6. The consultants assumed that game receipts and concession income would grow at a 5 percent annual rate and that local television and radio income would grow at 10 percent per annum. Since future revenue from the national broadcast contract was known, the actual amounts were employed. Using the unaudited financial data from the Ernst and Whinney report, over the period 1978 to 1983, game receipts actually grew at 10 percent, concessions at 15 percent, and local broadcast fees at 28 percent annually. The actual growth rate of local broadcast fees over the period 1984–87 was 15 percent. If the revenue projections are revised based on the growth rate of game receipts and concession income over the period 1978–83, which is an extremely conservative assumption, and the known value of the broadcast rights added, the average club had estimated 1987 revenue in the range of $34–$35 million, or $5 million more than projected by Ernst and Whinney. Cost projections aside, the adjustment in revenue is sufficient to yield a condition of break-even for the clubs in 1987. For club expenses, Ernst and Whinney assumed an increase of 8 percent in most categories. Player salaries were assumed to rise at 15 percent per year. In reality, player salaries did not rise at nearly the projected rate. In fact, in 1987 average salaries were lower than in 1986 (see table 8.1). The pessimistic forecast on player salaries led to projections of team costs that were several million dollars higher per club than actual expenses. As a result of these gross errors, the gruesome forecast of growing financial losses among the clubs turned out to be glaringly inaccurate. At the Winter Meetings in Dallas in December 1987, Peter Ueberroth was able to tell the owners that while 80 percent of them lost sizable sums in 1984, three-quarters of them either made money or broke even in 1987.[7] There is even some thought of eventually expanding to 32 teams in four four-team divisions in each league by the year 2000.[8] The reports of the financial death of baseball are greatly exaggerated.

7

Profitability, Survivability, and League Expansion

The sporting public remains rightly confused about whether baseball is profitable or not. Press releases from league and team front offices would have you believe that owning a baseball club is a form of philanthropy. Players' union spokesmen claim that all teams make large profits but hide behind statements of poor financial returns simply to hold the line on player salaries. To the researcher the analysis of profit in baseball is a particularly difficult undertaking, because uniform audited financial data from the clubs generally is not available, because expended items frequently cover some portion of profits, and because the financial return to ownership is multifaceted. To determine whether ownership is profitable, and ultimately to measure this profit at least in a crude fashion, requires that a charted course be steered through the labyrinth of team cost accounting and the tax treatment of profits and capital gains.

Sports Tax Treatment, Ownership Structure, and Cost Accounting

Owners claim that operating a baseball team is at best a break-even proposition. It is argued that only a privileged few earn profits from their operations and that overall this is offset by large losses incurred by most other franchises. Estimating the profit potential of clubs is very difficult. The usual procedure in examining profitability of any industry is to analyze the audited balance sheets of the firms and compare current income with current expenses and assets with liabilities. Such an analysis for baseball is difficult, because nearly all of the clubs are held privately and the owners are quite secretive about their financial affairs. Yet even with the data at hand[1] it remains extraordinarily difficult to compare the profit of one club with that of another. Current book profits measure only a small portion of the total economic returns of ownership. Franchises are owned for at least three other economic reasons: (1) to earn capital gains through the eventual sale of an asset, which historically has appreciated in value; (2) to increase the profits of

129

other affiliated businesses held by the owner; and (3) to reduce income tax liability by offsetting any book losses due to team ownership against other sources of income. Unless these other economic dimensions are understood, the ownership of what often appears to be a money-losing asset remains a paradox.

The Tax Treatment of Sports Franchises

Bill Veeck had two great passions: horses and baseball. Veeck owned clubs in Cleveland, St. Louis, and Chicago. Ingeniously, he reasoned that players were like horses or cattle in that they were a wasting asset. If the Internal Revenue Service permitted horses and cattle to be depreciated, why not the contracts of baseball players? In 1959, Bill Veeck became the first owner to notice and to exploit the tax shelter aspects of sports franchise ownership.

In purchasing a club, primarily three assets are acquired. First, the new owner acquires a roster of players, who each possess a rare playing talent. These contracts are of great value to a team and constitute the club's major asset. The second asset is the franchise itself, which conveys to the owner a property right to the exclusive promotion of games in its home territory. The third asset is a set of contracts, such as leases, concession and broadcast agreements, files of scouting reports and customer lists, and so on.

There are three salient tax characteristics of player contracts. First, and most importantly, under the IRS Code, player contracts may be treated as depreciable intangible assets. As such, sport franchises are unique in their tax treatment of employee contracts. While other businesses are free to capitalize and depreciate other intangible assets, such as customer lists, employee contracts are not depreciated. But player contracts normally are depreciated over the average career length of ballplayers. The percentage of the purchase price of a franchise that may be allocated to player contracts and the estimated useful life of the players are subject to negotiation with the IRS. Until the mid-1970s, generally 90 percent of the franchise purchase price was allocated to player contracts in baseball and the useful life was set at seven years.[2] In other sports (professional basketball, for example), up to 99 percent of the purchase price has been allocated to player contracts. In the mid-1970s, Congress curtailed excessive amortization in professional sports. Specifically, the law established a burden of proof on the amortization allocation formula. If less than 50 percent of the purchase price is allocated to player contracts, the burden of proof is on the IRS, should the allocation be challenged. If more than 50 percent is allocated, the burden is on the club. The courts have been inconsistent in their rulings on challenges to allowed amortization, sometimes reducing the amount well below 50 percent and sometimes allowing almost all of the purchase price as player contracts.[3]

The amortization allocation of the Chicago Cubs for 1982, shown in table 7.1, illustrates modern practice. Player contracts were allocated 38 percent of the purchase price and the franchise itself was allocated somewhat more than 5 percent. Player contracts constituted 45 percent ($9.8 million) of the allocation of the initial purchase price of the Chicago White Sox in 1981. On the other hand, Oakland allocated 63.8 percent ($8.123 million) of the initial purchase price in 1980 as player contracts.[4]

The second feature of the tax treatment of clubs was of greater importance prior to the passage of the Tax Reform Act of 1986, which did away with the differential taxation of ordinary income and capital gains. Upon resale of the club any appreciation in the value of the player contracts was taxed as capital gains. This was true of the contracts of other intangible assets as well (i.e., broadcasting and concession agreements, leases, etc.). However, there is a theoretical qualification. Where the sale price of these assets exceeded the original purchase price, the owner was subject to an excess depreciation recapture, which was taxed as ordinary income. But, at the time of sale, the original contracts virtually never would be in force. In the normal course of affairs,

Table 7.1 Amortization of the Chicago Cubs Baseball Club, 1982

Item	Allocation (in 000s)	%	Life (years)
Stadium	$7,611.6	32.3	20.0
Baseball Equipment	1,910.6	8.1	8.0
Office Equipment	207.2	0.9	10.0
Leasehold Improvements	12.6	—	18.0
Concession Agreement	595.4	2.5	12.0
Landlease Leasehold	1,389.3	5.9	31.0
Computer Software	5.5	—	5.0
Scouting Reports	258.0	1.1	3.5
Customer Files	223.3	0.9	5.0
Player Contracts	8,947.4	37.9	7.0
Franchise	1,250.3	5.3	40.0
Other Assets	1,186.8	5.0	—
Total	23,598.0	100.0	—

Source: Data provided by Roger G. Noll.

all of the players would have been reassigned or have left baseball and the other contracts would have expired as well. Hence, any realized gain from the sale of the club normally would be taxed as a capital gain.

The third tax aspect of player contracts is in the treatment of player development. Most players transit to the major leagues from the minors. Major league teams own or have working agreements with minor league clubs for the purpose of developing players of major league caliber. Baseball claims it costs several hundred thousand dollars to train a player. Since player contracts are treated as a depreciable asset, it might appear that clubs would capitalize the cost of player development and carry each player on the rolls at an initial book value equal to the training costs. Teams do not, however, capitalize player development, but treat player development costs as a current expense. The rationale for this treatment primarily is that it would prevent the teams from offsetting such costs against team revenues and, hence, increase their tax liability, and it would cause a tax on any profit realized from player cash sales.

The economic justification for a depreciation allowance to a business is the cost of replacing an asset that is being used up in the production process. In the case of physical assets like stadiums physical depreciation is obvious, although the economic rate of decline and the rate for tax purposes seldom bear a relationship to one another. In the case of some intangible assets, such as customer lists or a file of scouting reports, the economic basis for amortization is obvious also. But the economic basis for the amortization of player contracts, broadcast and concession agreements, stadium leases, the franchise, and so on is by no means obvious. None of these contracts really are wasting assets. As the contracts expire, they are renewed. Clubs have valuable rights to sell. As players are traded or retire, they are replaced with new players, much as in any business. Further, clubs already deduct the training expenses associated with player development as these costs are accrued. There is no economic justification for the amortization of player contracts and other intangible assets in sports. The only reason for amortizing these intangible assets in sports is to create a tax shelter, and as such this practice represents a taxpayer subsidy to franchise owners and consumers of sports.

There are financial implications of this special tax treatment. Clubs can suffer book losses but have positive cash flows. A club purchased today for $70 million easily could justify $7 to $10 million in annual amortization. With average club revenues in the $35 million range and direct costs of $30 million, the amortization added as an expense eliminates taxes and yields a positive cash flow. The asset will not waste away if the amortization is not reinvested, since the deduction has no economic justification. Thus, the tax shelter aspect of sports ownership is the tax value of the excess depreciation. The tax value of the asset is the excess depreciation times the owners marginal tax rate.

Ownership Structure

There are few family owned baseball clubs today. Partly, this is because the full capture of the tax advantages of ownership requires substantial income from other sources, if ownership is as an individual, or profit, if ownership is corporate. Additionally, and more importantly, many teams are owned because they increase the profits and asset values of other businesses. Part of the reason that August Busch owns the Cardinals is that it increases the sales of his beers. In the past, owners of construction and trucking firms have owned clubs and these businesses have prospered as a result. Today, broadcasters increasingly are owning baseball teams. Part of the increased asset value of clubs is due to the fact that they make stable sources of original programming upon which to build a loyal advertising audience. The value of this sports programming partly is measured by the great increase in broadcast fees, already documented. Since 1980, when the Federal Communications Commission effectively deregulated broadcasting, the rise of non-network broadcasting has increased the demand for original programming. Superstations like WTBS (Atlanta Braves) and WGN (Chicago Cubs) have used sports programming to break into the national market. Other stations have become dominant regionally or locally through sports programming. About half of the clubs in baseball are owned or associated with broadcasters or advertisers.

Joint ownership with affiliated businesses has implications for the analysis of sports profitability. The profits of the Cardinals, the Cubs, or the Braves are not independent of the profits of the parent companies. Theoretically, part of the profits of Anheuser-Busch Breweries, WGN, and WTBS ought to be allocated to the clubs, since in the absence of club ownership the parent companies would have had lower profits. Second, the revenues to the jointly owned clubs might be lower than their fair market value. For example, WGN or WTBS may pay local radio, television, and cable fees to the clubs lower than the market price for these rights. From a corporate viewpoint, profits from joint economic activity can emerge in the club or in the parent company. To the extent that the parent company internally transfers profits to itself, the club will appear less financially viable than it would as a free-standing economic entity. There seems to be no way of allocating these joint profits among the teams transacting with affiliated businesses, but one must view the financial operating statements of such affected clubs with suspicion.

Sports Accounting

The financial operating statements of the clubs are distorted by the tax law and the problem of affiliated ownership. Roger Noll points out: "The reason is that the law alters the value of different forms of income, and in particular, devalues profits relative to salaries, interest, and capital gains."[5] Corporate strategy determines where the profits from baseball emerge in the accounts of clubs owned jointly with other businesses. To the extent that the motives and the structure of ownership differ among the clubs, interteam comparisons of financial viability are complicated.

The residual from baseball can be taken in several ways. Most directly, economic return is collected as profits. In the case of affiliation with a related business, profit from club ownership can be transferred in all or in part to the parent company. The simplest means of transferring this profit is by underpricing to the club the jointly utilized rights purchased by the parent company (e.g., broadcast fees). A result of the transfer is a darkened financial picture of the club. A third economic return derives from utilizing the excess depreciation for tax avoidance and by accruing capital gains. Book loss from club operations shelters nonbaseball income from taxation. Over the lifetime of ownership, the amortization of these intangible assets is deducted at ordinary income tax rates. At the time of sale, the gain is subject to capital gains tax (now the same as the rate on ordinary income). If there is any recapture of the amortization due to the gain, the club owner has received an interest-free loan of tax liabilities, reducing the capital gains tax. A fourth way of capturing economic returns is for the owner to make a loan to the club and collect interest off the top. Roger Noll writes:

> One common means of acquiring a team is to establish a corporation that will own the team, and then to lend the corporation the funds necessary to purchase the team. This means that the team owes its owner the interest on the loan. From an economic standpoint, there is no significant difference between a corporation that was established by having the owner buy $40 million of stock versus a corporation that had $1 million in stock and $39 million in loans; in each case, the owner spent $40 million. But obviously the latter corporation is far less likely to show a profit—it must first cover interest on $39 million before a profit can be shown. Consequently, the books of the latter corporation will appear more shaky than the books of the former, even though from the point of ownership the two situations are almost the same.[6]

Finally, returns can be collected through salary payments to owners in excess of the market value of their managerial services, salary bonuses, fringe benefits, and perquisites. Most owners participate in club operations and receive a salary. Running a $35 million baseball operation requires some skill. But the actual salary payment need not be related to a market valuation of these managerial services. Frequently, owners take salary bonuses during years when the club does well. A common practice is for the club to purchase life insurance, retirement annuities, or other fringe benefits for the owner. Moreover, travel and entertainment expenses for the owner and other perquisites need bear no relationship to the cost of doing club business.

Thus, interclub financial comparisons are enormously complicated by tax law and ownership structure and their effect on how the economic returns of ownership are collected. Matters are made even more complex by an increase in nonbaseball economic activities that is appearing in the financial returns of some clubs (e.g., George Steinbrenner's hotel in Tampa).

Estimates of Club Profits, 1980–84

For the three years during 1980–84 reported in tables 6.2 and 6.3, average club net book losses were $953,000, $4,033,000, and $2,188,000, respectively. Of the three years, 1982 was the year of the largest reported losses, some $104.9 million for all of baseball. Losses were high in that year because attendance had not yet recovered from the players' strike, the new and lucrative $1.125 billion six-year national television contract was not yet in effect, and the growth rate in players' salary was not yet under control. Other than 1981, this was the worst financial year for the clubs. For this reason, the financial statement for 1982 are singled out for scrutiny. If 1982 was atypical financially, the analysis here will exaggerate the financial weakness of the clubs. Financial data from other years will be incorporated to complete the picture.

A first step in the analysis of baseball profits is to eliminate to the largest extent possible financial data not related to baseball. Largely, this is accomplished by restricting club revenues to "Revenues from Baseball Operations" and by adding General and Administrative Expenses (G & A) to the Operating Expenses. Clearly, front office expenses (G & A) ought to be related to baseball operations. The revenue

Table 7.2   Revenues, Costs, and Net Income from Baseball (000s), 1982

Club	Revenue (1)	Cost (2)	Income (3)	Cash Flow (4)	Adjustments (5)	Profit (6)
Baltimore	13610	14113	(503)	(918)	0	918
Boston	18106	16832	1274	2720	157	2877
California	21171	22632	(1461)	(609)	1830	1221
White Sox	17235	21677	(4442)	(1143)	754	(389)
Cleveland	9357	13677	(4320)	(3586)	0	(3586)
Detroit	15682	14818	864	1396	0	1396
KC	17911	18170	(259)	667	0	667
Milwaukee	18144	18127	17	552	0	552
Minnesota	9359	9306	53	422	0	422
Yankees	28245	31574	(3329)	456	3488	3944
Oakland	13477	23750	(10273)	(6668)	1213	(5455)
Seattle	7961	11067	(3106)	(1322)	0	(1322)
Texas	10528	15614	(5086)	(3717)	1376	(2341)
Toronto	13377	13826	(449)	805	1270	2075
Atlanta	14188	14967	(779)	282	1725	2007
Cubs	12933	18554	(5621)	(1373)	611	(762)
Cincinnati	14923	16848	(1925)	1075	0	1075
Dodgers	37340	28029	9311	10094	3183	13277
Houston	20824	25824	(5000)	(2608)	1176	(1432)
Montreal	19112	24848	(5736)	(5140)	0	(5140)
Mets	15328	22169	(6841)	(3667)	5465	1798
Phillies	21712	26192	(4480)	2007	1728	3735
Pittsburgh	12468	16291	(3823)	(3795)	0	(3795)
San Diego	12110	13802	(1692)	(936)	0	(936)
Giants	11996	16710	(4714)	(2283)	0	(2283)
St. Louis	14727	16104	(1377)	(989)	3570	2581

Source: See note in table 6.2.

and cost data for each club in 1982 is presented in table 7.2. Net income from baseball appears in column 3 of the table. The financial statements indicate that 5 clubs made money and 21 lost money from baseball in 1982. Except for the Los Angeles Dodgers, with measured profits above $9.3 million, the positive net returns were modest. Of the money losers, Oakland's reported $10.3 million loss was the largest, but numerous clubs reported losses over $4 million.

Book losses are not out-of-pocket costs when depreciation is allowed. In column 4 of the table amortization of intangible assets has been added to net income (expense). The amortization includes that allocated to the initial player roster and franchise, player acquisition costs (but, not signing bonuses), and other intangible assets that could be identified. Adding the amortization allowance to net income (expense) is one measure of cash flow to a club. The effect is quite dramatic. The number of clubs with positive economic returns rises to 12 and the financial losses of the remaining 14 clubs are cut quite substantially.

Next, certain idiosyncratic adjustments for particular clubs need to be made. The adjustments that will be made by no means are exhaustive. The alterations reflect a certain amount of analytical detective work, but much remains hidden in the quagmire of team financial accounting. The amount of the adjustment is shown in column 5 of table 7.2. The rationale for the modifications are as follows.

California Angels. The Angels are owned by Gene Autry and were at that time affiliated in a partnership with Golden West Broadcasters (Autry sold Golden West in 1986). The club received from its parent company $940,000 for local television rights, $1,035,000 for local radio rights, and $449,000 for local cable rights. While the Angels are not dominant in the Los Angeles market, the value of their broadcast rights is much lower than the Dodgers' ($6.713 million). The estimated value of the Angels' local television rights in 1982 is $2.85 million.[7] The difference between the estimated fair market value of these rights and the amount paid by Golden West was $1.7 million. The radio and cable fees appear closer to their market value. Additionally, insurance premiums are about $130,000 above the baseball average. Total adjustments to operating income were $1.83 million.

Chicago White Sox. The club established Sportsvision and sold television rights to 112 games for the 1982–88 seasons. The club invested $3.4 million in the venture. But nearly all of the money was paid back as payment ($1.8 million) for a loan it had guaranteed, $390,000 in interest, and $1.18 million as a loan to the club. According to the agreement the club receives fees only if Sportsvision turns a profit, but the club bears the production costs ($787,000 in 1983–84). These costs should be eliminated from club costs. The White Sox in effect have foregone current local cable fees and gotten nothing from Sportsvision in return. Lost cable revenues for 1982 were estimated at $220,000.[8]

The White Sox had an excessive amount of General and Administrative Expense: $2.810 million versus $2.352 for an average club. This may represent excess salary or bonus payments to the partners. If the average G & A expense in baseball is the true economic cost of the front office, the excess payment is $458,000. The total adjustment for the White Sox is $754,000.

New York Yankees. The Yankees had G & A expenses that were $3.294 million above the baseball average and they also had $194,000 in excess expenditures for insurance. The total adjustment to baseball operating income is $3.488 million.

The total losses shown by the Yankees ($6.312 million in 1982 and $9.39 million in 1984) are among the highest in baseball. Partly this is due to excessive cost across all expense categories. Partly the loss is due to hidden nonbaseball activities such as the Tampa hotel and to charitable contributions ($650,000 in 1984). Partly it is due to the fact that George Steinbrenner takes some of the economic returns as interest payments on loans to the club—$2.389 million in 1982.

Oakland Athletics. The club suffered the largest losses of all in baseball in 1982 and 1984, a two-year total of $28.381 million. The only adjustments that can be made to 1982 operating income are for excessive G & A expenses ($1.052 million) and excessive entertainment expense ($161,000).

Undoubtedly, Oakland has been a money loser. But, the extent of the financial loss is overstated. In 1982, Oakland reported payments of $1.432 million in interest to its owner. In 1984, the club reported a loss of $831,000 on the sale of marketable securities. Salaries of front office personnel were substantially above the league average. Oakland had signing bonuses ten times greater than the league average. In 1983, the club spent $600,000 on a Diamondvision scoreboard, an extraordinary amount if it represents amortization. In 1982, the club spent $300,000 on photography. Some expenditures appear bizarre compared to other clubs.

Oakland and San Francisco share the same market and had comparable records over the period. Oakland's combined loss in 1982 and 1984 was 2.4 times greater than the Giants' loss, a difference that is not due to higher revenues in San Francisco. Quite the contrary, club revenues were marginally higher in Oakland. Most of the difference is due to higher costs in Oakland: $45.415 million versus $34.169 million for the two-year period. The largest cost differences are in Team Replacement, Sales and Promotion, and General and Administrative Expense. Player amortization "costs" also are higher in Oakland, since the club was purchased in 1980.

Texas Rangers. While the local television rights of the Rangers appear to be fairly valued, the club reported no radio or local cable revenues for 1982. Bob Short sold the ten-year broadcast rights for a lump sum when he moved the club to Texas. The City of Arlington held the broadcast rights with the sales handled by the Texas Rangers Baseball Network. KXAS-TV and WBAP (AM) broadcast the games. Since Gaylord Broadcasting purchased 35 percent of the club, KTVT became the TV originator. The estimated value of the 1982 radio rights was $690,000 and the local cable rights was $210,000. Additionally, the Rangers reported $476,000 in non-player salary bonuses. The total adjustment to operating income is $1.376 million.

Atlanta Braves. WTBS and the Braves are jointly owned. WTBS is the TV rights holder, but the club retains the radio rights (WSB historically has radiobroadcast Atlanta games). Turner paid the club $747,000 for local TV rights in 1982. Local broadcast rights for Atlanta are 40 percent of the baseball average. The local television rights appear to be severely underpriced. While Atlanta is a relatively small urban area, the Braves have a monopoly on baseball in the Southeast. It was estimated that the local TV fees were undervalued by $1.1 million, while radio and local cable together were underpriced by $625,000.

New York Mets. WOR-TV has had a partnership arrangement with the Mets since the club was established. While local rights were comparably priced with the Yankees in 1987 ($16.5 versus $17.5 million), historically the club has gotten a third of what the Yankees received. It was estimated that the local television rights of the Mets were underpriced by $4.725 million. Additionally, the Mets had excessive G & A expenses of $740,000.

St. Louis Cardinals. The Cardinals are owned by August A. Busch, Jr., and are a main advertising tool in selling the brewery's beers. Anheuser-Busch controls the broadcast rights. The local TV rights seem undervalued. But the most unique aspect of the financial statement is the absence of any concession revenue. The Cardinals rent Busch Stadium from the Civic Center Redevelopment Corporation (CCC), a wholly owned subsidiary of Anheuser-Busch. In addition to paying stadium rent ($676,000 versus a league-wide average of $427,000), all concession and parking revenues accrue to CCC. The estimated value of the net concession income transferred from the club to CCC in 1982 was $3.57 million.[9] The arrangement is quite profitable for CCC. In 1984, CCC's pretax profit from baseball operations was $2.555 million.[10]

Other adjustments to operating income by club briefly were as follows.

Boston Red Sox. Excessive G & A expenses and insurance: $157,000.

Toronto Blue Jays. Excessive bank charges: $1.27 million.

Chicago Cubs. Excessive advertising expenses to its affiliate WGN-TV ($820,000 versus a league average of $209,000).

Los Angeles Dodgers. Excessive G & A expenses ($5.535 million versus a league average of $2.352 million).

Houston Astros. Excessive G & A expenses of $1.176 million.

Philadelphia Phillies. Excessive G & A costs of $1.728 million.

No anomalies were found in the 1982 operating statements of the 12 other clubs. Hence, no adjustments to operating income were made. These clubs were: Baltimore, Cleveland, Detroit, Kansas City, Milwaukee, Minnesota, Seattle, Cincinnati, Montreal, Pittsburgh, San Diego, and San Francisco.

The last column in table 7.2 is an estimate of club net income after making these crude adjustments to operating income. The results indicate that 15 clubs made profits and 11 lost money in 1982. Recall that stated losses in 1982 were $4.033 million per club or $104.9 million for all of baseball. After adjusting for amortization of intangible assets and undervalued rights or excessive expenses (hidden profits), clubs on average had profits of $427,000 or $11.1 million for baseball as a whole. In the analysis we did not consider the effect of interest income and interest expense connected with ownership. If all of the interest expense arose from owner loans to purchase the club, the "expenses" should be treated as an economic return. If this assumption is made and average interest income added to the cash flow, club profits would average $1.34 million or $35 million for baseball. And, recall that 1982 was a particularly financially stressful year in baseball.

Club Profit, Team Quality, and Market Size

Club revenues and costs have been shown to be related statistically to team quality and city size. If clubs are rationally pricing their rights and choosing the optimal level of team quality, profits ought to be correlated with team quality and market size. However, certain factors weaken any correlation among these variables. First, costs are incurred for a planned level of club performance, which may differ significantly from realized quality. Second, the adjustments that have been made to operating income in table 7.2 are subject to error. The estimated club net revenue may be a poor measure of actual profit.

The adjusted cash flow or profit data in table 7.2 was regressed against the club record for 1982 and the population size of the franchise city. The record for the previous season was not included because it was the year of the players' strike. The result was as follows.

$$\text{Profit} = -11{,}356.0 + 13{,}1190.0 \times \text{Win percentage} + 1.85 \times \text{Population.}$$

Both club quality and population size positively affect measured club profits and both variables are statistically significant at the 5 percent level, and some 53 percent of the variation in club profits was associated with these variables. At the mean, each additional game won is worth \$81,000 in further profit. [This figure is obtained by dividing 1000 points by 162 games per season to get a factor of 6.2 points per game. Multiplying 13,110 by 6.2 points gives a profit of approximately \$81,000 per game.] Each additional one million in the population of the area in which the team is located is worth \$1.85 million in profit. That is, the gains from franchise location are larger than those from team quality.

The profit equation is a useful analog in assessing the profit potential of the clubs. Predicted club profit on the assumption of a .500 season appears in table 7.3. Profitability differs among clubs because of differences in size of city of franchise location. Playing .500 baseball, 7 clubs were predicted to lose money in 1982, 12 were predicted to break even, and 7 were predicted to make money. Of course, actual club quality varied substantially among the clubs. Estimated profit outcome for 1982 (from table 7.2) based on the clubs' actual records also appears in table 7.3 as do estimates of 1984 profit potential prepared by Roger Noll for the Players Association.

The evidence from 1980–84 suggests the following. Four clubs have sustained significant financial losses: Cleveland, Oakland, Montreal, and Pittsburgh. Cleveland played .475 baseball throughout the period and is located in a comparatively small population center. Amortization of intangible assets is 40 percent of the league average. The club would produce a positive cash flow if it were sold to a new owner and if it improved its record to .500. Oakland is very unprofitable. If the team were efficiently managed and it played .500 baseball, the club should be about as unprofitable as San Francisco. Apparently, the San Francisco Bay Area is not large enough to support two viable clubs. Despite its average win record and population size, Montreal lost a lot of money in 1982 and 1984. The club should be viable if efficiently run. The Pirates are located in a small market and have played below .500 baseball. The club should be losing a small amount of money or breaking even, but it has suffered large financial losses. Pittsburgh had the

Table 7.3   Estimated Club Profit Potential, 1982 and 1984

Club	Profit at .500 Wins	Record 1982	Profit 1982	Record 1984	Profit 1984
Baltimore	Break Even	.580	Small Profit	.525	Profit
Boston	Break Even	.549	Profit	.531	Profit
California	Break Even	.574*	Profit	.500	Break Even
White Sox	Break Even	.537	Small Loss	.457	Profit
Cleveland	Small Loss	.481	Large Loss	.463	Small Loss
Detroit	Profit	.512	Profit	.642*	Large Profit
KC	Loss	.556	Small Profit	.519*	Profit
Milwaukee	Loss	.586*	Small Profit	.416	Large Loss
Minnesota	Break Even	.370	Small Profit	.500	No data
Yankees	Profit	.488	Large Profit	.537	Large Loss
Oakland	Small Loss	.420	Large Loss	.475	Large Loss
Seattle	Loss	.469	Loss	.457	Loss
Texas	Small Profit	.395	Loss	.429	Loss
Toronto	Break Even	.481	Profit	.549	Profit
Atlanta	Break Even	.549*	Profit	.494	Break Even
Cubs	Break Even	.451	Small Loss	.596*	Profit
Cincinnati	Loss	.377	Profit	.432	Small Loss
Dodgers	Large Profit	.543	Large Profit	.488	Large Profit
Houston	Small Profit	.475	Loss	.494	No data
Montreal	Break Even	.531	Large Loss	.484	Large Loss
Mets	Profit	.401	Profit	.556	Profit
Phillies	Profit	.549	Large Profit	.500	Profit
Pittsburgh	Break Even	.519	Large Loss	.463	Large Loss
San Diego	Break Even	.500	Small Loss	.568*	Large Profit
Giants	Loss	.537	Loss	.407	Loss
St. Louis	Break Even	.568*	Profit	.519	Profit

Note: *denotes divisional winner. Profit estimates for 1984 are from Roger G. Noll, "The Economic Viability of Professional Baseball: Report to the Major League Baseball Players Association," July 1985, 40–43.

lowest depreciation allowance of any baseball club and was a candidate for a change in ownership.

At the other end of the profit spectrum stands the Los Angeles Dodgers. The club is extremely profitable. Three clubs are solidly profitable: Boston, the Yankees, and Philadelphia. Boston's profitability is partly due to a good record on the playing field. The high net income of the Yankees and the Phillies is partly due to amortization that is two or three times the baseball average. Noll concluded that Detroit was very profitable in 1984. The club won the division title that year with a .642 win percentage. In 1982, the club's record was mediocre and profit was not nearly as large.

Other clubs fall between the extremes. They are much more dependent on team standing for financial success. Some clubs incur financial losses playing .500 baseball: Kansas City, Milwaukee, Seattle, Cincinnati, and San Francisco. Kansas City and Milwaukee played about .530 baseball over the period and were in the black or broke even. Seattle had an average record of .413 and lost money. Its losses were relatively small because its costs were the lowest in baseball. Cincinnati had an average record of .485 but had a small cash flow due to an above-average level of amortization. San Francisco lost money with an average record of .481.

The remaining 13 clubs generally will either break even or be profitable playing .500 baseball (i.e., Baltimore, California, Chicago White Sox, Detroit, Minnesota, Texas, Toronto, Atlanta, Chicago Cubs, Houston, New York Mets, San Diego, and St. Louis). Based on their actual win percentages over the period, the amount of amortization available to the clubs, the size of their geographical markets, and an analysis of their financial operating statements from 1980 through 1984, California, Minnesota, Texas, and San Diego probably suffered small financial losses over the period. The other clubs made money.

Capital Appreciation of Franchises

The historical appreciation of franchise values is the most convincing testament of the economic returns to ownership. During the 1950s the ten baseball clubs that were sold brought an average price of $3.5 million. The range in the exchange price was from $2.0 million for the Pirates to $5.5 million for the Tigers. During the 1960s, when Veeck's tax shelter discovery for sports franchises was beginning to play a role, the ten clubs that were sold brought an average price of $6.5 million, with a range from $1.8 to $14 million. The average growth rate of the capital gains was 6.5 percent per annum. During the 1970s clubs sold for around $10.4 million.[11] Clubs now are being sold for $40 to $100 million. The Minnesota Twins were sold for $36 million in 1984. The Gaylord Broadcasting purchase of a share of the Texas Rangers suggested a value of $40 million for the club.[12] Eddie Childs put his remaining 58 percent share of the club up for sale in 1988. The offer of a group of investors led by the wealthy Mack family and Tampa business interests implied an exchange value of the Rangers of $138 million, although real estate holdings in Arlington, Texas, are included in the deal.[13] The New York Mets were sold in 1986 for $100 million.[14] If the O'Malleys would part with the Dodgers, the club easily would bring in excess of $100 million.[15] These increases in capital values imply compound growth rates between 9 and 15 percent. What economic forces are driving up the value of these clubs?

The price of an income-producing asset is the discounted present value of the stream of net income arising from the economic use of the asset. Net income increases when revenue rises faster than cost or when taxes decline. Factors contributing to the growth of profits in baseball have been rising attendance and broadcast fees, the antitrust exemption and the tax shelter aspects of club ownership, and affiliation with related business, principally in broadcasting. Additionally, there are nonpecuniary aspects of ownership. Some owners get great pleasure from personal involvement with their club and take civic pride in their ownership. The tax reform of the mid-1970s, which restricted the fraction of the franchise price that could be allocated to player contracts, had a depressing effect on franchise values. But creative tax accountants found a sufficient number of other intangible assets to offset the limits on amortization of player contracts. The tax shelter and antitrust benefits of ownership remain. The advent of free agency in 1976 led to a doubling of the players' share of revenues. Modification of the reserve clause reduced the asset value of the clubs, although overall revenues appear to be rising faster than club costs and the growth rate of player costs has been drastically reduced.

Finally, expansion has dampened franchise values for several reasons. Expansion reduces each club's share of the network television contract. On the assumption that the supply of stars is fixed, there are fewer quality players to go around per team. Since expansion clubs are generally weak competitors, the quality of the games they play in declines. Moreover, expansion absorbs excess demand for franchises in nonbaseball cities that might otherwise have led to intercity bidding for club relocation. For example, in the spring of 1988 the White Sox, which have been playing baseball in Chicago since 1901, triggered a subsidy bidding war between Chicago and St. Petersburg. Governor Bob Martinez of Florida offered a $120 million package to the club to come to St. Petersburg to play in a new domed stadium. Governor James Thompson offered a revised lease on a new stadium that would save the club $60 million over ten years. Such action required legislative approval.[16] On the other hand, expansion has brought divisional play and the league championship series, which have contributed to the growth of revenues. Additionally, expansion has absorbed excess demand that could have resulted in the rise of a rogue league outside of the Major League Agreement. Such a development would have accelerated competition for players and shrunk net income markedly. Historically, interleague wars have been anathema to sports financially.

Expansion Possibilities in Baseball

Since the early 1980s, several plans for league expansion have been broached. The most ambitious calls for 32 teams by the year 2000 or so, with four four-team divisions per league, a 154-game schedule, and two rounds of play-offs prior to the World Series. But expansion, if it comes, likely will occur in stages. The most obvious and compelling suggestion is to extend the American League to 16 clubs, distributed in four four-team divisions. A second stage might add two teams and shift one club from the American to the National League. This would result in two 15-team leagues, organized in three five-team divisions. Play-offs would presumably be with three division leaders and a wild card team.[17] Later, two additional teams would yield two 16-team leagues.

A number of U.S. and Canadian cities have been campaigning aggressively for a major league team. The most frequently mentioned cities are Buffalo, Denver, Indianapolis, Nashville, New Orleans, Phoenix, St. Petersburg, Tampa, Washington, and Vancouver. Some of the potential owners of these expansion clubs are financially credible. Jack Kent Cooke, formerly chairman of Teleprompter Corporation, is majority owner of the Washington Redskins (Edward Bennett Williams is a minority owner of the Redskins and owner of the Baltimore Orioles) and has the personal fortune to subsidize a team in Washington. Edward J. de Bartolo, a shopping mall developer whose son owns the San Francisco 49ers, wants to bring a team to New Orleans. Martin Stone, a New York real estate developer and principal owner of the Class AAA Phoenix Giants, wants a major league team for Phoenix. Jack Beach, president of Molson Brewery in Vancouver, covets a club for Vancouver so that his beer can compete with Labatt (owner of the Toronto Blue Jays) and Carling (Montreal Expos).

To assess the prospects for expansion, two crucial questions need to be addressed. First, are any of the proposed expansion sites financially viable? Second, is it in the interest of the current clubs to agree to expansion?

The populations of the proposed expansion sites appear in table 7.4. Compare these locations with the seven smallest cities on the current circuit (Cleveland, Kansas City, Milwaukee, Oakland, Seattle, Cincinnati, and San Francisco). The average population in these seven major league cities is 1.6 million, with a range from 1.4 million in Cincinnati and Milwaukee to 1.9 million in Cleveland and Oakland. The average population of the other 19 major league cities is 3.3 million. Thus, the small major league cities are about half as populous as the large major league cities. On average the population in the proposed expansion cities is 1.75 million. Five of these sites have populations below that of the smallest major league city (Buffalo-Niagara, Indianapolis, Nashville, New Orleans, and Vancouver, B.C.). Clearly, two of the proposed expansion cities have sufficiently large populations (Miami-Ft. Lauderdale and Washington, D.C.). But it is an open question

Table 7.4   1984 Population of Potential Expansion Sites

Expansion Site	Population
Buffalo-Niagara	1,200,000
Denver-Boulder	1,800,000
Indianapolis	1,200,000
Miami–Ft. Lauderdale	2,800,000
Nashville	900,000
New Orleans	1,300,000
Phoenix	1,800,000
Tampa–St. Petersburg	1,800,000
Washington, D.C.	3,400,000
Vancouver, B.C.	1,300,000

Source: U.S. Bureau of the Census, Statistical Abstract of the United States: 1986 (106th edition) Washington, D.C., 1985.

whether the Washington-Baltimore area can support two clubs. The area may have a problem in that respect like San Francisco's. Since two clubs have fled Washington (in 1960 to Minnesota and in 1971 to Texas), one is not sanguine about the staying power of a Washington club. The Denver-Boulder, Phoenix, and Tampa–St. Petersburg areas have population sizes that are marginal (similar in size to Cleveland and Oakland).

Between 1980 and 1984 the seven small-city clubs in the major leagues had average records of .485. Their revenues were three-fourths of the larger city clubs (an average of $14.2 million versus $18.7 million). Cleveland and Seattle had revenues that were half of the other clubs. The Cleveland-Seattle experience may be the lower bound for financial survivability in baseball.

Typically, the win percentage of expansion clubs averages about .440 for the first decade of their existence.[18] Given such a win record, which would likely be even more dismal during the first three to five years of a new club's existence, and the population size of these cities, only half of the proposed sites would produce revenues comparable to the clubs located in the seven smallest cities on the major league circuit.[19] If the proposed clubs in Denver, Miami, Phoenix, Tampa, and Washington had .440 records, the clubs would be about as financially viable as Cleveland, Kansas City, Seattle, etc. Proposed clubs in Buffalo, Indianapolis, New Orleans, and Vancouver would have to play .500 baseball from the start to produce revenues comparable to baseball's small city clubs.

With costs comparable to the small city major league clubs, the expansion teams would suffer losses similar to Cleveland, Milwaukee, Cincinnati, or San Francisco. But, for the existing clubs to agree to expansion they would have to be indemnified for lost profits. The addition of six clubs to the major league circuit would reduce each existing club's revenues from the network contract by $1.75 million in 1989. While the networks surely will offer more in the next contract bargaining round, there is little prospect that the networks will subsidize the expansion. Furthermore, expansion clubs play notoriously poor baseball and gate revenue will almost certainly in consequence decline for the established clubs.

If $2 million is taken as the annual profit loss to each of the existing clubs, each of the six expansion teams would have to pay $8 to $9 million per year in compensation payments. Adding this sum to the costs of the clubs and taking amortization into account, a number of these expansion sites would be no more viable than Oakland. Financial instability of that sort would damage baseball.

Pay television and affiliated ownership are the keys to expansion beyond 28 teams in baseball—expansion in the American League to 16 clubs is too compelling to be denied. Pay television offers the opportunity of a large increase in broadcast revenues. The price to be paid is lost attendance and the encouragement of "studio" baseball. Affiliated businesses are also a key to expansion, because club financial losses can be offset by increased profit in the parent company. In all likelihood, Ted Turner does not care very much if the Atlanta Braves lose money. The trend towards club ownership by broadcasters and consumer product firms seems inexorable. The effect of these trends on the quality of baseball is not known.

3

THE BASEBALL PLAYERS' MARKET

8

Pay and Performance in Major League Baseball

Depending upon how sundry real estate deals and deferred salary payments are valued, Eddie Murray, Dan Quisenberry, or Jim Rice was the highest paid player in 1987. By conservative estimates Quisenberry earned $2,293,509, but an alternative valuation of the real estate deal in his contract raises this figure to $3.5 million. Eddie Murray was paid $2,246,887, and Mike Schmidt received $2,127,333. A total of 59 players were paid one million dollars or more.[1] For the 1989 season some 108 players were in the millionaire's circle, with 21 players at or above the $2 million level.[2] On average, players were paid $400,000 in 1987 and $450,000 in 1988. Even some novice players with only two or three years of irregular play were making $250,000.

Many both in and out of baseball genuinely seem appalled that ballplayers receive that kind of money for what many think of as summer play among overgrown boys. This kind of grumbling about player salaries has been heard throughout baseball's history. While admiring the play of a Reggie Jackson or a Babe Ruth or a Ty Cobb, many found their contract demands and their salaries to be a wonder. In 1974, Jackson obtained through arbitration what Finley denied him in negotiation—$135,000 (about $300,000 in today's prices). During the depth of the Depression Ruth was paid $80,000 (about $665,000 today). In 1912, after a disagreeable contract-holdout maneuver, Ty Cobb suited up for Detroit for $11,300 (about $130,000 today). Converting these salaries to today's prices makes it clear that today's players receive a salary that is a multiple of past player salaries.

Like singers and actors, baseball players possess a rare talent. The great demand for scarce talent bids up the price, often outrageously. The supply of talented ball players is very inelastic. Mike Schmidt is paid more than $2 million because his performance and resultant fan following contributes that sum and more to the pockets of Bill Giles and his partners. Bill Cosby, if the present value of his syndication rights from the 28 episodes of his 1987 show are included, earned nearly $100 million in 1987 and is certain to become a billionaire. Cosby commands that kind of money because his shows are highly rated. In 1988, 1,820 30-second segments of commercial time in reruns

151

of "The Cosby Show" were sold for $60 million ($33,000 a segment) to Procter and Gamble and to General Foods.[3] Bob Hope has made more than Bill Cosby. Both men are loved by nearly all Americans and no complaint is heard of their good fortune. Merv Griffin ($80 million), Sylvester Stallone ($53 million), Madonna ($26 million), Michael Jackson ($31 million), and other entertainers earned enormous sums for their talent without public complaint.[4] Yet, the supply of rare athletic ability is no more elastic than that of the ability to entertain.

In the last ten years player salaries have escalated dramatically. In table 8.1, average player salaries are presented. From 1951 to 1975 player salaries rose from $13,300 to $46,000, a compound growth rate of 5.3 percent per year. Player salaries grew at the same rate as club revenues. In 1950, clubs had revenues of $2 million on average.[5] In 1975, they made $6.8 million.[6] In 1977–78 player salaries nearly doubled, while club revenues rose about 35 percent. From 1979 to 1984, player salaries were rising about 25 percent per year, while club revenues rose about 15 percent per annum. Since 1982, there has been a very considerable slowdown in the growth of player pay. In 1987, average salaries actually declined compared to 1986, although they re-

Table 8.1   Major League Average Player Salaries, 1951–1988

Year	Average Player Salary	Percentage Change
1951	13,300	
1967	19,000	5.3[a]
1975	46,000	
1976	51,500	12.0
1977	76,066	47.7
1978	99,876	31.3
1979	113,558	13.7
1980	143,756	26.6
1981	185,651	29.1
1982	241,497	30.1
1983	291,108	20.5
1984	329,408	13.2
1985	371,157	12.7
1986	410,517	10.6
1987	402,094	−2.1
1988	449,826	11.9

[a]This figure is for the compound growth rate for player salaries from 1951 through 1975.

Sources: Organized Baseball, House Report no. 2002, 82d Congress, 1st sess., 1952, 110; Major League Baseball Players' Association; New York Times, 8 November 1987; Dallas Times Herald, 15 January 1984.

covered in 1988. On the other hand, club revenues have been rising steadily at 15–20 percent per year.

Two events govern the path of player salaries over this time period: from 1976 to 1983 competitive bidding for free agents was in full swing and during 1984–88 there is evidence that club owners colluded to suppress free agency. In 1976, players became free agents simply by playing out their option year. Free agency was replaced by veteran free agency and, until 1985, by the free agent draft. Prior to the Messersmith decision players were paid just a small fraction of their actual contribution to team revenues, since there was only one buyer of their services.[7] With the coming of free agency, clubs bid against each other for rare talent, making rational decisions about the value of the player to the club relative to his market price. More or less, players began to be paid their expected net contribution to club revenues. The 1981 players' strike appears also to have been a critical event, uniting the owners in an alliance of perceived mutual self-interest and solidifying a determination to restrain the growth of player salaries by controlling the appetite for free agents. Their resolve was demonstrated when they hired Peter Ueberroth, the strongest commissioner since Landis.

Their lack of interest in the 1985 crop of free agents was the first real evidence that owners were colluding to restrict the market for free agents. Yet, anecdotal evidence suggests that the collusion began shortly after the 1981 strike. Indeed, by 24 February 1982, Marvin Miller was already testifying before Congress that,

based upon information supplied to the Players Association by free agent players and their agents, in addition to the results of the signings of this year's group of free agents, there is considerable evidence that the clubs have embarked upon a concert of action in violation of the Basic Agreement, in an attempt, inter alia, to limit the length of contracts, to force players to re-sign, in most instances, with their former clubs, and to affect salaries adversely by preventing operation of a free market for free agent players' services."[8]

If the conspiracy is sustainable, owner collusion will function like the pre-1976 reserve clause. By refusing to bid on free agents and by offering one year contracts the owners implicitly are reinstituting the reserve clause.

Player Contributions to Team Revenues

Major league baseball sells club contests. The quality of the games is determined strictly by the quality of the clubs competing on the playing field. Club quality mainly depends on the level of skills of the players, although managers, coaches, facilities, team spirit, and other inputs also contribute.

Club revenues arise from two main sources: gate receipts and broadcast fees. As we have seen in previous chapters, team revenues are directly related to the club's win percentage and to the size of the market from which it draws fans. While fans derive great satisfaction from individual player performance, it is the home team's prospects for victory that draws them. Previous research documents the effect of club standing and market size on attendance and broadcast fees.[9]

The contribution of the players to club revenues is estimated in a simple two-equation model developed earlier by the author. The first equation is a production function which relates team win percentage (output) to team hitting and pitching (inputs). The second equation relates team revenue to club standing and to the size of the market in which the team plays. The effect of team hitting or pitching on club revenue is determined by substituting their effects on win percentage from the first equation into the effect of win percentage on revenues in the second equation. This recursive approach to estimating the relationship between team hitting and pitching on revenues is justified because fans do not come to the park primarily to see hitting and pitching; rather, they come to see their team win. Finally, by making assumptions about the level of contribution of individual players to team hitting and pitching, it is possible to crudely measure individual player (or, rather, skill-level) contributions to team revenues.

Performance is best measured by the slugging average and the strikeout-to-walk ratio. These are not the performance measures that first come to mind. Many would conjecture that batting average, home-run percentage, runs batted in, on-base percentage, etc., would measure hitting performance more suitably.[10] For pitchers, games won per season, innings pitched, or earned run average also appear relevant. All of these measures capture important elements of player quality. All are related to club wins and to player salaries. But, the slugging average for hitters and the strikeout-to-walk ratio for pitchers have been and remain the best single predictors of player quality.

The club win percentage is hypothesized to be related to the team slugging average and the team strikeout-to-walk ratio. Data on these measures for the 1984 season is available in *The Baseball Encyclopedia*. Statistical estimation of the relationship revealed that a 1-point increase in the team slugging average (say, from .385 to .386) raised the club win percentage by 1.09 points (e.g., from .500 to .50109). A .01-point increase in the team strikeout-to-walk ratio (e.g., 1.68 to 1.69) raised the win percentage by .65 points (e.g., .500 to .50065). But there is considerable error in each estimated coefficient. The standard error of the coefficient of team slugging on team win percentage was ± .43, which means that one cannot reject the hypothesis that the coefficient is any different from 1.0. Adding the standard error to the coefficient yields a range from .66 to 1.52, which obviously includes 1.0. A similar exercise with the coefficient of team strikeout-to-walk ratio on win percentage produces pretty much the same result. In my earlier study, using 1968–69 data, the coefficients of the team slugging average and the team strikeout-to-walk ratio were .92 and .90, respectively. The respective standard errors of the coefficients were ± .21 and ± .15. *The evidence supports the assertion that basically there is a unit relationship between either team slugging or team strikeout-to-walk ratio and team win percentage.* Each point increase in either measure raises club win averages by a point.

Team revenue is estimated as a linear equation, with club win percentage and population size as the determinants. Revenues are for 1984, the most recent official data. The data is available for all clubs except Houston and Minnesota. Revenue includes game receipts, broadcast fees, concession income, parking receipts, play-off and World Series shares, and other baseball-related revenues. The hypothesis is that fan support is affected by club wins. Adjusted for market size, the coefficient of win percentage on team revenue is a measure of the marginal revenue of team quality across teams. Market size is a proxy for the monopoly income that arises from exclusive territorial rights. Accordingly, the 1984 population size of the city is included in the revenue function to adjust for the magnitude of monopoly rents.

The statistical results established that a 1-point increase in the team win record raised 1984 team revenues by $31,696 (this result is slightly different from the result in chapter 6, because the win percentage for 1983 is not included as a regressor).[11] Thus, the effect of city size held constant, a .400 club earned $12.68 million and a .600 club earned $19.02 million for their respective performances, a difference of $6.34 million. A win out of a 162-game schedule is equal to an additional 6.2 points in club win percentage. Thus, an extra victory was worth $195,653. Now, consider the effect on revenues of adding a hitter of the quality of Andre Dawson, the National League MVP of 1987, or a pitcher like Roger Clemens, the Cy Young Award winner in the American League in 1986. In 1987, Dawson had a slugging average of .568 over 621 at-bats. Chicago had a team slugging average of .432 over 5,583 at-bats. Dawson contributed 11.1 percent of the at-bats and .063 of the team slugging average. Given the relationship between slugging average and wins those 63 points conservatively were worth 11 games to Chicago. The marginal revenue of 11 games was about $2.2 million. Roger Clemens posted a 24–4 record in Boston in 1986. Assuming Clemens was the source of the margin of victory in those net 20 games, his performance was worth $3.9 million in revenue. Players of the caliber of Dan Quisenberry and George Brett of Kansas City, Jim Rice of Boston, Eddie Murray of Baltimore, Mike Schmidt of Philadelphia, and Gary Carter of the Mets, all of whom had salaries above $2 million, individually are worth 10 to 15 games ($2 to $3 million) per season to a club. By this economic standard such players are not overpaid.

Of course, the proximity of salary and marginal revenue is a recent phenomenon in baseball, brought about by free agency. In an earlier study, I found an enormous difference between a player's pay and his contribution to team revenue. Superstars like Bob Gibson, Willie Mays, Roberto Clemente, Reggie Jackson, and Carl Yastrzemski were paid $100,000 to $125,000. Individually, they were worth 10 to 15 wins per season to their clubs. In 1968–69, a win was worth about $64,000 in additional revenues. These players, then, each contributed $640,000 to $1 million to team revenues but were paid only 10 to 20 percent of their contribution. Since the reserve clause prevented interclub competition for player services, this discrepancy between pay and performance hardly is surprising.

Player Pay and Performance

Four factors are crucial to the determination of player salaries: the overall quality of player performance; the weight or fraction of the player's contribution to team performance; the experience of the player; and, the popularity or recognizability of the player to the fans—"star" or "superstar" status, if you like.

For hitters, the preferred measure is career slugging average. Career slugging average is a better measure than that of the previous season because hitting fluctuates from season to season. A career average contains more information about ability than performance in a single year. A case can be made that both current and past average performance should be included in the analysis so that changes in performance can be captured. However, career and current performance are sufficiently correlated to cloud an empirical analysis. Slugging average is preferred to batting average because its predictive power is greater. All hits are counted equally in the batting average measure, although extra base hits produce more runs and higher win percentages. The weight of the hitter's contribution to team performance is his total career at-bats divided by his years in the majors times 5,500, the average season at-bats for a team. This variable measures the average percentage contribution to team performance. A superstar in the regular lineup like Dawson, Raines, or Schmidt will contribute about 10 percent or so of the team at-bats and more of the team hits. Average players contribute half or less of that percentage.

Pitching performance is measured by the career strikeout-to-walk ratio. Interseason performance fluctuates more for pitchers than for players. Partly this is due to disability or injury, and partly it is caused by aging and subsequent adjustment to a new inventory of pitches. The contribution of individual pitcher performance to team pitching is measured as the career average percentage of innings pitched out of the team total (approximately, 9 times 162 times career years). Primary starting pitchers like Roger Clemens or Charlie Hough pitch 19 to 20 percent of team innings. More frequently, starters hurl about 200 innings or 13 to 14 percent of the schedule. Of course, relief pitchers work fewer innings: Steve Bedrosian, the National League Cy Young Award winner, pitched only 89 innings in 1987, but had 40 saves in 65 appearances. Of course, less talented pitchers and rookies work fewer innings.

Veteran players earn more than rookie players of essentially the same ability, which is to say that salaries rise automatically over time. This independent effect of experience on salary is not just a seniority effect. We have seen that a player's level of performance predictably increases over his career, up to a point (recall figure 3.1, the career batting profile). It is also true that a veteran's expected contribution to the team can be known with more certainty than can a rookie's. The relatively high pay of veteran players is also an incentive for younger players to perform at their very best.

Finally, great players command salaries apparently in excess of their relative contribution to team performance. This fact introduces a nonlinearity into the relationship between salary and performance. The nonlinearity might be caused by their greater bargaining strength, but this seems unlikely in the era of free agency. Alternatively, great players have a following of fans that gives them greater value to a team. For example, Reggie Jackson in 1987 was not half the player that he was in 1973 (in 1987 he hit .220 with 15 home runs, while in 1973 he hit .293 with 32 homers), but Oakland paid him over $500,000 in 1987 to boost attendance. Some fans go to the Coliseum just to see him play. To account for this star effect, the salary relationship is estimated nonlinearly.

There were two primary sources for the data used in the estimated

Table 8.2   Player and Pitcher Salary Regressions, 1986 Season

Variable	1986 Salary Hitters	1986 Salary Pitchers
Intercept	10.06	10.53
1985 Career slugging average or strike-to-walk ratio	1.90	0.23
Career Years	0.56	0.60
1985 Career at-bat or innings pitched percentage	17.56	10.02
1985 Free agent	−0.29	−0.99
$\bar{R}^2$	.78	.60
(N)	(345)	(260)

Note: The salary data and career years are in logarithms. All of the other variables are arithmetic.

Sources: The 1986 salary data is from *USA Today*, 19 November 1986, p. 5C, and 20 November 1986, p. 6C. Performance and career years are from *The Baseball Encyclopedia*. 1985 free agent status is from *Baseball Register* (St. Louis: The Sporting News, 1986).

player salary equations reported below. The 1986 salary data is from published newspaper accounts, which contained contract information on 605 major league players. Thus, a very large fraction of all of the players who appeared on Opening Day rosters is represented. All of the independent variables were obtained or constructed from *The Baseball Encyclopedia*.

The salary regressions appear in table 8.2. First, note that all of the independent variables, which were hypothesized to have an effect on salary, are statistically significant at above the 1 percent level. Second, the coefficient of determination ($\bar{R}^2$ Adj.) is high for the size of the sample: 78 percent in the hitter salary equation and 60 percent in the pitcher salary equation. Thus, 60 to 78 percent of the variance in player salaries is associated with the variance in the independent variables. Undoubtedly, if more variables that are related to player salary are added to the equation, somewhat more of the variation in player salaries would be determined. But my experience with salary models of this sort is that additional independent variables produce very rapidly diminishing returns.

For hitters, each 1-point increase in career slugging average yielded a 1.9 percent increase in salary in 1986. The average hitter in the sample had a .385 career slugging average and earned $475,000. At the mean salary and slugging average a 1-point increase in career slugging average added $902.50 in 1986 salary. The mean at-bats for hitters was approximately 300 per season. A rise in the career slugging average from .385 to .386 for a 300 at-bats per season player is equivalent to an increase of about one-third of a base per season. Thus, an additional base hit per season over one's career for the average player was worth $2,700 per year. An extra home run was worth $12,030. Little wonder hitters leap joyously around the diamond after hitting a home run!

The relationship between the career slugging average and salary is illustrated in figure 8.1. All of the independent variables in the salary equation other than 1985 slugging average were set equal to their respective means. Thus, the figure describes the salary structure for average career length and average percent at-bat players arrayed by skill at power hitting. Salaries range from $386,000 to $467,000 for below average sluggers (.270–.370), and from $485,000 to $683,000 for above average power hitters (.390–.570).

For each one percent increase in career time in the majors, salary rises by about one-half of a percent. The average career is seven years. Thus, an extra year for the average player is about 14 percent of career time. Holding performance and fraction of team hitting constant, average hitter salaries rise nearly 8 percent per year. At the average salary, this amounts to $38,200 per year. The independent effect of experience on player salary is illustrated in figure 8.2. All of the independent variables other than career years have been set to their mean levels. Thus, the graph illustrates the profile of average player salary across career length.

For pitchers, each one hundredth point increase in the career strikeout-to-walk ratio yielded a 0.23 percent increase in 1986 salary. The mean salary for pitchers was $431,000 and the mean strikeout-to-walk ratio was 1.73. At the means a .01-point increase in the career

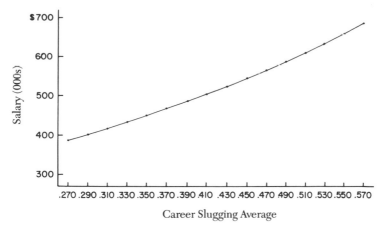

Figure 8.1   The Effect of the Career Slugging Average on Hitter Salary, 1986

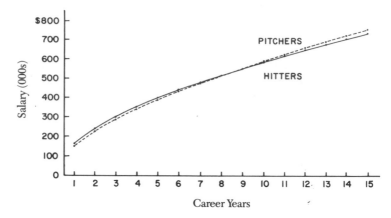

Figure 8.2   The Effect of Career Length on Player Salary, 1986

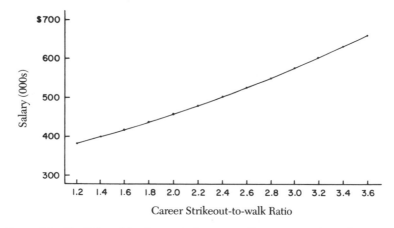

Figure 8.3   The Effect of the Career Strikeout-to-walk Ratio on Pitcher Salary, 1986

strikeout-to-walk ratio added $987 to salary. The average pitcher pitches 7.3 percent of his team's total innings. On the average a pitcher will amass 70 strikeouts and give up 40 walks during a season. A record of 71 strikeouts to 40 walks per season raises the strikeout-to-walk ratio by 0.025 points. Therefore, at the means an extra strikeout per season is worth $400 to a pitcher. The profile of pitcher salary for various levels of skill is illustrated in figure 8.3.

Final Offer Arbitration in Baseball

An important feature of the Basic Agreement in 1973 was the establishment of a binding arbitration procedure for salary and other contract
disputes between players and management. The procedure is available
for all players with three years (previously two years) to six years of
major league experience and it went into effect in 1974. In 1974 and
1975, there were 500 players eligible for salary arbitration. More recently, 200 or so players become eligible each season. About half of
those eligible will file and more than half will settle with their clubs
prior to the deadline. For example, of the 111 players who filed for arbitration in 1988, 93 resolved the disagreement before the deadline.
(Frequently, negotiations go down to the last minute. In 1985, relief
pitcher Bill Caudill had demanded $1.3 million against the Blue Jay's
offer of $850,000. General Manager Pat Gillick placed a five-year, $7
million offer on the table the night before the hearing. Caudill signed
the contract eight minutes before the hearing).[12]

In theory, arbitration is an impartial process designed to equalize
salaries among players with similar stature and experience. The criteria
to be used by the arbitrator are completely objective. Player salaries
are strictly related to performance. Hence, to a large degree, there is
an expectation that the decision is based on the facts, or at least is not
random. Both owners and players have access to the same information
(collusion?) as the arbitrator. The low utilization rate for the procedure
in a milieu of intensive, personalized, and often bitter negotiations
points to the indirect pressure that arbitration brings to the bargaining
table. Since its inception fewer than a 1,000 cases have been filed out
of a group of 3,000 eligible players. Of those eligible, only about 8 percent saw the procedure through.

In an earlier study, I pointed to several problems with binding arbitration in baseball.[13] First, it appeared that relatively weak drawing
clubs were using the process disproportionately. Each club was expected to have 4 percent of the arbitration cases in 1974–75. Yet,
Oakland and Minnesota accounted for half of the cases, and the A's
alone for one-third. This imbalance remains today. Over 1974–87, the
American League, which historically has had a larger share of weak
drawing franchises, accounts for 62 percent of the arbitration activity.[14]
Oakland has a 13 percent share of the cases, compared to a 3.8 percent
expected share. Minnesota has a 7.8 percent share. Other clubs utilizing the procedure much above average are Cincinnati (6.9 percent) and
California (6.0 percent). These four clubs account for one-third of the
arbitration cases. There is a rationale for the high incidence among the
weaker franchises, which will be given momentarily.

Table 8.3   Arbitration Cases Filed and Settled, 1974–1988

Year	Cases Filed	Club Decision	Player Decision
1974	54	16	13
1975	55	10	6
1978*	16	7	2
1979	40	6	8
1980	65	11	15
1981	96	10	11
1982	103	14	8
1983	88	17	13
1984	80	6	4
1985	97	7	6
1986	162	20	15
1987	108	16	10
1988	111	11	7

*No cases were heard in 1976–77 because of the changes arising from free agency.

Source: The Sporting News, annually in the March issue.

An important issue concerning arbitration is whether the decisions are based on merit. Of the 269 arbitration decisions recorded in table 8.3, the players won 118 (44 percent) and the clubs won 151 (56 percent). The arbitration process is thus pretty much a random process, basically no different from flipping a coin. Based on historical evidence, the owner and player can go to arbitration confident that the outcome is about an even bet.

There is some evidence to support the conclusion that the decisions in arbitration are not based on merit but on an even splitting among the adversaries. Most observers of the decision-making process in arbitration suggest that arbitrators split the difference where they can: even if they cannot split the difference between salary demand and salary offer (a stipulation the owners insisted on), arbitrators can split the number of decisions between players and owners, and thereby emerge with a reputation of fairness. Players who lose in one year can come back and win in the following year. Of the fraction of player repeats in arbitration a very substantial number obtain just the opposite ruling a year later, despite the fact that changes in their performance data were not dramatic. For the weak clubs a large sum in player salaries can be saved by going to arbitration. Oakland has saved about $1 million in salary costs as a result of winning in arbitration. When these clubs lose they tend to trade the players.

The stakes for both the player and the club have grown as salaries have escalated. Table 8.4 presents data on the arbitration decisions over the period 1986–88. A total of 381 cases were filed during the pe-

Table 8.4   Arbitration Positions and Outcomes, 1986–1987

Player	Club	Previous Salary (000s)	Owner Offer (000s)	Player Demand (000s)	Relative Spread	Outcome
1986						
W. Boggs	Bos	1,000	1,350	1,850	37.0	Club
O. Hershiser	LA	212	600	1,000	66.7	Player
R. Gedman	Bos	478	650	1,000	53.8	Club
G. Ward	Tex	720	865	930	7.5	Club
B. Saberhagen	KC	160	625	925	48.0	Player
B. Butler	Cle	425	600	850	41.7	Player
C. Leibrandt	KC	225	550	770	40.0	Player
J. Franco	Cle	455	575	740	28.7	Club
B. Smith	Mon	290	500	700	40.0	Player
G. Gaetti	Minn	415	515	675	31.1	Club
F. Viola	Minn	375	525	674	28.4	Player
R. Darling	Mets	230	440	615	39.8	Club
D. LaPoint	Det	380	410	550	34.1	Player
A. Davis	Sea	225	400	550	37.5	Club
M. Moore	Sea	228	400	530	32.5	Club
E. Lynch	Mets	330	400	530	32.5	Player
E. Milner	Cin	300	350	530	51.4	Club
S. Balboni	KC	205	350	525	50.0	Player
R. Kittle	Sox	300	400	500	25.0	Club
P. Bradley	Sea	125	375	475	26.7	Player
K. McReynolds	SD	150	275	450	63.6	Club
G. Brock	LA	150	325	440	35.4	Club
M. Barrett	Bos	273	325	435	33.8	Player
B. Dawley	Hou	295	325	435	33.8	Club
W. Backman	Mets	200	325	425	30.8	Club
G. Pettis	Cal	125	300	425	41.7	Club
R. Romanick	Cal	147	250	425	70.0	Player
F. DiPino	Hou	255	280	380	35.7	Club
T. Teufel	Mets	110	200	350	75.0	Club
B. Kearney	Sea	183	215	300	39.5	Player
R. Horton	St. L	110	215	275	27.9	Player
J. Dedmon	Atl	150	200	270	35.0	Club
T. Laudner	Minn	145	155	250	61.3	Club
D. Van Gorder	Cin	60	75	150	100.0	Player
A. Knicely	Phi	60	80	140	75.0	Club
1987						
D. Mattingly	Yank	1,375	1,700	1,975	16.2	Player
J. Morris	Det	875	1,350	1,850	37.0	Player
O. Hershiser	LA	1,000	800	1,100	37.5	Club
R. Darling	Mets	440	800	1,050	31.3	Player
B. Butler	Cle	850	765	875	14.4	Club
D. Cox	St. L	400	600	875	45.8	Club
C. Leibrandt	KC	770	725	850	17.2	Player
B. Hurst	Bos	495	700	845	20.7	Club
B. Doran	Hou	550	625	825	32.0	Club
K. McReynolds	Mets	275	625	825	32.0	Club
P. Bradley	Sea	475	550	750	36.4	Player

(continued)

Table 8.4   (*continued*)

Player	Club	Previous Salary (000s)	Owner Offer (000s)	Player Demand (000s)	Relative Spread	Outcome
O. Boyd	Bos	375	550	695	26.4	Club
K. Bass	Hou	310	560	630	12.5	Player
J. Howell	Oak	530	530	630	18.9	Club
G. Harris	Tex	310	575	620	7.8	Player
T. Power	Cin	500	500	610	22.0	Club
D. Walling	Hou	367	450	595	32.2	Player
G. Pettis	Cal	300	400	550	37.5	Club
K. Schrom	Cle	275	450	545	21.1	Club
A. Hawkins	SD	300	450	535	18.8	Player
K. Gross	Phi	355	420	530	26.2	Club
K. Phelps	Sea	235	300	515	71.7	Club
D. Schofield	Cal	210	305	475	55.7	Player
J. Acker	Atl	368	350	450	28.6	Club
A. Pena	LA	350	280	368	31.4	Club
D. Motley	Atl	258	210	258	22.9	Club
1988						
A. Dawson	Cubs	700	1,850	2,000	8.1	Club
D. Gooden	Mets	1,500	1,400	1,650	17.9	Club
F. Tanana	Det	663	800	1,100	37.5	Player
T. Henke	Tor	331	725	1,025	41.4	Club
J. Franco	Cin	300	675	925	37.0	Club
B. Boone	Cal	747	710	883	24.4	Player
T. Burke	Mon	210	625	850	36.0	Club
M. Gubicza	KC	450	525	635	21.0	Player
M. Pagliarulo	Yank	175	500	625	25.0	Club
M. Moore	Sea	536	482	565	17.2	Club
Z. Smith	Atl	250	450	550	22.2	Club
J. Acker	Atl	350	435	495	13.8	Club
G. Redus	Sox	400	370	460	24.3	Player
M. Thurmond	Det	370	370	435	17.6	Player
G. Perry	Atl	225	375	425	13.3	Player
D. LaPoint	Sox	65	265	425	60.4	Player
C. Brown	SD	215	265	410	54.7	Club
J. Oquendo	St. L	100	275	360	30.9	Club

Sources: Sports Illustrated, 3 March 1986, 32; *The Sporting News*, 2 March 1987, 37; *The Sporting News*, 28 February 1988, 35.

riod, with a record 162 in 1986. Of the 79 cases arbitrated, 47 were won by the clubs and 32 by the players. The relative spread between owner offer and player demand is quite large. Between 1986 and 1988, on average, the players and the owners were apart by amounts from $151,000 to $164,000. Some players won large salary increases, others failed. Wayne Boggs made $1 million at Boston in 1985 and demanded $1.85 million in 1986. Boston offered $1.35 million and won in arbitration. In 1987, Boggs was paid $1.72 million. Orel Hershiser, after a record year of 19 wins and 3 losses in 1986, demanded $1 million from the Dodgers and won. In 1987, after finishing with 14 wins and 14 losses, Hershiser demanded $1.1 million; the Dodgers offered $800,000 and won. Rich Gedman demanded $1 million at Boston in 1986 and got $650,000, which was better than his $478,000 in 1985. Gedman hit .295 in nearly 500 at-bats. In 1986, his batting average fell to .258 and he became a free agent. He got not a single offer from other teams and re-signed with Boston for $773,000. Don Mattingly who hit .352 with 31 homers for the Yankees and Jack Morris who won 21 games for Detroit in 1986 were the big winners in arbitration in 1987. Ron Darling's 15 wins and 6 losses for the Mets gave the fourth-year pitcher an extra $610,000 for 1987. In 1988, Andre Dawson became the first player with prospects of gaining a salary of $2 million through arbitration. However, arbitrator Stephen Goldberg ruled in favor of the club's $1.85 million offer, thereby leaving Don Mattingly's $1.975 settlement in 1987 the all-time arbitration record.

Are Club Owners Colluding to Suppress Free Agency?

Bidding for Players in a Competitive Free Agent Market

A source of supply of veteran players is the free agent market. Star players are allocated in the free agent market according to their value to alternative franchise locations and subject to any locational preference constraints of the players (e.g., Los Angeles and New York offer higher endorsement revenue, San Diego has a pleasant climate, etc.). While star players are worth more to big city franchises than to those located in small population centers, it does not follow that all of the star players are clustered on the rosters of the rich clubs.

Clubs want the best playing talent that they can get at the lowest price. The upper bound price that a club will offer for a free agent is the expected marginal revenue of that player to that club. Expected marginal revenue is expected player performance to team win production times the marginal revenue that team win production brings to the club. Clubs base their offers to free agents on their estimate of the players' contribution to the enterprise's revenues.

Given a distribution of playing talent among the clubs, a player of the caliber of Andre Dawson might be worth $3.5 million to a New York or a Los Angeles club, $2.5 to Houston or Philadelphia, and $1.5 to Cincinnati or Cleveland. It is thus not in the interest of any club other than the Dodgers, the Mets, or the Yankees to bid for Dawson, since they would presumably have to pay a price above his worth to the club. The successful bid would undoubtedly have to be in the range of $2.5 to $3.5 million. However, if another player of the same quality is added to the free agent market, because the incremental revenue of winning declines as winning increases, the second such player no longer is worth to New York or Los Angeles the $3.5 million that they had to pay Dawson to sign him. Suppose now that this second star is worth $2.5 million in New York or Los Angeles. Such a player, however, is also worth that amount in Houston or Philadelphia, and thus there is no guarantee that the second star player will wind up in New York or Los Angeles. Houston or Philadelphia rationally can bid an amount similar to the big city clubs and get the star player. Now add a third star player. The third star may be worth $1.5 million in New York or Los Angeles, in Houston or Philadelphia, but now also in Cincinnati or Cleveland.

In general, while it is true that big city clubs will have more star players than small city franchises, the movement of a star player in the free agent market will not necessarily be to a big city team. Andre Dawson probably would contribute less extra revenue in New York than in a number of other locations. The Yankees, for example, have four veteran players with higher batting averages than Dawson (C. Washington, D. Winfield, R. Henderson, and D. Mattingly).

Owner Collusion in the Free Agent Market

The Players Association filed grievances on behalf of the 1985, 1986, and 1987 crop of free agents charging that the owners colluded to block the market for free agents. Club owners deny the allegation, but arbitrators have ruled for the players. The fact that no free agent received an offer *at any price* was sufficient evidence for arbitrator Thomas Roberts to conclude that the owners had acted in concert. Will salary levels decline in baseball? What is the evidence that clubs are colluding to reimpose restraints on player movement?

Interest in the effect of free agency on the baseball players' labor market supported a small cottage industry of economists writing on the topic. All of the papers agreed and documented a substantial positive impact on salary during the period of study, 1976–79.[15] In 1976, the crop of free agents averaged salaries just over $1 million, compared to a major league average of $51,500. The average salary of 14 free agents in 1977 was $1.73 million and that of 10 free agents in 1978 was $1.56 million.[16] Further, average baseball salaries rose very rapidly after free agency occurred. Note in table 8.1 the 47.7 percent and 31.3 percent rise in salaries in 1976–78. Clearly, free agents and players in general were experiencing enormous benefits from the interclub competition for their services.

A variable not discussed previously but included in the salary regressions in table 8.2 is 1985 Free Agent. This binary variable is equal to 1 for all players who were free agents in 1985 and 0 otherwise. The coefficient in the regressions indicates the percentage change in 1986 salaries arising from the status of free agency, holding performance, experience, and player utilization constant. The coefficient is negative and is statistically significant for both free agent hitters and pitchers. Evaluated at the means and converting back to arithmetic values, the 1986 salary of the hitters who took free agency was $120,000 lower than those who did not. For the pitchers, the 1986 salary of the free agents was $271,000 lower.

Perhaps, the outcome for the 1985 free agents was anomalous. In table 8.5, the effect of free agency on 1987 salaries is shown. All the players in this sample ($N = 479$) were in the 1986 sample ($N = 605$). Thus, comparisons of the same cohort of players over the two-year period are possible. While there are some changes in the sizes of the coefficients, our interest is in the effect of free agency on 1987 salaries.[17] The coefficient 1986 Free Agent is negative and is statistically significant in both salary equations. The mean salary of the hitters was $551,374. Naturally, the mean is higher, because most of the 66 players who were in the 1986 sample but not in the 1987 group were rookies

Table 8.5   Player and Pitcher Salary Regressions, 1987 Season

Variable	1987 Salary Hitters	1987 Salary Pitchers
Intercept	9.46	10.57
1986 Career slugging average or strikeout-to-walk ratio	3.25	0.19
Career years	0.71	0.80
1986 Career at-bat or innings pitched percentage	14.58	7.32
1986 Free agent	−0.47	−0.71
$\bar{R}^2$	.71	.54
(N)	(279)	(200)

Note: The salary data and career years are in logarithms. All of the other variables are arithmetic.

Sources: The 1987 salary data is the *New York Times*, 12 April 1987, p. 24, and *Sports Illustrated*, 20 April 1987. Performance and career years are from *The Baseball Encyclopedia*. 1986 free agent status is from *Baseball Register* (St. Louis: The Sporting News, 1987).

who did not survive. The players who opted for free agency in 1986, holding the effects of performance, experience, and contribution constant, had 1987 salaries that were $206,000 lower than non–free agents. The mean salary of the pitchers was $508,624. Holding pitching performance, fraction of team innings pitched, and experience constant, free agent pitchers received $259,000 less than non–free agent pitchers in 1987.

Perhaps, the decline in free agent salaries reflects nothing more than a decline in performance or frequency of play. The changes in slugging average and percentage of team at-bats for the hitters and the changes in strikeout-to-walk ratios and percentage of team innings pitched for the pitchers between 1985 and 1986 was computed for the sample of ballplayers. The free agents were not found to have had a significantly different level of performance in 1986 than in 1985. Clearly, salary reduction because of poorer performance is not justified.

Another approach to determining if the owners were colluding is to compare salary of the free agents to their contribution to team revenue. If certain assumptions are allowed, player marginal products crudely can be calculated.

Data on the Elite Six hitters who were free agents in 1986 and 15 of the most highly paid hitters who were not free agents in 1986 are presented in table 8.6. Performance is measured with two variables: the slugging average over 1985–86 and the average total runs produced over the period. Runs produced is runs scored plus runs batted in. To calculate the hitter contribution to games won, runs scored was regressed against team wins.[18] The coefficient of runs scored on wins was 0.11. Thus, it takes about 9.45 runs produced to win a game. Dividing the hitter's runs produced by 9.45 gives the expected number of games won in 1987 due to his run production. We have already established the effect of a win on 1984 team revenues. A forecasting report from Major League Baseball projected revenue growth of 24.6 percent between 1984 and 1987, which is very conservative.[19] Using this figure, a win in 1987 was worth $244,000 to a team. Multiplying this sum by the number of expected games won through the player's performance yields the estimated contribution to team revenue (MRP) in table 8.6. Two facts stand out sharply. Player marginal revenue products exceed salary by a large margin. One needs to be cautious about the result, since the estimates of player marginal products are crude. Nevertheless, these estimates are not so crude as to conclude by any means that players are overpaid. That matter aside, comparison of the ratio of player salary to player contribution to team revenue reveals a very interesting difference between the elite free agents and the elite non–

Table 8.6 Performance, Pay, and Marginal Revenue Products of the Elite Hitters: Free Agents vs. Non–Free Agents, 1986

Player	SA 85–86	RUNS 85–86	SAL86 (000s)	SAL87 (000)	MRP87 (millions)	SAL87/ MRP87
Free Agents						
B. Boone	.311	95	853	747	2.45	.30
A. Dawson	.460	150	1,047	700	3.87	.18
R. Gedman	.455	130	650	773	3.36	.23
B. Horner	.485	154	1,800	750*	3.98	—
L. Parrish	.480	126	850	1,000	3.25	.31
T. Raines	.476	155	1,515	1,666	4.00	.42
Non–Free Agents						
J. Barfield	.548	197	725	1,525	5.09	.30
W. Boggs	.482	182	1,350	1,720	4.70	.37
G. Brett	.539	182	1,471	2,175	4.70	.46
G. Carter	.465	185	2,161	2,099	4.78	.44
P. Guerrero	.573	102	1,370	1,520	2.63	.58
R. Henderson	.491	211	1,570	1,670	5.45	.31
K. Hernandez	.438	178	1,650	1,800	4.60	.39
D. Mattingly	.570	241	1,375	1,975	6.22	.32
D. Murphy	.395	113	900	1,925	2.92	.66
E. Murray	.495	190	926	2,247	4.90	.46
J. Rice	.489	198	1,984	2,222	5.11	.43
M. Schmidt	.540	199	2,137	2,127	5.14	.41
O. Smith	.347	123	1,940	1,940	3.18	.61
W. Wilson	.387	126	1,175	1,933	3.25	.59
D. Winfield	.467	157	1,887	1,911	4.05	.47

*Horner's salary in Japan.
Source: Salary and performance data are cited in tables 8.2 and 8.5.

free agents. *The free agents' salary is a much smaller fraction of their contribution to team revenues than is the case of the non–free agents.* The average of the free agents is 29 percent; the average of the non–free agents is 45 percent. If the free agents were paid 45 percent of their marginal revenue in 1987 their salaries would have averaged $1.52 million, rather than the actual $977,000. This exercise offers some support for the conclusion that owners colluded to suppress the market for free agents.

A final calculation is due to a suggestion by Roger G. Noll. Noll believes that salaries as a fraction of team revenues peaked in professional team sports in the late 1970s and early 1980s.[20] In the NFL, the demise of the United States Football League ended the only serious alternative source of bidding for players. In the NBA, the team salary cap, the right of first refusal, and the college draft have slowed salary relative to revenue growth.[21] In baseball, the players' strike of 1981 deeply angered owners. Implicitly, free agency may have been lost at this point. Unable to restrain competition among themselves for free agents by significantly raising the compensation price, collusion became an alternative. Noll believes that this collusion may have begun in 1981 but was not obvious until bids failed to materialize for Gibson, Niekro, Fisk, Raines, Dawson, et. al., in 1985 and 1986. Some evidence for this view is revealed in table 8.1. In 1981 and 1982, average player salaries grew at about 30 percent. Thereafter, the rate of salary increases declined. The percentage change in salary in 1987 actually was negative. The average salary change for the 1988 season was similar to the increments from 1984 to 1986. In 1982, player salaries were 45 percent of club revenues. In 1984, they were 40 percent.[22] In 1987, total player compensation was about $256 million.[23] Estimated revenues for 1987 conservatively were $774 million. Player salaries have shrunk to 33 percent of revenues. In 1976, before the effects of free agency on player salaries, players received 25 percent of revenues.[24] For all of the talk about exorbitant player salary demands, the benefits of free agency to players appear to be eroding away through club collusion. If player salary in 1987 was the same fraction of baseball revenue as in 1982, aggregate player salary would be $100 million more than the 1987 level.

9

Race Discrimination in Baseball

A segment of Ted Koppel's "Nightline" show of 6 April 1987 was devoted to a commemoration of the 40th anniversary of the breaking of the color ban in baseball. The 1987 season then unfolding was dedicated to the memory of Jackie Robinson, who had become the first black major league player since Moses Fleetwood Walker and his brother Welday in 1884.[1] Koppel's guest that evening was Los Angeles Dodgers' vice-president Al Campanis, who was in charge of player personnel and who had played with Robinson in Montreal in 1946. Koppel asked about the absence of black managers and general managers and the paucity of black executives in the front offices of organized baseball. Campanis replied: "I truly believe that they may not have some of the necessities to be, let's say, a field manager, or perhaps a general manager. . . . Well, I don't say all of them, but they certainly are short. How many quarterbacks do you have—how many pitchers do you have—that are black? Why are black men, or black people, not good swimmers? Because they don't have the buoyancy." Chairman of the Board of Directors Peter O'Malley and Manager Tom Lasorda sought to protect him but under some prodding from Ueberroth, Campanis resigned on 8 April.[2]

Apparently, learning nothing from the firestorm which surrounded Campanis's remarks, Jimmy ("the Greek") Snyder, a CBS Sports commentator, in an interview on 16 January 1988 with WRC-TV in Washington, said that if blacks "take over coaching jobs like everybody wants them to, there's not going to be anything left for the white people." Snyder's theory of black athletic success was that "he's been bred to be that way because of his thigh size and big size."[3] On the following day CBS fired him.

Campanis's and Snyder's insensitive public remarks opened a wound that had been closed for nearly two decades. As blacks came to dominate professional team sports and earned handsome salaries, complaints of racism seemed ungracious. Nevertheless, it remains a fact that blacks largely have been confined to the playing field. Baseball has taken on the appearance of a white man's game which employs well-paid black gladiators. Despite low ticket prices and an historic reputation as a working man's game, few blacks attend games. A 1986 survey by Simmons Market Research Bureau found that black attendance was 6.8 percent of the total in baseball, compared to 7.5 percent in football and 17 percent in basketball.[4] In 1987, there were a total of 84 Latin and black professional employees in the front offices in the major leagues, or on coaching staffs in the majors or the minors.[5] Blacks represent less than 5 percent of the front office personnel. Partly as a result of Campanis's remarks and partly under Ueberroth's prodding there were 180 new hires of minorities in the front office and on the field in 1988. All of the hires were for relatively low-level, nondecision-making jobs.[6] As of the date of writing, there is one black manager in the majors. Of the 130 coaching positions, minorities hold a total of 16. There are no black trainers. There is no black umpire in the American League, and only six in the minors.[7] After the Campanis calamity, Peter Ueberroth urged the clubs to hire blacks as field managers and general managers. Between April and November of 1987, 9 of the clubs appointed 13 new managers, general managers, and presidents. None were black.[8]

Race Discrimination in Baseball before 1947

Black baseball always was separate from white baseball. By the end of the Civil War there was a formal ban against playing black clubs or using black players. At the National Association of Base Ball Players in Philadelphia in 1867, the following formal ban was adopted. "It is not presumed by your committee that any club who have applied are composed of persons of color. . . . They unanimously report against the admission of any club which may be composed of one or more colored persons."[9] The ban was effectively enforced and resulted in racially segregated leagues.

However, for a brief time limited opportunities for blacks in white baseball arose. The aforementioned Moses Fleetwood Walker, an Oberlin College graduate, caught 41 games for Toledo in the old American Association in 1884, making him the first black major leaguer. At the end of the season his less talented brother Welday, an outfielder, played five games at Toledo. In 1885, only Fleet Walker and Bud Fowler were playing in the white leagues.[10] In 1886, George Stovey and Frank Grant played on white teams.

The few black players on white teams in the 1880s were not well received by either the fans or the players. At Richmond, Fleet Walker had to sit out a game for fear of a lynching.[11] Adrian (Cap) Anson, a founding father of professional baseball, refused to field his White

Stockings against Toledo in 1884, because of the presence of Walker in the lineup, and in Newark, in 1887, because of Stovey and Walker.[12]

By 1887, pressure was building from the players to ban blacks from the minor leagues. At the International League Meeting in Buffalo, agreement was reached not to extend contracts to black players.[13] The Ohio State League followed suit in 1888.[14] After 1888, very few blacks appeared in organized baseball. Attempts were made to hire blacks in the 1890s but were blocked. In 1898, the Acme Colored Giants played in the white Iron and Oil League, but the league folded in mid-July. These ballplayers were the last to play white teams in organized baseball.[15]

By the 1930s influential sports writers like Heywood Broun, Jimmy Powers, and Shirley Povich began to speak out against baseball's "gentleman's agreement" to keep blacks out of the game. The great talent in the Negro Leagues, they suggested, would add to the caliber of play in the major leagues. Indeed, the skills of Leroy (Satchel) Paige, James ("Cool Papa") Bell, Walter (Buck) Leonard, and Josh Gibson were generally recognized as outstanding.

From 1933 to 1945 pressure built against baseball's color ban and the response was incoherent. J. Louis Comiskey, President of the Chicago White Sox, in an advanced case of Stengelian (Casey Stengel) logic commented on the ban in 1933: "You can bet your last dime that I'll never refuse to hire a great athlete simply because he isn't the same color of some other players on my team if the alleged bar against them is lifted."[16] In 1942, William Benswanger of the Pirates promised Roy Campenella a tryout. It was never held. In 1943, tryouts for black players were promised by two Pacific Coast League teams, but were withdrawn.[17] Finally, in 1945, Terris McDuffie, a 36-year-old pitcher, and Dave (Showboat) Thomas, a 39-year-old first baseman, were given trials at the Dodgers' spring training camp at Bear Mountain, New York.[18] Neither player was major league caliber. Jackie Robinson, Sam Jethroe, and Marvin Williams got tryout offers from the Red Sox and the Braves. After the players worked out with the Red Sox, they concluded that there was no serious interest.[19]

Six months after the Red Sox fiasco, Branch Rickey signed Robinson to play in the Dodger organization at Montreal. Organized baseball was furious at both the agitation for racial integration and at Rickey's maneuver. At their Boston Meeting on 8 July 1946, they appointed a steering committee to look into the matter. The report of the committee warned that integration would not be good for the game, that droves of black fans would drive white fans from the park, that black ballplayers were inferior to whites, that segregation profited the Negro leagues, and that integration would bring financial ruin to the clubs.[20] Despite virulent fan and player abuse, Jackie Robinson comported himself as a gentleman on Opening Day in 1947. Rickey had chosen wisely.

Do Blacks Face Entry Barriers in Baseball?

The Percentage of Black Players

Evidence of racial entry barriers might include the underrepresentation of black players relative to the population, higher performance requirements for blacks, and racial segregation by position. Aaron Rosenblatt was the first scholar to measure the extent of such barriers in baseball.[21]

Blacks constitute about 12 percent of the U.S. population. The historical percentage of black baseball players is illustrated in figure 9.1. The percentage of black players rose steadily until the mid-1970s,[22] and by the late 1950s blacks were represented in baseball about as in the population. Thereafter, blacks became overrepresented in the sport.

Racial Performance Differentials

Simple comparisons of racial percentages may, however, be misleading. Rosenblatt argued that numbers do not imply equality of opportunity, since superior performance may be a requirement for entry and retention.[23] In fact, Rosenblatt showed that there was a substantial dif-

Figure 9.1   The Percentage of Black Players in the Major Leagues, 1950–1986
Source: See notes in table 9.1.

ference between black and white lifetime batting averages over the period 1953–65. In 1965, more than a third of the black players hit .270 or better and well over half hit above .250. The overall average in baseball during that period was .246. Among the players starting the 1986 season, 32 percent of the blacks but only 15 percent of the whites had career hitting averages of .280 or greater. On the other hand, only 10 percent of the blacks compared to 28 percent of the whites had averages of .241 or less. Among pitchers, 40 percent of the blacks but only 11 percent of the whites had ERAs less than 3.00, while 13 percent of the blacks and 27 percent of the whites had ERAs over 4.00.[24]

Besides discrimination, two other factors have been argued to explain the racial performance differential: (1) the existence of racial differences in the distribution of playing skills; (2) racially different supply elasticities due to wage discrimination in society as a whole. While the first argument is popular there is no evidence whatsoever to support it. The second argument asserts that societal discrimination causes relative wages of blacks to be higher in baseball. But if the distribution of playing skills is racially invariant, there is no reason to expect that the black players attracted to baseball will have higher average performance levels. The superior financial opportunities in baseball would attract mediocre as well as superior black players, so that the net effect on racial performance differentials is unclear. The supply of players at any given ability level is determined by the elasticity at that level of ability. Given societal wage discrimination the supply of black players relatively will be greater than that of whites. So, the higher fraction of black players is expected. However, as one goes up the ability distribution, the baseball-nonbaseball wage differential widens and the supply elasticity declines. At the level of "star" the supply of talent of both races is perfectly inelastic with respect to salary, which is to say that owners cannot produce additional stars simply by raising salary. If ability distributions are racially invariant, the proportions of "stars" are racially invariant.

Thus, we are drawn back to the argument that blacks have to be better than whites to make the clubs initially and to stay in the majors. There is, however, some evidence that the performance differential is narrowing. In figure 9.2, the ratio of black to white batting averages from 1953 to 1980 is presented. From 1954 to 1972 black batting averages were 7 to 8 percent higher than those of whites. Since 1972, there has been a steady decline in the performance differential. The remaining difference is partly due to the positional distribution of blacks, since they are overrepresented in the outfield.

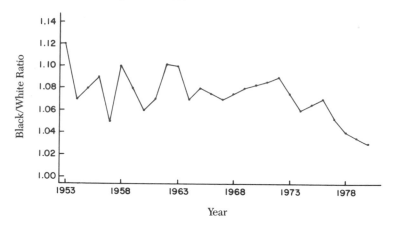

Figure 9.2   Racial Batting Differences: The Ratio of Batting Averages of Black to White Players, 1953–1980

Source: Aaron Rosenblatt, "Negroes in Baseball: The Failure of Success," *Transaction* 4 (September 1967): 51–53; John C. Phillips, "Race and Career Opportunities in Major League Baseball: 1960–1980," *Journal of Sport and Social Issues* (Summer/Fall 1983): 1–17.

Racial Entry Barriers by Position

Blacks have historically been distributed unevenly by playing position, and this maldistribution is not improving over time (see table 9.1). Blacks today are predominantly outfielders. The upward trend in black dominance in the outfield has been steady. On the other hand, since the late 1960s blacks have held only about 25 percent of the infielder positions, primarily first base and shortstop. There were no black catchers and very few black third basemen in 1986.[25] Blacks have never constituted more than 11.3 percent of the pitchers,[26] and the fraction of black pitchers has been declining in the 1980s.

Several hypotheses have been advanced to explain the positional distribution of blacks. Opportunities for supervised amateur and semi-professional baseball are more readily available to whites than to blacks. Accordingly, defensive and pitching skills probably would be less highly developed among blacks. Hitting probably develops more fully without supervision and independently of the quality of the play-ing field. Consequently, the poorer environment in which blacks learned the game might have contributed to their distribution on major league teams. But this explanation is inconsistent with the dominance of blacks among fielding leaders. Another hypothesis is that racial

Table 9.1   Percentage Black by Position, 1960–1986

Year	Outfield	Infield	Pitching
1960	33.3	16.0	6.0
1965	50.0	16.3	9.0
1970	59.2	24.6	9.2
1972–78	69.1	23.3	9.1
1986	70.0	25.5	7.7

Sources: Gerald W. Scully, "Discrimination: The Case of Base-ball," in *Government and the Sports Business,* edited by Roger G. Noll, (Washington, D.C.: Brookings, 1974), p. 242; James Richard Hill and William Spellman, "Pay Discrimination in Baseball: Data from the Seventies," *Industrial Relations* 23 (Winter 1984): 104; Brent Staples, "Where Are the Black Fans?" *The New York Times Magazine,* 17 May 1987, p. 29.

prejudice among white managers and coaches in both the majors and the minors causes blacks to be assigned to the outfield, where they would not require the intensive coaching infielders and pitchers normally receive. Perhaps, since leadership cannot be exercised in the outfield, it is an unwillingness to assign leadership responsibilities to blacks.

Or, perhaps it is because the real drama of baseball takes place in the infield. It is true that outfielders more frequently are the super-stars, but they are not the featured actors in the game. To the stadium fan, his proximity to the outfielder is inversely related to the price of his seat; the inexpensive seats are closer to the outfield than to home plate. The television fan sees the outfielder only when he bats and fields. If the pitching is at all effective, this exposure is a tiny fraction of that which the battery and the infielders get. Skin color and non-Caucasian features were found to be good predictors of the positional distribution of black players in an earlier study.[27]

Two final hypotheses attribute the problem to blacks themselves. First, pitching and the infield positions are said to require "thinking and decision making," while the outfield requires "speed." According to this hypothesis, then, black players are apparently unable to run and think simultaneously. Like genetic explanations of hitting ability, the hypothesis is rubbish. Alternatively, since the black superstar heroes tend to be outfielders, young black players emulate outfielders as role models. Such sociological explanations are, however, not very satisfying, nor do they explain the original maldistribution. The positional distribution of blacks in baseball thus remains an open question.

Black-White Pay Differentials in Baseball

In 1986, the average black player made $531,000 compared to $450,000 for whites. But since blacks outperform whites, this is not startling. Higher average salaries for blacks is not a guarantee that baseball is free from salary discrimination. What is required is that racial salaries be equal after adjustment is made for any performance differentials.

In an earlier study I found some evidence to suggest that in 1968–69 black players received less pay per unit of contribution to team productivity than did whites.[28] Specifically, whites got more pay per point in slugging or batting average or in strikeout-to-walk ratio than did blacks. A study on black-white salary differentials among 516 major leaguers in 1976 concluded that racially based pay discrimination had disappeared.[29] Further, under free agency the propensity to discriminate is restricted. Since players are free to choose between teams, discriminating employers wind up with weak teams.

Salary regressions by race were estimated for the 1986 players. The results appear in table 9.2. In the first regression in the table a binary variable for race is included (black = 1, 0 otherwise). This race dummy captures any salary differential which may remain after average performance differentials have been taken into account. The coefficient is not statistically different from zero. We can conclude that *holding performance constant, black and white players are paid the same on average.*

Player salaries were estimated separately by race. The procedure permits interracial comparisons of the salary-performance coefficients. The coefficients of 1985 Salary and Log Career on Log 1986 Salary are higher for the blacks. The racial difference between these coefficients is not statistically significant. We conclude that black and white players

Table 9.2   Player Salary Regressions by Race, 1986

Variable	All Players 1986 Salary	Whites 1986 Salary	Blacks 1986 Salary
Intercept	10.07	10.20	10.02
1985 Career Slugging average	1.89	1.52	2.13
Career years	0.53	0.46	0.60
1985 Career at-bat percentage	17.89	20.61	15.41
Black	0.01*	—	—
$\bar{R}^2$	.78	.77	.80
(N)	(345)	(216)	(129)

Note: See notes in table 8.2 for variable definitions and data sources.

are paid the same per unit of performance in baseball. Salary discrimination is not a feature of modern baseball.

Why Have There Been So Few Black Managers in Baseball?

In 1988, there was one black manager in major league ball and only a few blacks in coaching positions. The gross underrepresentation of blacks in these decision-making positions is associated with and perhaps caused by certain factors that fix the background of managers by region of birth and playing position as a major leaguer. From 1947 to 1967, there were 88 managers of major league teams (of course, some managed more than one team). The regional origin of managers conforms closely to that of ballplayers (see table 9.3). About 74 percent of the managers came from non-southern states. About 74 percent of the 9,659 players in major league ball from 1871 to 1968 were born outside of the South.[30] On the other hand, about 63 percent of the North American born blacks playing in 1969 were born in the South.[31]

A player's positional background probably has much more of an effect on his chances of becoming a field manager. Nearly 80 percent of all managers over this period were infielders as players, and the situation remains unchanged today. In table 9.4, the playing positions of all major league managers in the 1986 season are given. Only four of the managers were major league outfielders: Whitey Herzog, Lou Piniella, Pete Rose, and Dick Williams. Except for three who were pitchers, all of the rest were infielders.

Recall our findings concerning the positional distribution of North American blacks. Infielders amount to about 40 percent of the regular season roster, as do pitchers. Blacks occupy roughly a fourth of these infield positions. Thus, blacks are outnumbered by about 4 to 1 in possessing that which appears to be most useful for managers—infield

Table 9.3   Characteristics of 88 Major League Managers, 1947–1967

Position Played	Percentage	Born	Percentage
Outfield	12.2	Northeast	24.1
Infield	79.3	South	26.4
First base	13.4	Midwest	35.6
Catcher	23.2	West	13.5
Other infield	42.7		
Pitcher	8.5		
Nonplaying manager	8.5		

Source: Calculated from data in *The Baseball Encyclopedia,* 1969.

Table 9.4   Player Positions of Managers, 1986 Season

Manager	Position as Player
Sparky Anderson	Second base
George Bamberger	Pitcher
Steve Boros	Third base
Pat Corrales	Catcher
Chuck Cottier	Second base
Roger Craig	Pitcher
John Felske	Catcher
Mike Ferraro	Third base
Jim Fregosi	Shortstop
Jimmy Frey	Not in majors
Whitey Herzog	Outfielder
Dick Howser	Shortstop
Davey Johnson	Second base
Tom Kelly	First base
Hal Lanier	Shortstop
Tony LaRussa	Second base
Tommy Lasorda	Pitcher
Jim Leyland	Not in majors
Gene Mauch	Second base
John McNamara	Not in majors
Gene Michael	Shortstop
Ray Miller	Not in majors
Jackie Moore	Catcher
Jeff Newman	Catcher
Lou Piniella	Outfielder
Doug Rader	Third base
Buck Rogers	Catcher
Pete Rose	Outfielder
Chuck Tanner	Not in majors
Tom Trebelhorn	Not in majors
Bobby Valentine	Shortstop
John Vukovich	Third base
Earl Weaver	Not in majors
Dick Williams	Outfielder
Jimy Williams	Shortstop

Source: *The 1987 Baseball Encyclopedia Update* (New York: Macmillan Publishing Company, 1987).

experience. Further, most managers have had previous coaching experience. Of the five coaches on a team, the majority devote their time to infielders and pitchers. It is reasonable, then, that coaches be predominantly selected from the infield positions. Of the five black coaches in the 1969 season, all were former infielders. (On the other hand, two of the three black managers were former outfielders: Larry Doby and Frank Robinson. Maury Wills had been a shortstop.)

That former infielders rather than pitchers tend to become managers probably stems from the fact that infielders have leadership responsibilities. Most team captains are infielders. On the other hand, pitchers play at most 20 percent of the innings and are segregated from the rest of the team during the game. Furthermore, they are relatively passive in team decision-making on the field, as are outfielders.

There were 84 minorities employed in administrative, managerial, or coaching positions within organized baseball in 1987. Of these positions, 55 were team-related rather than front office jobs. A total of 17 minorities were coaching or instructing on major league teams. Ten of these were hitting instructors. Only five personnel could be said to be in positions that might lead to managing a major league club: Frank Robinson, coach (and subsequently manager) at Baltimore and a former major league manager; Jose Martinez, third base coach at Kansas City; Willie Stargell, first base coach at Atlanta; Manny Mota, coach at Los Angeles; and Bill Robinson, first base coach and hitting instructor for the Mets.[32]

If it is correct that infield experience is a valuable asset for a manager, then the lack of black managers is a supply problem, not a demand problem. The source of the problem of the inadequate supply of black coaches and managers lies in the historical racial pattern of positional segregation in organized baseball. That is, there is a shortage of blacks with the necessary infield training and past decision-making authority to serve as managers. The baseball commissioner and Dr. Harry Edwards, the University of California sports sociologist hired to advise on minority hiring, may be able to encourage some black candidates into managerial roles. But, the problem is structural and one is not sanguine that black managers will be very common in the game in the near future.

10

Managerial Quality in Baseball

Baseball managers are much maligned. Indeed, when a club is slipping in the standings, it is the manager who will usually be fired. The implication of this maneuver is that another manager can organize the existing player inputs in a somewhat different fashion to produce more output (wins). If this is possible, it is a less costly solution for a club owner than going into the players' market for additional expensive playing talent.

The conceptual importance of managing as organizing the inputs for team production is well known, but nothing is known empirically about the actual effect on output of variations in the skill of managers. Partly, this is due to the fact that firms treat their data as proprietary. It is also due to the fact that it is difficult to measure the inputs and the outputs in complex production processes.

In baseball the outputs (wins) and inputs (player skills) are unambiguously measured and the production process is simply specified. By employing a concept known as the "frontier" production function, efficiency can be measured by manager and by club, the rate of change in managerial efficiency over time can be determined, and the managerial marginal revenue product estimated.

Measuring Managerial Quality[1]

Previously, it was established that the output of a club is wins and that player skills such as pitching and hitting are the inputs (see chapter 8). The quality of a team is measured by its win percentage. Player inputs are best measured by the team slugging average and the team strike-out-to-walk ratio.

Club managers have the responsibility of transforming player inputs into team victories. In addition to recruiting new playing talent, training and motivating players, and maintaining club morale, managers make field decisions that affect the chances of winning. These decisions include such matters as the composition of the club's roster, the order of the lineup, the choice of the starting pitcher and the relief pitchers, substitutions in the hitting lineup, and a variety of other strategic choices made during the game. How satisfactory these decisions are determines the quality of the manager.

But there is considerable dispersion among teams in the quality of the players fielded during a season (see chapter 4). It is easier to achieve victory with a club of talented players. Hence, the efficiency of a manager must be measured independently of the level of team playing strength. Managerial quality must be measured in terms of the difference between the club's actual performance and what the club could have achieved under "best" management practice technique. To remove the effect of variations in playing talent among clubs, the variables are normalized by dividing them by the club win percentage. Thus, inputs now are expressed as "unit inputs," i.e., the number of inputs necessary to produce one unit of output.

The normalized production function (the "unit isoquant") is drawn as the hyperbola $w-w'$ in figure 10.1. If all managers were equally efficient in transforming their unit inputs of player skills into unit wins, they would lie along the unit isoquant $w-w'$ in the figure. However, given the level and complexity of skill required to manage a major league baseball club, it is likely that few managers will achieve this level of efficiency. To measure the degree to which managers fail to realize maximum possible output for their given player inputs, the concept of the frontier unit isoquant is employed.

Managers that fail to attain the most wins possible for their inputs of playing skill lie to the northeast of the frontier unit isoquant along rays through the origin 0. Such managers require greater quantities of inputs per win than is indicated by the frontier unit isoquant $w-w'$. In

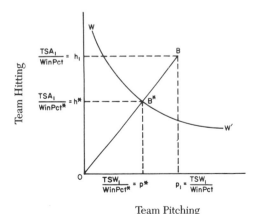

Figure 10.1   Rating Managerial Skill Using a Normalized Production Function

the figure, B represents the actual performance of a hypothetical manager of Team 1, utilizing team hitting (TSA_1) and team pitching (TSW_1) inputs to produce the club's win percentage (WinPct). B^* is the best possible performance of a manager with those player inputs. WinPct* is the win record that actually satisfies the equation for the frontier unit isoquant, $w-w'$, for those levels of hitting and pitching inputs. Managerial performance is measured as the distance OB^*/OB.

Suppose the value of OB^*/OB in figure 10.1 for a hypothetical manager is 0.5. Then, the manager is using twice (1/0.5) as many player inputs to produce the win record as would be needed under "best" management practice. Alternatively, given the player inputs, the manager is winning half the number of games that would be possible under best practice technique.

Estimates of Managerial Quality

Employing normalized values of hitting and pitching inputs, empirical estimates of the frontier unit isoquants for the National and the American Leagues and for each of the years from 1961 to 1980 were obtained using a linear programming technique. In particular, the linear programming technique required that all observations of unit inputs lie on or above the isoquant and minimized the sum of the squared deviations from the observations to the isoquant along rays through the origin. The parameter estimates of the isoquants are of no interest here, although they seemed plausible and were reasonably well behaved. What is of interest are the efficiency estimates of managers, which are presented in table 10.1.

In the table, major league baseball managers are ranked by mean lifetime efficiency. Also presented in the table are their respective standard deviations of efficiency, their years of experience, and the teams which they managed. Earl Weaver ranks as the best manager in the period: Not only is Weaver's average efficiency level extraordinarily high at .987, his performance is very consistent. With a standard deviation of only .023, Weaver's efficiency level over his 13 years of managing was between 0.964 and 1.00. Earl Weaver continued to manage in Baltimore through the 1982 season, when the club finished with a .580 record. Weaver was out of managing in 1983–84, but was hired back in Baltimore in 1985 to replace Joe Altobelli. Interestingly, this premier manager never played in the major leagues.

The second most efficient manager is Sparky Anderson, with a mean efficiency rating of .961 ± .049. Anderson has managed in Cincinnati and Detroit and by now has been managing continuously for 18 years. Anderson had one full year of major league experience, having played

Table 10.1   Performance Measures of Major League Baseball Managers with Five or More Years of Experience, 1961–1980

Manager	Team(s)	Years of Experience	Years in Sample	Mean Efficiency	Standard Deviation
Weaver, E.	Bal.	13	13	.987	.023
Anderson, S.	Cin., Det.	11	11	.961	.049
Alston, W.	Bkn., L.A.	23	16	.945	.089
Virdon, B.	N.Y., Hou.	7	7	.936	.062
Schoendienst, R.	St. L.	12	12	.933	.060
Murtaugh, D.	Pit.	14	10	.931	.057
Lopez, A.	Chi.	6	6	.918	.089
Walker, H.	Pit., Hou.	9	8	.916	.087
Dark, A.	S.F., Cle., Oak.	9	9	.913	.091
Martin, B.	Min., Det., Tex., N.Y., Oak.	11	11	.912	.068
Williams, D.	Bos., Oak., Cal., Mon.	13	13	.909	.068
Bauer, H.	K.C., Bal.	7	7	.909	.081
Ozark, D.	Phi.	7	7	.907	.045
Rigney, B.	L.A./Cal., Min., S.F.	17	12	.905	.078
Tanner, C.	Chi., Oak., Pit.	10	10	.902	.082
Franks, H.	S.F., Chi.	7	7	.900	.045
Berra, Y.	N.Y., N.Y.	5	5	.898	.078
Houk, R.	N.Y., Det.	16	16	.886	.107
Hodges, G.	Was., N.Y.	9	9	.886	.074
Mele, S.	Min.	7	7	.877	.109
Mauch, G.	Phi., Mon., Min.	21	20	.874	.104
Lemon, J.	Was., K.C., Chi., N.Y.	7	7	.870	.060
Bristol, D.	Cin., Sea., Atl., S.F.	11	11	.869	.078
Dorocher, L.	Bkn./L.A., N.Y., Chi.	24	7	.856	.071
Harris, L.	Bal., Hou., Atl.	6	6	.837	.075
Zimmer, D.	S.D., Bos.	7	7	.831	.081
Westrum, W.	N.Y., S.F.	5	5	.822	.107
Johnson, D.	Bos., Sea.	7	7	.793	.099
Other active			<5	.881	.093
Other inactive			<5	.824	.094

Source: Philip K. Porter and Gerald W. Scully, "Measuring Mangerial Efficiency: The Case of Baseball," *Southern Economic Journal* (January 1982).

second base for Philadelphia in 1959 and hitting .218 for the season. The third most efficient manager was Walt Alston, who managed the Dodgers continuously for 23 years before retiring in 1976. Walt Alston appeared in one game as a major league player in St. Louis in 1936. He struck out in his only time at bat. The mercurial Billy Martin ranks only tenth in terms of efficiency. Martin's lifetime career record was .553. Had he been frontier-efficient, the records of the clubs that he managed would have averaged .606. If Earl Weaver had managed the players that Martin did, his clubs would have had records averaging .598 (.987 times .606). Thus Weaver as compared to Martin was worth .045 points or seven to eight wins per season. Alternatively, Earl Weaver's lifetime record was .583. If he had been frontier-efficient, his club would have had an average record of .591. If Billy Martin had managed Weaver's players at Baltimore, the club would have had an average record of .532 (.912 times .591).

The Managerial Learning Curve

Independent of natural ability, skill is improved by experience or "learning by doing." The longer a manager directs a baseball club the better he becomes at the task. This is largely a consequence of the time necessary not only to determine what game strategies work, but also to learn player abilities and how to employ them most effectively. But learning in the management of baseball teams as in that of other organizations is subject to diminishing returns. Therefore, managerial efficiency is expected to rise more rapidly in the early years of a career.

A managerial efficiency learning curve was estimated from the year-by-year efficiency measures discussed previously.[2] The efficiency learning curve is shown in figure 10.2. The average manager completes his first year with a performance level of about .90 percent of potential and improves his efficiency 0.8 percent after the first year and at a decreasing rate the following years. Average managerial efficiency reaches a maximum of .945 between the 12th and the 13th year of experience. Also considered was the effect on managerial efficiency of changing teams. Managers who change teams during their careers have efficiency levels 5 percentage points below those who do not change clubs. Theory would suggest that some managerial skills are general, and hence transferable between teams, while some skills are team specific. For example, game strategy is transferable, but knowledge of the specific talents of the players on a given team is not. As can be seen in table 10.1, the most efficient managers have tended to stay with their original teams, while the less efficient have not.

Some teams keep their managers for a very long time (e.g., Weaver at Baltimore, Anderson at Cincinnati and Detroit, Alston at Los Angeles, Schoendienst at St. Louis, Murtaugh at Pittsburgh, and so on), while other clubs change managers frequently. It is useful, therefore, to estimate mean managerial performance by club. The average and standard deviation of managerial performance, along with the club record, is presented by team, ranked by efficiency, in table 10.2. Cincinnati, Los Angeles, and Pittsburgh dominate the National League,

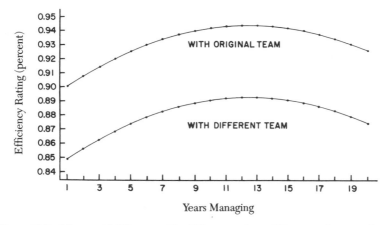

Figure 10.2   Managerial Efficiency: The Effect over Time of "Learning by Doing"

Table 10.2   Managerial Performance Measures by Team 1961–1980

Team	Mean Efficiency	Standard Deviation	Mean Win Percentage
National League			
Cincinnati	.968	.049	.581
Los Angeles	.942	.081	.557
Pittsburgh	.924	.069	.544
St. Louis	.919	.067	.519
San Francisco	.899	.059	.525
Atlanta	.857	.081	.488
Philadelphia	.856	.115	.497
Montreal	.846	.096	.460
Houston	.836	.108	.470
Chicago	.825	.077	.471
New York	.804	.121	.418
San Diego	.800	.107	.410
American League			
Baltimore	.965	.046	.580
New York	.930	.073	.554
Kansas City	.921	.083	.526
California	.875	.087	.474
Boston	.869	.090	.520
Oakland	.868	.109	.480
Detroit	.863	.090	.522
Chicago	.853	.094	.492
Minnesota	.849	.077	.521
Cleveland	.837	.072	.470
Milwaukee	.834	.079	.459
Texas	.834	.070	.444
Seattle	.714	.032	.381
Toronto	.703	.053	.361

Source: See table 10.1.

Table 10.3 Mean Managerial Performance by Year for Expansion Teams, 1961–1980

Year	Montreal	Houston	New York	San Diego	Kansas City	Milwaukee	Seattle	Toronto	Average All Expansion Teams
1	.637	.645	.496	.669	.749	.709	.686	.615	.650
2	.855	.764	.719	.689	.813*	.767*	.717	.718	.755
3	.885	.832*	.666	.774	.998	.902	.767	.723	.759
4	.868	.683	.659*	.722*	.855	.848	.688	.759*	.760
5	.840	.817*	.916	.661	1.000*	.915*			.858
6	.902	.700	.753	.761*	.860	.837			.802
7	.800	.854*	.827*	.787	.888*	.826			.830
8	.685*	.754	1.000	.909	.955	.769*			.845
9	.844*	.864	.959	.859	.936	.717			.863
10	.897	.967	.980	1.000*	1.000	.944*			.965
11	.973	.851	.817*	.815	1.000	.950			.901
12	.972	.844*	.944	.955*	1.000*	.824			.923
13		.927*	.798						.862
14		.666*	.843						.754
15		.988	.761*						.874
16		.896	.756*						.826
17		.858	.792						.825
18		1.000	.808						.904
19		.983	.783						.883

*First year under new manager.
Source: See table 10.1.

while Baltimore, New York, and Kansas City dominate the American League. Not surprisingly, these teams are among the top winning clubs. Nevertheless, the correlation of efficiency and win percentage is by no means perfect: note the figures for San Francisco in the National League and Boston, Detroit, and Minnesota in the American League, among others. In general, the expansion clubs (e.g., Montreal, Houston, New York, San Diego, Kansas City, Milwaukee, Seattle, and Toronto) finished poorly and were managed inefficiently.

Learning by Doing for Expansion Clubs

Generally, it is thought that expansion teams are noncompetitive, because of the initial low quality of the playing talent fielded. But operating a new franchise efficiently may require learning in much the same way that managing does. New franchises require inside information, which is costly to acquire. Existing clubs have no incentive to share this information. Indeed, since profits depend on club records there are gains to not divulging such knowledge.

By focusing attention on expansion clubs, a rough estimate of the time necessary to bring a new firm up to a league-efficient level of performance can be obtained. Efficiency estimates for the expansion clubs were calculated annually and are presented in table 10.3. All of the clubs began as highly inefficient organizations, with the New York Mets in 1962 under Casey Stengel the least efficient team of all. The Mets had a record of .250. Of course, Stengel had managed the league-leading New York Yankees from 1949 to 1960, and the inefficiency of the Mets organization cannot be blamed on him. All of the expansion clubs have been relatively inefficient in their early years, but there is a rapidly rising learning curve. The evidence suggests that efficiency rises over the first ten years of a club's existence. By the tenth year, expansion clubs are about as efficient as the existing league clubs. In terms of managerial efficiency, it takes about a decade for an expansion club to transform its player inputs into output as competitively as the average club.

Pay and Performance of Baseball Managers

In chapter 8, the marginal revenue of a win was estimated. In 1987, a win was worth about $244,000 to a club. For an average club, a 1 percent increase in managerial efficiency increases the club win percentage by .005 points (.500 times .01). The increased efficiency is worth $198,000 to an average club. A manager of the caliber of Earl Weaver is

Table 10.4   Salaries of Managers, 1987 Season

Manager	Salary ($)
Pete Rose	750,000
Tommy Lasorda	500,000
Whitey Herzog	450,000
Chuck Tanner	400,000
Tony La Russa	333,000
Davey Johnson	325,000
Lou Piniella	300,000
Sparky Anderson	275,000
Buck Rogers	250,000
Pat Corrales	200,000
Jim Fregosi	200,000
John McNamara	200,000
Dick Williams	200,000
Hal Lanier	175,000
Gene Mauch	175,000
Roger Craig	160,000
Gene Michael	150,000
Bobby Valentine	130,000
Larry Bowa	125,000
John Felske	125,000
Billy Gardner	125,000
Jimy Williams	120,000
Tom Kelly	100,000
Jim Leyland	100,000
Cal Ripkin	100,000
Tom Trebelhorn	100,000

Source: *Sports Illustrated*, 20 April 1987, 81.

13.1 percent better than the average manager. Hence, his marginal product is .065 points to the club win percentage or 10 to 11 games to the club's wins. In 1987, those extra victories were worth $2.6 million to a club. Thus, a manager of the quality of an Earl Weaver or a Sparky Anderson or a Red Schoendienst or a Danny Murtaugh contributes as much to team revenues as does a superstar player like a Mike Schmidt.

How well are managers paid? The salaries of a large number of the 1987 managers are presented in table 10.4. Pete Rose, at $750,000, is the highest paid, but he also was a player. The top salary for strictly managing was that of Tommy Lasorda. Sparky Anderson earns $275,000 at Detroit, which seems low given his skills. Many managers make $100,000 to $150,000, which is less than a majority of novice players make.

11
Summary and Conclusions

Historically, organized baseball has sought to restrict competition in its various markets. New teams require the permission of the existing clubs to enter the league, clubs are assigned exclusive territories, revenues are divided by formula, and so on. Elaborate procedures have been devised for moving players within and between leagues. Baseball's unique antitrust exemption makes these collusive practices perfectly legal; indeed, the public policy toward baseball has been that the public interest is served if the industry operates as a self-regulated cartel. Clearly, the rules governing league operations affect both the absolute and the relative quality of play on the field—as well as profit—but baseball has always claimed that these practices are necessary in bringing about team equality and in preventing the financial collapse of franchises located in smaller population centers.

The myth that the reserve clause and other collusive practices have been required for reasons of playing competitiveness has been a source of much mischief in baseball. Formal models of sports leagues have established that equalization of playing strengths within a league occurs only through the equalization of revenue among the clubs or, lacking that development, through a system of player reservation, reverse order drafting, and a ban on the cash sale of player contracts. Playing talent always migrates toward its highest-valued use. The assignment of the property right (by reservation or free agency) only determines who obtains the value in use; hence, the restrictive labor market practices have been devices by the clubs to extract the monopsony rents from player services, that is to keep the lion's share of the cash value from player services in the hands of the owners. The dominance of the New York Yankees, the Brooklyn Dodgers, and the New York Giants testified to the impotence of the reserve clause as a device for equalizing the distribution of playing talent. The lack of big city dominance in the period of post–free agency is further evidence of the fact that player reservation per se has nothing to do with the distribution of playing talent. The near ten-fold increase in average player salaries, since the advent of free agency, is some measure of the financial exploitation of the players under the reserve clause.

Complaining about the lack of profit in baseball is a perennial avocation of club owners. This posturing has helped foster an image of owners as sportsmen and has deflected any serious public inquiry into the antitrust exemption. The complex motives of ownership, ownership structure, and the accounting distortions induced by the tax laws make an analysis of profit in baseball hazardous. But, certainly since World War I, baseball has been a profitable business, and, despite free agency, remains so today. Indeed, major league baseball has entered a golden era of wealth and prosperity. Attendance, broadcast fees, and the exchange value of franchises are at record levels. Tickets are priced and broadcast agreements structured so as to maximize revenue. The spread of cable television promises to usher in a very large increase in revenues in the 1990s. Partly as a result of increased revenue potential, franchises are selling for $100 million or more. Clubs have contained costs largely by colluding to boycott veteran free agents. Both the incidence and the length of multiyear contracts have been reduced. Whether the owners can reimpose a de facto reserve clause, through the imposition of single-year player contracts and a gentlemen's agreement not to compete for free agents, is an open question.

Nevertheless, the case for self-regulation in organized baseball is more compelling today than it has ever been. This is so as a consequence of the rise and successes of a powerful and militant players' union and the influence of the television industry. These developments significantly eroded owner control in the players' market and in the output market. Moreover, alternative policies such as the repeal of the antitrust exemption or government regulation are neither realistic nor attractive. The players are better off in baseball with the antitrust exemption than they are in football with the protection of the Antitrust Act. League control in the output market is as pervasive in football and basketball as it is in baseball, and the affairs of too many people would be affected by a change in the exemption. In 1972, Senator Marlow Cook introduced a bill that would have created a federal agency to regulate franchise and player movements and sports broadcasting, but the public interest would not have been served by the passage of such a bill: experience shows that government regulation is not benign.

The Major League Baseball Players Association succeeded in its quests for binding salary arbitration and veteran free agency. Prior to 1976, players negotiated exclusively with the reserving club. The lack of interclub competition greatly lowered salaries from the level that would have prevailed in an open and free labor market. The successes of the players' union greatly reduced, if not eliminated, the monopsony power of the clubs. The financial exploitation of the players in the regime of the indefinite term reserve clause was the most important abuse associated with the antitrust exemption. The players obtained the protection that was denied by the courts through collective bargaining. The players' interests are now well protected by the union. Collective bargaining is the self-regulating mechanism for solving labor-management disputes.

The effect of television on baseball has been mixed, but its beneficial effects are greater today than in the past. Television greatly expanded the size of the baseball audience: nearly everyone in America can now see a game on TV. But televised games helped decimate the minor leagues and vast differences in local rights fees increased revenue inequality among the clubs. As a result, the ability of the minor leagues to supply major league playing talent of the highest caliber has been reduced. Further, the comparatively large local rights fees to the big city clubs contributed to their dominance on the playing field, and thus some of the financially weak franchises have sought to increase revenues by shifting locations. Larger local broadcast fees, stadium rental concessions, and the "honeymoon" attendance effect of a newly relocated franchise induced the shift of ten franchises between 1953 and 1972.[1]

By 1980, the fees from the sale of national broadcast rights exceeded those from the sale of local rights and broadcast income as a fraction of baseball revenues rose sharply. While local rights fees vary among the clubs, national rights fees are evenly split. A decade ago, broadcast fees were about 20 percent of club receipts. Now, they are about 35 percent of revenue. Rising national television revenue has contributed to a trend toward revenue socialization among the clubs. Coupled with greater urban population diffusion, which has reduced the dispersion in gate receipts, the variance in club revenues has declined. This trend toward reduced revenue inequality has contributed to a reduction in the inequality of playing strengths among the clubs. And the increased socialization of revenues has greatly reduced, but not eliminated, the threat of franchise relocation. Broadcast deregulation and the size of the cable television network offer impressive financial prospects for baseball in the 1990s. To capitalize on these opportunities, local club rights to both home and away games will have to be collectivized, as with the national network television contract.

The effectiveness of the players' union and the marketing demands of the television industry have significantly eroded owner autonomy. Clubs no longer are able to trade players like bushels of corn or dictate the terms of employment. Part of the value of the network TV contract arises from the assumption that the games will be reliably supplied.

This requirement puts pressure on the owners to resolve disputes through collective bargaining rather than to precipitate players' strikes. Matters regarding scheduling, league expansion, league realignment, divisional play-offs, and so on are influenced by the television industry. The current pressure for league expansion, increases in divisional play-offs, and league realignment partly is coming from broadcast interests.

As a cartel, baseball is not efficient. The rules governing the clubs are hardly designed to maximize joint profits. Quite the contrary. Exclusive territorial rights and the high fraction of revenue arising from the local market have guaranteed that the clubs would seek to maximize club profits even at the expense of other clubs. Such structural incentives within the agreements are a major source of the historical instability within the cartel and for the continuous tinkering with league governance. The complex motives of ownership and the supramajority voting rules governing league operations have made league responses to both internal and external challenges weak and inept.

Despite a rule against the practice, and the presence of a strong commissioner with broad powers, the majority of owners were unable to stop Branch Rickey's reimposition of the practice of farming. The farm system permitted the monopolization of playing talent and paved the way for the era of big city club dominance. As a result, many of the clubs in smaller population centers were nearly driven to ruin. Such clubs were forced either to establish farm teams of their own to obtain new playing talent or to buy what they could from Branch Rickey. The farm system thus choked off the competitive supply of players to these clubs. Television and expansion subsequently undermined the farm system, not consensus among the clubs in the cartel.

Baseball's response to external challenges has been equally incoherent. Blacks and sportswriters agitated for integration for more than a decade before the color ban was formally broken. Branch Rickey was castigated by other owners for bringing Jackie Robinson into the Dodger organization. There never has been a league policy on racial integration. The hiring of black players was a matter left entirely to club discretion, and as a result, there were wide differences in the degree of integration among the teams. The Boston Red Sox, for example, did not integrate until 1959 when they hired Elijah ("Pumpsie") Green.

League wars, demands for expansion, television, the role of the minor leagues, and the demands of players constitute challenges that the cartel has not handled well. These challenges remain unresolved and are recurrent threats to the fans' enjoyment of the game. For example, the owners won the Mexican League War because the players were intimidated by their threats of retribution and because Don Jorge Pasquel, the Mexican League promoter, had neither the money nor the stomach to go head to head with organized baseball. The cartel then ignored the excess demand for franchises—particularly in the West—after the threat from the Mexicans passed. The emergence of the Continental League prompted the flight of the Dodgers and the Giants to California and the 1961–62 league expansions. No consideration of its effect on the minor leagues was given in the decisions to expand. The cartel was badly damaged by the conflicts surrounding expansion.

Even after the cartel's three decades of experience with the medium, it took a strong commissioner to exploit the revenue potential of television. Broadcast income had been treated as a nice supplement to road income and was a club prerogative. Despite both an antitrust exemption in 1961, which permitted clubs to collude in negotiating national broadcast contracts, and the example of the television-stimulated rise in the popularity of football, baseball was slow in exploiting network television opportunities. Clubs with large local broadcast rights were reluctant to surrender autonomy for an expanded pool of collective broadcast revenue. Such attitudes again will have to be overcome if further large increases in the network TV contract are to be negotiated in the future and if the financial prospects of pay-TV are to be exploited.

Lastly, consider the cartel's response to free agency. Freed to compete for veteran players, the clubs chose reckless interclub competition rather than a collective solution through good faith bargaining with the players' union. Clubs outdid one another with long-term guaranteed contracts at salaries that were a multiple of pre-1976 pay levels. These types of contracts severed the important link between player pay and performance. Play suffered as a result. By the time average salaries reached $250,000 the clubs concluded that unrestrained competition in the free agents' market was dangerous to their financial health. The owners demanded that the union agree to higher compensation for clubs that have lost a free agent. The players balked, seeing in the demand the beginnings of a return to the reservation system; at some compensation level free agency is of no value to the players. An alternative method of accommodating free agency and containing club salary costs is, however, available. Basketball has had free agency for a long time. Because of the 100-0 gate split and the relatively small amount of television revenues, club revenues are more unevenly divided than in baseball. Thus the dominance of club over league interests is even stronger in basketball. Nevertheless, owners and players agreed to a system of club salary caps. Teams are free to compete for free agents as they see fit, subject to an overall limit on team salary. The salary limits are a collective bargaining matter. Financial stability in a league can be assured through good faith collective bargaining on the level of the salary caps. And inequality of team playing strengths can be reduced by reducing the spread in team salaries. The introduction of such a scheme of player compensation in baseball would require that the cartel favor the overall strength of the league over the special financial interests of a minority of the clubs. There is no evidence that the owners have such a vision.

In 1989–90, a number of agreements that shape the financial structure of baseball will expire. A new agreement with the players will have to be negotiated in an environment in which the owners have violated the current collective bargaining agreement by colluding to boycott free agents. Future television contracts will have to be negotiated within the framework of network proddings for league expansion, league realignment, and expanded divisional play-offs. League expansion will be destabilizing to the cartel. To capture significantly expanded cable income the owners will to some extent be required to collectivize current local broadcast rights and to televise some home games. The Major-Minor League Agreement will be negotiated at a time when league expansion and expanded television coverage threaten to further damage what remains of minor league baseball. These challenges will be resolved only if the clubs surrender further autonomy. The cartel's response to such challenges in the past has not been such that one is sanguine that the blocking minorities will surrender their autonomy in the collective interests of baseball. The period 1989–90 and after promises to be turbulent. Yet baseball is in its second century. History suggests that the leagues will, at the very least, blunder through and that the game which is our national pastime will endure.

Notes

Chapter One

1. *Organized Baseball*, Report of the Subcommittee on the Study of Monopoly Power of the Committee of the Judiciary, House Report no. 2002, 82d Congress, 1st sess., 1952, 16.

2. For the economic aspects of baseball in its formative years see *Organized Baseball* and also Harold Seymour, *Baseball: The Early Years* (New York: Oxford University Press, 1960).

3. *Organized Baseball*, 29–30.

4. Ibid., 31.

5. Ibid., 36–41.

6. Ibid., 44–45.

7. Ibid., 66.

8. Ibid., 57.

9. Ibid., 86–110.

10. Ibid., 209.

11. Ibid., 210.

12. Simon Rottenberg, "The Baseball Players' Labor Market," *Journal of Political Economy* 64 (June 1956):242–58.

13. Mohamed El-Hodiri and James Quirk, "An Economic Model of a Professional Sports League," *Journal of Political Economy* 79 (November–December 1971):1302–19.

14. Gerald W. Scully, "Pay and Performance in Major League Baseball," *American Economic Review* 64 (December 1974):915–30.

15. David A. Kaplan, "What's Killing the Umps?" *The New York Times Magazine*, 20 March 1988.

16. David Nightingale, "The Commissioner's Empire," *The Sporting News*, 11 April 1988, 30.

17. Tracy Ringolsby, "Baseball," *Dallas Morning News*, 29 May 1988, 10–B.

Chapter Two

1. "Statement of Bowie K. Kuhn, Commissioner of Baseball," in *Antitrust Policy and Professional Sports*, Hearings before the Subcommittee on Monopolies and Commercial Law of the House Committee on the Judiciary, 97th

Congress, 1st and 2d sess. (Washington, D.C.: GPO, 1984), 432. Cited hereafter as *Antitrust Policy and Professional Sports*, 1984.

2. For a recent restatement of the owners' view, see the testimony of Bowie Kuhn in *Antitrust Policy and Professional Sports*, 1984, 425–38 and 458–73.

3. See the testimony of Marvin Miller, the Executive Director of the Players Association, in *Antitrust Policy and Professional Sports*, 1984, 473–500.

4. See Roger G. Noll, ed., *Government and the Sports Business* (Washington, D.C.: The Brookings Institution, 1974).

5. See Lance E. Davis, "Self-Regulation in Baseball, 1909–71," in *Government and the Sports Business*, edited by Roger G. Noll, 349–86.

6. "Major League Agreement," in *Baseball Blue Book 1987* (St. Petersburg, Fla.: Baseball Blue Book, Inc., 1987), 501–10.

7. "Major League Rules," in *Baseball Blue Book 1987*, 511–90.

8. "National Association Agreement," in *Baseball Blue Book 1987*, 701–810.

9. "Professional Baseball Agreement," in *Baseball Blue Book 1987*, 601–6.

10. "Professional Baseball Rules," in *Baseball Blue Book 1987*, 607–71.

11. Harold Seymour, *Baseball: The Golden Age* (New York: Oxford University Press, 1971), 8.

12. "New TV Contracts Push Baseball Rights to $268 Million," *Broadcasting*, 27 February 1984.

13. *Baseball Blue Book 1987*, 514.

14. Simon Rottenberg, "The Baseball Players' Labor Market," *Journal of Political Economy* 64 (June 1956): 242–58; Mohamed El Hodiri and James Quirk, "An Economic Model of a Professional Sports League," *Journal of Political Economy* 79 (November–December 1971): 1302–19; and Gerald W. Scully, "Pay and Performance in Major League Baseball," *American Economic Review* 64 (December 1974): 915–30. For a minority view, see Jesse W. Markham and Paul V. Teplitz, *Baseball Economics and Public Policy* (Lexington, Mass.: Lexington Books, 1981).

15. *Baseball Blue Book 1987*, 519.

16. Ibid., 560.

17. For Class AAA and Class AA clubs, seventeen-player contracts may be optionally assigned. For Class A clubs, eight optional assignments are permitted.

18. *Inquiry into Professional Sports*, Hearing before the House Select Committee on Professional Sports, 94th Congress, 2d sess., Part 1 (Washington, D.C.: GPO, 1976), 143. Hereafter cited as *Inquiry into Professional Sports*.

19. "New TV Contracts Push Baseball Rights to $268 Million," *Broadcasting*, 27 February 1984, 45; and "Baseball Rights Approach $350 Million," *Broadcasting*, 2 March 1987, 47–48.

20. Ira Horowitz, "Sports Broadcasting," in *Government and the Sports Business*, edited by Roger G. Noll, 279–80.

21. Calculated from data in Seymour, *Baseball: The Golden Age*, 106.

22. Based on data in Seymour, *Baseball: The Golden Age*, 117.

23. Ibid., 228–29.

24. Lee Allen, *100 Years of Baseball* (New York: Bartholomew House, 1950).

25. Seymour, *Baseball: The Golden Age*, 171.

26. Ibid., 176.

27. Ibid., 206.

28. Ibid., 173–74.

29. James G. Scoville, "Labor Relations in Sports," in *Government and the Sports Business*, edited by Roger G. Noll, 206.

30. Ibid., 206–7.

31. *Inquiry into Professional Sports*, part 1, 380.

32. "Major League Baseball Players Benefit Plan—Monthly Retirement Benefits," in *Inquiry into Professional Sports*, part 1, 381.

33. From the 1976–78 Basic Agreement, reprinted in *Owners Versus Players: Baseball and Collective Bargaining*, by James B. Dworkin (Boston: Auburn House Publishing Co., 1981), 187–90.

34. Gerald W. Scully, "Binding Salary Arbitration in Major League Baseball," *American Behavioral Scientist* 21, no. 3 (January–February 1978): 438–41.

35. Murray Chass, "Arbitration Time Gives Clubs Something to Worry About," *New York Times*, 3 January 1988, Sports Pages.

36. James R. Hill and William Spellman, "Professional Baseball: The Reserve Clause and Salary Structure," *Industrial Relations* 22, no. 1 (Winter 1983): 3.

37. *Professional Baseball Clubs*, 66 LA 101 (1975).

38. Testimony of Marvin Miller, in *Inquiry into Professional Sports*, part 1, 369.

39. In 1976, 25 players became free agents. Thereafter, the number of free agents rose—1977, 39 players; 1978, 42 players; and 1979, 44 players. Dworkin, *Owners Versus Players: Baseball and Collective Bargaining*, 113–16.

40. Donald P. Doane, "Batter Up! Baseball Aims for Big Year," *U.S. News and World Report*, 9 April 1984, 69.

41. "Excerpts from the Ruling," *New York Times*, 22 September 1987, Sports Pages, 54.

42. Ibid.

43. Dave Nightingale, "Dawson: A New Beginning in Chicago," *The Sporting News*, 11 May 1987, 7.

44. Bob Verdi, "Will Owners Bite Dust in Collusion Collision?" *The Sporting News*, 14 September 1987, 8.

45. Marty Kuehnert, "Horner is 'Mr. Hom-ah' in Japan," *The Sporting News*, 29 June 1987, 12; "Braves Seek Horner," *New York Times*, 5 December 1987, Sports Pages.

46. "Huge Baseball Pay Loss is Reported," *New York Times*, 17 March 1988, Sports Pages, 49.

47. Murray Chass, "Arbitrator Finds Baseball Owners in Second Free-Agent Conspiracy," *New York Times*, 1 September 1988, 1.

Chapter Three

1. Armen A. Alchian first observed the "learning by doing" phenomenon. During World War II aircraft were manufactured with a certain fixed technology, fixed capital stock, and fixed labor force. Yet, output rose the longer a particular model was manufactured. The experience of doing similar tasks repetitively improved productivity. See Armen A. Alchian, "Reliability of Progress Curves in Airframe Production," *Econometrica* 31, no. 4 (October 1963): 679–93.

2. The performance profile in figure 3.1 is derived from the following regression equation:

$$BA_t = .0083* + .948 \text{ Lifetime } BA + .00233 \text{ Career Year}$$
$$- .00017 \text{ Career Year Squared}, R^{-2} = .42, N = 564.$$

Only the intercept term is not statistically significant at the .95 percent level (throughout the text statistical insignificance is denoted by an asterisk (*) next to the coefficient). Lifetime batting average adjusts the profile for individual differences in hitting performance among the players.

3. Gerald W. Scully, "Pay and Performance in Major League Baseball," *American Economic Review* 64, no. 6 (December 1974): 925.

4. Lance E. Davis, "Self-Regulation in Baseball, 1909–71," in *Government and the Sports Business,* edited by Roger G. Noll, 361.

5. "National League Franchises and Their Minor League Affiliates," *Amusement Business,* 9 May 1987; "American League Franchises and Their Minor League Affiliates," *Amusement Business,* 16 May 1987, 15–16.

6. Murray Chass, "A Shortage of Rookies in the Major Leagues," *New York Times,* 14 April 1988, Sports Pages.

7. *Baseball Blue Book 1987* (St. Petersburg, Fla.: Baseball Blue Book, Inc., 1987), 37–41, 56–62.

8. U.S. Bureau of the Census, *Statistical Abstract of the United States: 1976,* 97th ed. (Washington, D.C.: GPO, 1976), 219.

9. Leonard Koppett, "Baseball's Offensive Figures Continue to Slide," *The Sporting News,* 14 October 1972, 6.

10. U.S. Bureau of the Census, *Statistical Abstract of the United States: 1986,* 106th ed. (Washington, D.C.: GPO, 1985), 229.

11. Based on calculations from data in "Rights Go Out of the Park," *Broadcasting,* 10 March 1980, 34.

12. "Gate Tops 52 Million," *The Sporting News,* 19 October 1987, 32.

13. "Baseball Rights Approach $350 Million," *Broadcasting,* 2 March 1987, 47.

14. Stan Isle, "A Redefined Strike Zone: Addition by Subtraction," *The Sporting News,* 21 December 1987, 45.

15. The slugging average is singles plus doubles plus triples plus home runs divided by at-bats. The batting average weights all hits equally.

16. In 1927, when Ruth hit sixty home runs and Gehrig hit forty-seven, the Yankees reached an all-time high team slugging average of .489.

17. Henderson stole 100 bases in 1980 and 108 in 1983, which places him

fifth and third on the all-time, single-season list (through the 1984 season). In 1986, at New York, he stole eighty-seven bases.

18. Sandy Koufax was a Cy Young recipient in 1963 and 1965 as well.

19. In 1894, the batter was charged with a strike for hitting a foul bunt. In 1895, a strike was charged to the batter for a foul tip. In 1897, an earned run was scored by the aid of hits only. In 1901, any foul caught on the fly became a strike, unless the batter had two strikes on him. In the American League the rule was changed in 1903.

20. The source on glove design changes in major league baseball is the illustration contained in *The Sporting News*, 5 April 1969, 28.

21. Originally adopted on a three-year experimental basis, the DH rule became permanent in the American League in December 1975.

22. Statistical testing on the league differences in batting and pitching showed that the DH rule produced significant inter-league differences.

23. The coefficients of the regression equation were statistically significant at or above the .99 percent level, with better than three-fourths of the variance in runs per game associated with the two performance measures.

Chapter Four

1. To verify that P_M is the profit-maximizing quality adjusted ticket price, choose a higher or lower price than P_M in the diagram and observe that the profit rectangle shrinks.

2. "1987 World Series Financial Figures," *The Sporting News*, 9 November 1987, 56.

3. "$85,581 Each for 26 Twins," *New York Times*, 13 January 1988, Sports Pages.

4. Ira Horowitz, "Sports Broadcasting," in *Government and the Sports Business*, edited by Roger G. Noll, 289–90.

5. "Baseball Rights Approach $350 Million," *Broadcasting*, 2 March 1987, 49. The Yankees' fee from WPIX is overstated slightly, since it includes radio rights to WABC (AM) Radio.

6. Roger G. Noll, "The Economics of Sports Leagues," in *The Law of Professional and Amateur Sports*, edited by Gary A. Uberstine (New York: Clark Boardman, 1988).

7. From a memo to all major league clubs from Bowie Kuhn, Eddie Einhorn, and Bill Giles, dated 15 April 1983, pp. 1–3 of the "Summary: Combined NBC/ABC Contract Terms."

8. While these fees are large, they remain small in comparison with the fees charged by the NFL. ABC-TV pays the NFL some $7 million a game, Michael Goodwin, "Policy on TV is Under Scrutiny," *New York Times*, 5 November 1987, Sports Pages, 51.

9. Kuhn Memo, 4–5.

10. Noll, "Economics of Sports Leagues," 32.

11. Ibid., 33.

12. Despite editorial support (*San Francisco Chronicle*, 2 November 1987)

and other backing, owner Bob Lurie did not convince the voters to approve Proposition W, a bond proposal for the park.

13. Noll, "Economics of Sports Leagues," 31.

14. Ronald H. Coase, "The Problem of Social Cost," *Journal of Law and Economics* 3 (October 1960): 1–44. For an elaboration of the Coase theorem see Harold Demsetz, "When Does the Rule of Liability Matter?" *Journal of Legal Studies* 1 (January 1972): 13–28.

15. Simon Rottenberg, "The Baseball Players' Labor Market," *Journal of Political Economy* 64 (June 1956): 248–49.

16. William H. Holahan, "The Long-Run Effects of Abolishing the Baseball Player Reserve System," *Journal of Legal Studies* (1978): 129–37.

17. Michael E. Canes, "The Social Benefits of Restrictions on Team Quality," in *Government and the Sports Business,* edited by Roger G. Noll, 81–113; George Daly and William J. Moore, "Externalities, Property Rights and the Allocation of Resources in Major League Baseball," *Economic Inquiry* 19 (January 1981): 77–94.

18. Mohamed El-Hodiri and James Quirk, "An Economic Model of a Professional Sports League," *Journal of Political Economy* 79 (November–December 1971): 1302–19.

19. James Quirk and Mohamed El-Hodiri, "The Economic Theory of a Professional Sports League," in *Government and the Sports Business,* edited by Roger G. Noll, 33–80.

20. Ibid., 46–47.

21. Daly and Moore, "Externalities, Property Rights and the Allocation of Resources," 93.

22. See note 39 in chapter 2.

23. Christopher R. Drahozel, "The Impact of Free Agency on the Distribution of Playing Talent in Major League Baseball," *Journal of Economics and Business* 38 (1986): 113–21.

24. Ibid., 117.

25. Roger G. Noll concludes that free agency may improve the balance of league competition by allowing free reign of locational preferences of players to affect their choice of teams. Noll, "Economics of Sports Leagues," 47–48.

Chapter Five

1. Roger G. Noll, "The Economics of Sports Leagues," in *The Law of Professional and Amateur Sports,* edited by Gary A. Uberstine (New York: Clark Boardman, 1988).

2. Based on data in an Ernst and Whinney report to the baseball Commissioner, dated 1 April 1985, tables 1–3.

3. "Network Sports Audience Trends, Household Ratings," *Sports, Inc.,* Premier Issue, 1987, 33.

4. Ibid., 34.

5. A claim offered by Bill Veeck, in Bill Veeck, with Ed Linn, *Veeck—as in Wreck: The Autobiography of Bill Veeck* (New York: Putnam, 1962).

6. "Network Sports Audience Trends," 34.

7. See Ira Horowitz, "Sports Broadcasting," in *Government and the Sports Business,* edited by Roger G. Noll, 310–19 for a historical treatment and its implications.

8. Roger G. Noll, "Attendance and Price Setting," in *Government and the Sports Business,* edited by Roger G. Noll, 115–31.

9. Ibid., 121.

10. The simple correlation between Standard Metropolitan Statistical Area (SMSA) per capita income and 1984 attendance was $r = .31$. For the number of degrees of freedom the minimal correlation required for statistical significance at the 95 percent level is $r = .38$.

11. The simple correlation between the number of sports franchises and club attendance was $r = .12$, which is not statistically significant. Multiplying this variable and SMSA per capita income by population as Noll did only weakens the correlation.

12. The simple correlation of the percentage black population on attendance was $r = .35$, which is not significant and is of the wrong sign, while the correlation coefficient of previous championship status was $r = -.04$.

Chapter Six

1. Alternative nonlinear specifications were estimated. These equations had less explanatory power than the linear regression and are not reported here.

2. Population alone is a significant predictor of club costs. The statistical result is not reported here. Thus, big city teams have higher costs. But, there is collinearity between 1984 Population and 1983 Win Percentage, which precludes the inclusion of 1984 Population as a regressor. Therefore, there is some evidence that at least for 1984, club standing and city size are correlated. However, the statistical ground on which this finding rests is shaky and the finding should not be interpreted as a refutation of the conclusion of a historical narrowing of the range of club playing strengths, which was documented in chapter 4.

3. *Organized Baseball,* Report of the Subcommittee on the Study of Monopoly Power of the Committee of the Judiciary, House Report no. 2002, 82d Congress, 1st sess., 1952, 21.

4. House Committee on the Judiciary, Subcommittee on Study of Monopoly Power, *Study of Monopoly Power,* Pt. 6, *Organized Baseball.* Hearings. 82d Congress, 1st sess., 1952, 736.

5. Allan Sloane, "Wait 'til next year," *Forbes,* 4 August 1980, 46.

6. Nancy J. Perry, "A Big Winner, in Two Leagues," *Fortune,* 5 January 1987, 34.

7. Dave Nightingale, "Ueberroth a 1-Term Commissioner," *The Sporting News,* 21 December 1987, 44.

8. Dave Nightingale, "Looking Down Expansion Road: 15-Team Leagues," *The Sporting News,* 21 December 1987, 44.

Chapter Seven

1. I am grateful to Roger G. Noll of Stanford University for making this data available to me.

2. For an analysis of the tax treatment of professional sports, see Benjamin A. Okner, "Taxation and Sports Enterprises," in *Government and the Sports Business*, edited by Roger G. Noll (Washington, D.C.: The Brookings Institution, 1974), 159–83.

3. Roger G. Noll, "The Economic Viability of Professional Baseball: Report to the Major League Baseball Players Association," July 1985, 1–2.

4. Unpublished data provided by Roger G. Noll.

5. Noll, "The Economic Viability of Professional Baseball," 6.

6. Ibid., 13–14.

7. To obtain an estimate of the fair market value of the local television rights, 1982 local TV fees by club were regressed on market size. The predicted value of the local rights was the measure of fair market value. The regression equation was:

$$\text{Local TV Fees} = 64.67^* + .45 \text{ Market Size}, \ R^{-2} = .32,$$
$$N = 26.$$

As the asterisk indicates, the intercept was not statistically significant at conventional levels.

8. Cable fees were estimated from 1982 cable revenue by club regressed on market size. The predicted value of the cable rights was a measure of the foregone cable fees. The regression equation was as follows:

$$\text{Cable Fees} = -152.79^* + .11 \text{ Market Size}, \ R^{-2} = .37,$$
$$N = 22.$$

9. To estimate the fair market value of the St. Louis concession income, the concession income of the other 25 clubs was regressed on attendance. The predicted value for St. Louis was $3.57 million. The regression equation was as follows:

$$\text{Concession Revenue} = -882.81^* + 2.11 \text{ Attendance},$$
$$R^{-2} = .50.$$

10. Noll, "The Economic Viability of Professional Baseball," 22.

11. Data on sales prices from 1950 through 1974 is from Lance Davis and James Quirk, "The Ownership and Valuation of Professional Sports Franchises," California Institute of Technology, Social Science Working Paper number 79, April 1975.

12. Todd Mason, "For Eddie Chiles, Oil and Baseball No Longer Mix," *Business Week*, 21 July 1986, 72.

13. Robert McG. Thomas, Jr., "Sale Deal is Reached for Texas Rangers," *New York Times*, 27 August 1988, Sports Pages.

14. Nancy J. Perry, "A Big Winner, in Two Leagues," *Fortune*, 5 January 1987, 34.

15. Julie Flynn, "Win or Lose, The Dodgers are Power Hitters at the Gate," *Business Week*, 20 October 1988, 66.

16. "White Sox Set Their Terms," *New York Times*, 12 May 1988, Sports Pages, 48.

17. Allegedly this is the plan offered by Commissioner Ueberroth. Dave Nightingale, "Looking Down Expansion Road: 15-Team Leagues," *The Sporting News*, 21 December 1987, 44.

18. This is the average win percentage for all expansion clubs in baseball over the first ten years of the existence of the franchise.

19. The revenue equation in table 6.4 is the basis for the revenue projections of the expansion clubs.

Chapter Eight

1. The salary data is from Murray Chass, "Baseball's Bonus Beauties: '87," *The Sporting News*, 16 November 1987, 48–49. Steve Bedrosian won the Cy Young Award and got a $100,000 bonus, which pushed his earnings over the $1 million mark.

2. Murray Chass, "Hershiser's Contract Is Richest 3-Year Deal," *New York Times*, 22 February 1989, Sports Pages, 41.

3. Philip H. Dougherty, "Cosby Rerun Ad Time is Sold for $60 Million," *New York Times*, 6 May 1988.

4. Allan Dodds Frank and Jason Zweig, "The Fault is Not in Our Stars," *Forbes*, 21 September 1987, 120–21.

5. Calculated from data in *Organized Baseball*, Report of the Subcommittee on the Study of Monopoly Power of the Committee of the Judiciary, House Report no. 2002, 82d Congress, 1st sess., 1952, 6.

6. Ernst and Whinney Report to the Commissioner of Baseball, 13 August 1984, "Combined Summary of Operations (before Income Taxes), Major League Baseball."

7. Gerald W. Scully, "Pay and Performance in Major League Baseball," *American Economic Review* 64, no. 6 (December 1974): 915–30.

8. *Antitrust Policy and Professional Sports*, Hearings before the Subcommittee on Monopolies and Commercial Law of the House Committee on the Judiciary, 97th Congress, 1st and 2d sess. (Washington, D.C.: GPO, 1984), 484.

9. Roger G. Noll, "Attendance and Price Setting," in *Government and the Sports Business*, edited by Roger G. Noll, 115–57; Ira Horowitz, "Sports Broadcasting," in *Government and the Sports Business*, edited by Roger G. Noll, 275–323.

10. Knox Lovell has found that speed, as measured by stolen bases, contributes to team wins but not to player salaries. C. A. Knox Lovell, "More on Pay and Performance in Major League Baseball," University of North Carolina—Chapel Hill, photocopy, n.d.

11. The regression results were as follows:

1984 Revenues = $-1,877.2^* + 31,696.1$ 1984 Win

Percentage $+ 3.31$ 1984 Population,

$\bar{R}^{-2} = .69$, DF = 21.

12. Ivan Maisel, "Ball Park Figures? Better Believe It," *Sports Illustrated*, 4 March 1985, 24.

13. Gerald W. Scully, "Binding Salary Arbitration in Major League Baseball," *American Behavioral Scientist* 21, no. 3 (January–February 1978): 431–50.

14. Dropping Toronto and Seattle to make the leagues comparable in size reduces the percentage to 60 percent.

15. James Cassing and Richard Douglas, "Implications of the Auction Mechanism in Baseball's Free Agent Draft," *Southern Economic Journal* 47 (July 1980): 110–21; Paul M. Sommers and Noel Quinton, "Pay and Performance in Major League Baseball: The Case of the First Family of Free Agents," *The Journal of Human Resources* 17, no. 3 (1982): 426–35; Henry J. Raimondo, "Free Agent's Impact on the Labor Market for Baseball Players," *Journal of Labor Research*, 4, no. 2 (Spring 1983): 183–93; and, James R. Hill and William Spellman, "Professional Baseball: The Reserve Clause and Salary Structure," *Industrial Relations* 22, no. 1 (Winter 1983): 1–19.

16. Free agent salary averages based on data contained in Cassing and Douglas, "Implications of the Auction Mechanism," 111.

17. Rodney D. Fort and Roger G. Noll were the first to point out the different elasticities of salary with respect to performance between veteran and rookie players. See their study on "Pay and Performance in Baseball: Modeling Regulars, Reserves and Expansion," California Institute of Technology, Social Science Working Paper 527, May 1984.

18. The regression is:

Wins = 11.82* + .1058 Runs Scored − 6.97 American League, $\bar{R}^2$ = .35.

19. Ernst and Whinney, Report to the Commissioner of Baseball, "Assumptions Used in Forecasting Combined Summary of Operations for 1984–88," photocopy, n.d.

20. Roger G. Noll, "The Economics of Sports Leagues," in *The Law of Professional and Amateur Sports*, edited by Gary A. Uberstine (New York: Clark Boardman, 1988).

21. Players average about $520,000 in the NBA. On 26 April 1988, a six-year pact was announced between the NBA and the players' union. Under the terms of the agreement the college draft was to be reduced from seven to two rounds, the salary cap was to be increased in stages over the length of the agreement, and the right of first refusal was modified in the players' favor. Robert McG. Thomas, Jr., "N.B.A. in 6-Year Pact with Players' Union," *New York Times*, 27 April 1988, Sports Pages.

22. Based on data provided by Roger G. Noll, table titled "Financial Trends in Baseball, 1976–84," photocopy, n.d.

23. "$256,296,950," *Sports Illustrated*, 20 April 1987, 54.

24. Based on data from Noll, "Financial Trends."

Chapter Nine

1. The Walker brothers played for Toledo, which joined the American Association in 1884.

2. Gordon Verrell, "A Doleful Day for Dodger Blue," *The Sporting News*,

20 April 1987, 12; Pete Axthelm, "Baseball: A Crisis in Black and White," *Newsweek*, 20 April 1987, 71; "Racism at Bat," *Time*, 20 April 1987, 63.

3. "CBS's Snyder Causes Racial Storm," *New York Times*, 16 January 1988, Sports Pages.

4. Brent Staples, "Where Are the Black Fans?" *The New York Times Magazine*, 17 May 1987, 27.

5. *Dallas Times Herald*, 26 July 1987, D–12.

6. Michael Martinez, "Baseball's Upswing in Minority Hiring Is Followed by Clash of Interpretations," *New York Times*, 6 April 1988, Sports Pages, 46.

7. Reggie Jackson, "We Have a Serious Problem That Isn't Going Away," *Sports Illustrated*, 11 May 1987, 42.

8. Much of the approach to the material in this chapter is based on my "Discrimination: The Case of Baseball," in *Government and the Sports Business*, edited by Roger G. Noll (Washington, D.C.: The Brookings Institution, 1974), 221–73.

9. Harold Seymour, *Baseball: The Early Years* (New York: Oxford University Press, 1960), 42.

10. Robert W. Peterson, *Only the Ball Was White* (Englewood Cliffs, N.J.: Prentice-Hall, 1970), 24.

11. Seymour, *Baseball: The Early Years*, 334; Lee Allen, *100 Years of Baseball* (New York: Bartholomew House, 1950), 282.

12. *Sporting Life*, 21 September 1887, 3.

13. *Sporting Life*, 20 July 1887, 1.

14. *Sporting Life*, 29 February 1888, 1.

15. Peterson, *Only the Ball Was White*, 46–51.

16. *Pittsburgh Courier*, 11 March 1933, 2d sect., 5.

17. *Pittsburgh Courier*, 15 May 1943, 19.

18. Arthur Mann, *Branch Rickey, American in Action* (Boston: Houghton-Mifflin Company, 1957).

19. Carl T. Rowan with Jackie Robinson, *Wait Till Next Year: The Life Story of Jackie Robinson* (New York: Random House, 1970): 99–100.

20. "Report of Major League Steering Committee for Submission to the National and American Leagues at Their Meetings in Chicago," in House Committee on the Judiciary, Subcommittee on Study of Monopoly Power, *Study of Monopoly Power, Pt. 6, Organized Baseball*. Hearings. 82d Congress, 1st sess., 1952, 483–85.

21. Aaron Rosenblatt, "Negroes in Baseball: The Failure of Success," *Transaction* 4 (September 1967): 51–53.

22. The sources of the data in the figure are as follows: 1953–59, Rosenblatt, "Negroes in Baseball"; 1960–71, Scully, "Discrimination," 234–35; 1972–80, John C. Phillips, "Race and Career Opportunities in Major League Baseball: 1960–1980," *Journal of Sport and Social Issues* (Summer–Fall 1983): 1–17; 1986, author's calculation from published data.

23. On this point also see the following: Anthony H. Pascal and Leonard A. Rapping, "The Economics of Racial Discrimination in Organized Baseball," in *Racial Discrimination in Economic Life*, edited by Anthony H. Pascal (Lex-

ington, Mass: Lexington Books, 1972): 119–56; James Gwartney and Charles Haworth, "Employer Costs and Discrimination: The Case of Baseball," *Journal of Political Economy* 82 (July–August 1974): 873–81; Gerald W. Scully, "Economic Discrimination in Professional Sports," *Law and Contemporary Problems* 38, no. 1 (Winter–Spring 1973): 67–84; Scully, "Discrimination"; and Phillips, "Race and Career Opportunities."

24. Brent Staples, "Where Are the Black Fans?" 30.

25. Ibid., 29.

26. Scully, "Discrimination," 242.

27. Ibid., 245.

28. Ibid.

29. James R. Hill and William Spellman, "Pay Discrimination in Baseball: Data from the Seventies," *Industrial Relations* 23, no. 1 (Winter 1984): 103–12.

30. *The Baseball Encyclopedia* (Toronto: The Macmillan Company, 1969), 30.

31. Calculated from a sample of 159 black ballplayers in *Ebony*, June 1969.

32. Data from the *Dallas Times Herald*, 26 July 1987, D–12.

Chapter Ten

1. Much of the material in this chapter is based on a previously published paper. Philip K. Porter and Gerald W. Scully, "Measuring Managerial Efficiency: The Case of Baseball," *Southern Economic Journal* (January 1982): 642–50.

2. Statistical estimation yielded:

$$E_{it} = .8923 + .00828t - .00033t^2 - .0515\ ORIG.$$

E is the efficiency measure of the ith manager in year t; t is career year; and *ORIG* is a dummy equal to 1, if the manager changed teams one or more times over his career.

Chapter Eleven

1. "Prepared Statement of Gerald W. Scully," *Hearings before the House Select Committee on Professional Sports*, 94th Congress, 2d sess., part 2, 1976, 165.

Index

Accounting, club, 134; problems with, 135–37, 192

Acme Colored Giants, 173

Affiliate ownerships. *See* Broadcast rights; Revenue, club; Television

Amateur Free Agent Draft, 21

Amateurs: college players, 22, 23; eligibility of, 22; and minor leagues, 22

American Association, 3; and National League, 4, 14

American Baseball Guild, 34

American League: championships, 86–87; club revenues, 118, 120–21; cost of tickets, 106; expansion in, 145; and Designated Hitter Rule, 67–69, 72–74; managerial quality of, 184; and rate of attendance increase, 102, 104; and standard deviation of wins, 91–93

Amortization. *See* Costs, club

Arbitration, 36–37; decisions based on player merit, 162; decisions through (1986–88), 162–64; procedure of, 161. *See also* Uniform Players' Contract

Atlanta Braves, 139

Attendance at games, 101; determinants of, 111–15; increase in (1947–87), 102–3; and season ticket sales, 103–4; and strongest and poorest drawing clubs, 105. *See also* American League; Ticket prices

Autry, Gene, 137

Averages, player. *See* Player performance; Players

Basic Agreement, 8, 17; of 1967, 34–35; of 1969, 35; of 1973–75, 35–36, 161; and player reservation, 38

Blacklisting, 2

Broadcast rights, 18; actual financial gains from, 127–28; and broadcasters' ownership of clubs, 108–9; legal status of, 31–32, 195; local rights, 109–10, 139. *See also* Television; Quality of play, relative

Brotherhood of Professional Baseball Players, 32

Brush Classification Plan (1888), 32

California Angels, 137

Campanis, Al, 171

Canes, Michael, 84–85

Chicago White Sox, 137

Club management: decision-making and club quality, 182-83; estimates of frontier unit isoquants, 184–86; expansion clubs, 189; "frontier" production function, 182; learning curve, 186–89; normalized production function, 183; salaries and performance, 189–90

Coase, Ronald, 84

Cobb, Ty, 33

Collusion against players. *See* Free Agents; Major League Baseball Players Association

Comiskey, J. Louis, 173

Commercialization, 7–8

Commissioner of Baseball (office), 14–15, 194

Contracts. *See* Major League Baseball Players Association; Players, contracts with; Strikes; Uniform Players' Contract

Costs, club: average losses, 135; club operation at a loss, 126–27, 141–42; and depreciation, 132, 134; due to franchise expansion, 144; direct costs, 123; franchise taxation, 130–33, 134–35, 143–44; increases in (1974–84), 122–23; and player salaries, 124–25. *See also* Quality of play, relative

Craig, Peter S. See *Organized Baseball* (Craig)

Demand by fans. *See* Attendance at games, determinants of

Designated Hitter Rule. *See* American League; National League; Rules of play, fluctuation of

209